ETHNIC CONFLICT,
TRIBAL POLITICS

ETHNIC CONFLICT, TRIBAL POLITICS

A GLOBAL PERSPECTIVE

edited by
Kenneth Christie

CURZON

First Published in 1998
by Curzon Press
15 The Quadrant, Richmond
Surrey, TW9 1BP

Editorial Matter © 1998 Kenneth Christie

Typeset in Sabon by LaserScript Ltd, Mitcham, Surrey
Printed and bound in Great Britain by
TJ International, Padstow, Cornwall

British Library Cataloguing in Publication Data
A catalogue record of this book is available from the British Library

Library of Congress Cataloguing in Publication Data
A catalog record for this book has been requested

ISBN 0–7007–1097–3 (Hbk)
ISBN 0–7007–1118–X (Pbk)

*This is dedicated to Helen (for sisterly support) and
to Penny (for the HTB's)*

Contents

Acknowledgements

I would like to thank Jonathan Price of Curzon Press for his help and commitment to seeing this project finished. I would also like to thank Terese Zeil of the University of Bergen for help with the index and David McCarthy of LaserScript for his help in the final production.

Kenneth Christie
University of Bergen

Chapter One

Introduction: The Problem with Ethnicity and 'Tribal' Politics

Kenneth Christie

It was the former French President, Francois Mitterand who drew some of our attention to the ethnic, tribal threat to a 'civilised' Western Europe in a conference in 1992 entitled 'L'Europe et les tribus'. He saw a picture of a problematic post-Maastricht vision of Europe, a Community surrounded by barbaric sentiments occupying the peripheral space of European frontiers.[1] The imagery was startling; hostile tribes driven by ancient feudal ties and primitive allegiances were threatening the integrity of the European integration project. While one region of Europe appeared to be descending into the primeval sludge, another was paradoxically ascending the heights of supra-nationalism.

Previously and in other contexts, experts in various fields had located tribal and ethnic conflict in less developed regions of the globe; Africa, Asia, perhaps Latin America. Suddenly, and with great alacrity, the post cold war period had erupted into unprecedented ethnic violence in central and eastern Europe, prompting connotations of tribalism in previously communist states. It also appeared most vociferously in a federal state known most notably for its relaxed and democratic attitudes and policies of non-alignment; Yugoslavia. The world will not soon forget the horrific process of 'ethnic cleansing' entailing the creation of homogeneous populations by means of mass exile; here more than two million people were removed from areas in which for most of the time they classified as minorities.

Despite the end of the cold war and the promise of a 'New World Order' which would produce peace, stability and harmony on a global basis, liberal democrats have been severely disappointed. An end to history vis-a-vis a Fukuyamanian type analysis has not materialised; rather a return to history in the form of often genocidal ethnic conflict from Burundi to Burma has proved to be one of the most salient and disturbing agendas of the 1990's.

Ethnic unrest and communal strife proved fairly resilient in the Third World but also in developed societies during the 20th century. Why are such conflicts so important? One reason is that this type of conflict has produced more abject misery and loss of life than any other in the post second world war period. As Freeman has argued 'Tribes, states and empires are all agents of war' (Freeman, 1993: p. 27).

In a speech on the 9th of November 1993, Boutros Boutros Ghali, the Secretary-General of the United nations warned that global security was under threat because of the spread of ethnic conflicts in the post cold war period. He noted that since World War II there had been 127 wars most of them for ethnic reasons and made the point that borders and oceans could no longer insulate societies from the implications of this type of violence. And this is particularly so as ethnic groups do not necessarily align themselves with state borders.

New concepts concerning 'security' in the post-cold war period also started to focus less and less on the idea of an 'enemy' and the idea that there is a military threat (particularly in Europe for instance), and more and more on the intangible, 'soft' threats to security. These include areas such as the changing boundaries, race and ethnicity, mass migration, the question of national minorities, the question of Islam, Aids, and religion amongst others. And these threatening problems exist not only at certain national levels but on a global scale.

They are difficult to deal with because many politicians see them as unsolvable; they don't fit neatly into the political structure. And they represent dark underlying forces and currents threatening to disrupt and perhaps dismember the status quo. They are questions apparently without answers because they are seen as complicated and irrational. In short they are highly problematic. Boundaries are constantly in a state of flux in the wake of the Cold War. Yugoslavia, all of Eastern Europe, Russia and the CIS are just a few of the areas on the European continent that have been affected by the traumatic events following the end of the Cold war.

The changes to the world political map are greater now than at any other period in the 20th century with the exceptions of the two world wars and their immediate aftermath. The collapse of Communism as a system of rule in the Soviet Union and Eastern Europe has had enormous consequences for those areas and the rest of the world as well. In the former communist ruled systems, pre-communist attitudes, values, fears and hatreds have resurfaced with a vengeance. Chief amongst these factors is the resurgence of ethnic violence and extreme nationalistic tendencies. The increasingly fragmented societies of the Eurasian continent in turn have added another dimension to the ethnic animosities and strife already evident in the Middle east, parts of Asia (e.g. Indonesia and East Timor), Somalia, much of Sub-Saharan Africa and Cyprus.

Serious analysis of this phenomenon, its causes and consequences, is important and much needed in the new global 'disorder.' Analysts and commentators alike are concerned with the need to explain the sources of ethnic conflict, as well as its policy consequences. Even in established political systems, based in long-standing industrial democracies, separatism and regionalism are becoming more pronounced; examples are the United Kingdom, France and Spain. In these countries, important elements of the population now focus on their immediate localities and regions as political benchmarks, and they emphasize their local heritage in history, music, the arts and other cultural expressions. This is not a new phenomenon, but it appears to be more urgently expressed as the 20th century draws to a close. The drive for nation-building and the construction of regional entities, a dominant theme in much of the world for many decades (in the West, several centuries) is being overshadowed by a quest for smaller, more manageable, political and cultural units.

To what extent is this a result of historical development? For instance is this a natural consequence of the maturation of nation-building and the return to a different, pre-modern form of political organization? To what extent are these problems idiosyncratic and country specific? One of the aims of this volume is to show how ethnic conflict is a comparative phenomenon which shares similarities and exhibits differences and unique characteristics across the board. The expression of ethnicity may lead to strife within multi-ethnic societies for instance, but it also produces conflict between states.

With the break-up of the Soviet Union for instance at least 47 new international boundaries were created, out of which 22 are between the newly independent republics and the neighbouring countries in Eastern Europe and Central and Eastern Asia. Many of the disputes over territory and borders have of course already risen to the surface such as between Armenia and Azerbaijan over Nagorny Karabakh or between Russia and the Ukraine over the Crimea. The entire region has in fact become a geopolitical fault zone complete with religious, ethnic and national rivalries. In many of these cases there is a complete breakdown in law and order, a lack of democracy and an almost anarchical condition or state of affairs. And as the text addresses this is not simply limited to this particular part of the world; it has become part of a global condition.

The break-up of states, the creation of new 'nation-states', and the rise of ethno-nationalism and ultra-nationalist political forces in many parts of the world are posing many new security problems and crises for the international community. There is also a conflict between two important principles of the inter-state system since World War II, those of territorial sovereignty for existing states and self-determination for peoples living within those state territories.

The UN for instance will and has become more and more involved in many of these old and new ethnic conflicts; since 1988 for instance they have ventured into more peacekeeping missions than they did in the entire period since World War II up to that date. Moreover, the nature of the new peacekeeping ventures is far more broad-ranging including many of the ethnic conflicts and involves more ambitious mandates than the missions mounted in the Cold War period.

3

Various analyses propound the idea that the end of superpower rivalry unleashed uncontrollable forces of ethno-nationalism and tribal sentiments, but overwhelming evidence shows that these problems have been around for a fairly long time, many of them in effect caused by processes of decolonization at the end of the second world war. The partition of India, and the Arabs and Jews in Palestine, just two examples of this phenomenon. Eric Hobsbawm has argued that nationalism belongs with the study of political theory and ethnicity with sociology and/or anthropology. I disagree. Just as war is too important to be left to the generals, so ethnicity is too important to be left to sociologists. Political scientists must reclaim this territory which is filled with the 'political.'

Michael Freeman has a clear problem in viewing these conflicts in simple dichotomous terms as 'struggles between primitive and irrational forces on the one hand and the civilised international legal order on the other.' and as he further elaborates:

> The atrocities in the post-Yugoslav war are indeed 'barbaric'. Yet the primitive/civilised distinction is a barrier to understanding. It commonly rests upon a view of history, according to which once there was the primitive, the irrational and the violent, then there was progress towards the civilised, the rational and the orderly, a progress, however, that has been interrupted from time to time by reversions to primitive barbarism. This view of history is deeply embedded in our moral and political culture. It is, however, seriously misleading.[2]

In part the objective of this book is to examine the assumptions, controversy and views around such a framework of understanding in which this violent and disturbing social conflict is taking place.

How do we account for trends and the emergence of these apparently tribal passions and animosities in a comparative sense; what are some of the historical roots of such conflict? How and why is politics involved? The task of imposing a rigid structured framework on seven different academics is a nightmare that doesn't bear contemplating. Rather than applying such a straitjacket (which few would adhere to anyway), I decided to offer them a loose structure looking at the problem of tribalism and ethnicity and relating it to the particular case studies in which they have expert knowledge.

DEFINING TRIBE

There is little doubt (and this is a theme running through all the chapters), that Tribalism is a difficult and often misplaced term. Nevertheless it is a term which is used widely, particularly to explain what often seems to be irrational, violent ethnic conflict. And we shall see that throughout the text it appears to work in different contexts and cannot be confined to one area.

The term 'tribe' derives from the Latin term 'tribus', and was initially used in a biblical connotation.[3] Tribes were self contained groups; they were autonomous and based on kinship ties. Anthropologists and others define tribe as a groups with certain characteristics in common (self-sufficiency, a distinct language, culture and sense of identity including a shared set of mythologies, taboos, and heroes and villains, a defined set of relationships, including a clear hierarchy of power and definite rules of behaviour, and a loosely defined territory utilized for hunting and gathering). Relations between tribes are often marked by competition and outright animosity, but the low level of technology reduces casualties in the frequent inter-tribal skirmishes to a minimum. The main point here is the notion that tribes are an early form of human organization, preceding that of nation or state. Tribes, presumably, can be found hundreds, perhaps thousands, of years before the latter forms of human organization appear. If we accept these notions then we can argue that when we witness the breakdown of the nation-state into different components then we are seeing a return to a smaller tribal unit after the other forms of human organization have been experienced. We might call this a retribalization which denotes the breaking up of the nation-state into a set of smaller units. And the dismantling process is often perceived as nasty, brutish or in other words, tribalistic. The reason for current interest in this concept is the fact that this dismantling process now seems to be underway in certain parts of the world, while other parts are experiencing instability that may in the end lead to dismantling there, too. We look around for explanations and more often than not we find 'tribalism' as a convenient and appealing explanation. And again it should be stressed that this volume in part is an effort to illustrate the rich and varied complexity of such terms in the light of violent conflict.

More recent notions of the 'tribal' in tribe evoke images of savagery, barbarism and a primitive state. The concept is a controversial one to say the least; appeals to age old passions, myths and questionable histories are rarely uncontroversial. Tribalism may have emerged in the late twentieth century with pejorative associations, but tribes even in Africa share similarities in terms of historical formation, institutions, customs, traditions and belief systems. To some extent they are the product of contemporary political and economic forces; colonialism for administrative purposes actually invented certain tribes.

New symbols, forms of organization and interests were accorded to such groups including highly contested resources such as land. Competition for the latter reinforced and frequently elevated tribal consciousness. Classic colonial divide and rule strategies allowed for the exacerbation and enhancement of inter-group rivalries. The internecine conflict in Rwanda that erupted in the 1990's for instance has its roots in the colonial period when a strategy of indirect rule transformed an ascribed Tutsi superiority into an inherited one. This merely served to reinforce and exacerbate the already increasing Hutu resentment. Following independence the question of which group would assume power was a contested and contentious one given the taste of indirect rule by one group.[4] Despite the mythical quality of the tribe built on distinctive customs, traditions and cultural beliefs, its bases were clearly rooted in past and contemporary struggles for economic resources and political power.

Colson argues that the legitimacy and appeal of tribalism are by and large intellectual inventions by people who have had the opportunity to participate in the political and social world.[5] In this light it might be regarded as a ideological mechanism, a topic that Nergis Canefe dwells on at some length in her chapter on Turkey.

The concept tribalism has other connotations as well – connotations that, presumably, help define their characteristics in a discrete way. For example, tribes are seen as operating at a high level of internal conformity, coupled with external conflict, with little tolerance for others (others being those who have set themselves outside the collectivity, or have been excluded from it by characteristics or conscious decisions by those who are in). In other words, there is no civility in the tribe in the sense usually attributed to modern, pluralistic societies, where individual and subgroup autonomy, willingness to allow others to exist and even to prosper in their otherness are major characteristics. Hence, the notion of retribalization carries with it the idea that society is regressing from a higher form (e.g. civil society) to the older, more primitive form of the tribe.

The problem with this kind of conceptualization is that it does not clearly distinguish tribalism from other forms of societal behaviour which is much discussed in the literature. For example, there are definitions of nationalism, ethnonationalism, ethnochauvinism, and primitive nationalism that operate with similar characteristics and behaviour patterns as those used to define tribalism here. To some extent we use tribalism because it appears as the most used (and abused) term in the literature and the media. In his chapter, Michael Freeman seeks to discuss and comprehend the various theories and concepts on offer, illuminating in large part their significance for political theory.

This still does not help bridge the gap between tribalism and nationalism as concepts, however; it merely establishes some connection between the tribe, the state, the nation, and current political trends. If one assumes that tribes naturally developed into nations which then produced their own states, current events can only be explained by the notion that the inherent inclusiveness and exclusiveness of the tribes involved made it impossible to keep the larger unit, the state, together once a unifying symbol (such as a founding father or an overwhelming external threat has disappeared (e.g.

Yugoslavia); alternatively, it can be argued that a dominant tribe in a multitribal setting has hijacked the state for the purposes of utilizing this structure to discriminate against others in ways that we normally attribute to tribes.

Occasionally, other uses of the concept tribe can be found; of particular relevance here is the use made of it to describe the rootless groups of marginalized people whose lives have been turned upside down by political or economic change, without any direct action undertaken by them, and with no real possibility of remedial undertakings which can once again make their existence meaningful. There are hundreds of thousands of people in this category in contemporary Eastern Europe, many of them in the Balkans. They are older industrial workers whose livelihood has been destroyed by the privatization of state enterprises; young people with few skills that are needed in todays society; refugees from wars and upheavals, as well as the floating current of humanity from parts of Asia, Africa, and the Middle East who swell over the region, in search of the simplest of livelihoods, often merely in transition to the vaunted West. These are typically people without any stake in the systems in which they find themselves. As the miseries of the socio-economic transformation process in the region continues, these groups of marginalized people will become an ever greater problem.

Manning Nash has made a similar argument when he says:

> Ethnicity is a reservoir for unrest in a world where power, prosperity and rank are distributed in an unequal and illegal way between and within nations.[6]

This volume seeks to provide some of the answers about the nature of ethnicity and tribalism and its political context, drawing on the work of acknowledged experts in the field, from a global perspective. Thus ethnic strife is seen as not only confined to eastern Europe and the tragedy of the Balkans that Trond Gilberg describes in such detail, but also to other countries and regions. I have included comparisons of highly industrialised societies within such a context to demonstrate that ethnic politics is not specific to geographical and level of development criteria, occurring as it can in developed states like Scotland, Catalonia and Quebec equally as in underdeveloped African contexts. Ethnic attachments are not simply related to socio-economic stages of development in a global economy in other words.

OVERVIEWS

In this section a summary and overview of the various chapters, is offered in an effort to draw the common threads of comparison and highlight the individuality of each case also.

In his broad, theoretical overview of ethnic politics, Michael Freeman ponders such difficult questions as whether we are witnessing a 'return of the primitive?' If we thought the end of the Cold war would create a new, and improved world order under the humanitarian auspices of the United Nations and their principles and goals, then we were sadly mistaken. One of the most significant features of the 1990's is that ethnic violence has become a pervasive feature of most post cold war conflicts. Freeman is anxious to place this in the context of the problems this creates for liberal democracy and indeed the general nature of liberalism. Ethnicity and its supportive movements tend to threaten and undermine the liberal project which in essence was designed to guarantee the rights of the individual against authoritarian and traditional collectivities. He immediately notes the problems associated with the term 'tribalism', a problem which the other case study authors also dwell on.

Liberal scholars, as Freeman argues, have responded by reference to the 'new tribalism'; a topic that appears vague and ill defined. Tribalism in this sense is seen as a primitive form of politics often located in terms of a Darwinian evolutionary scale. And he stresses the pejorative connotations of this. He also goes onto discuss how flawed the nature of this pejorative association is, a theme reiterated in the detailed case studies. Tribes in other words are no less civilised than nation-states and certainly not as destructive. Moreover, he analyses the distinctions in the body of literature surrounding ethnic groups and nation states and the plethora of theories used to explain ethnic formation, persistence and change as well as how they mobilize on a political level and how they can act to subvert the state. These include primordialism, family values, sociobiology, political sociology and rational choice theory among others.

In Chapter 3, Michael Keating asks whether minority nationalism (in the cases of Quebec, Catalonia and Scotland) must be tribal? Following from Freeman, he also argues that the terms of ethnic group, nation and state are inherently problematic, and only contingently and not necessarily linked. Furthermore, they are fluid terms in the sense that they are subject to changing circumstances. All ethnic and civic nationalism to Keating are ideal types and they are normative and value laden. In each of his three cases, Keating provides three nationalist movements who, represent historical nations but whose movements have been tempered and moderated to fit contemporary realities. They are in effect very 'modern responses to the dilemmas of the contemporary era.' Ethnic movements are analyzed in a comparative sense in a world where borders are becoming increasingly meaningless and globalisation represents a powerful force for change. Movements in these countries are in broad terms both 'old and new.' They are civic rather than ethnic, free trading rather than protectionist and have accepted a multiple rather than an exclusive identity. As he argues 'Nationalist ideology bridges the past and the future, the imagined community and the daily reality in an effort to cope with the dilemma of modernity.'

It is a new form of minority nationalism which emerges in this scenario, and one in which identity has been re-invented and recharged by external pressures. None of these cases genuinely wants complete separation, but they maintain a strong from of ethnic nationalism in terms of self assertion. Keating also makes the valuable point that far from eroding ethnic minority nationalism, globalization and continued regional integration have actually encouraged it, a point which seems to apply across the board. Keatings chapter also brings out the difference factor. By and large these are developed nations, with long histories of cultural nationalism. They illustrate the fact that ethnicity and nationalism are not the exclusive concern of underdeveloped or post-colonial states.

Trond Gilberg continues with the useful definitional and analytical precedents embarked upon by Michael Freeman in his chapter and adds some terms of his own, reflecting the rich diversity of theoretical insight in the literature. He notes that ethnicity and associated behaviour in the region has increased in frequency as well as intensity and there are several reasons for this. Gilberg points to the collapse of the old order which has re-opened the opportunity for ethnic violence. Historical antecedents are also very strong and virulent in this juncture and there is an interesting degree of continuity between old and new. Moreover given the manufactured nature of tribalism and ethnicity, individual leaders like Karadzic and Mladic are more than willing to exploit this for self interest. And for this author, ethnicity represents a central feature of political behaviour in the Balkans and he explores attitudes which derive from the 'rich heritage of tribalist myth.' The region is replete with examples of where history and myth collide, coincided and appear at times inseparable. Gilberg analyses several crucial factors, including the 'notion of a glorious past that must be recaptured and the idea that others deprived the group of its rightful glory.' The examples of ex-Yugoslavia, Romania, Bulgaria and Albania are used again stressing the overall comparative nature of the text.

Finally, given these orthodox views, Gilberg poses an alternative view; what if this ethnic behaviour is simply a form of atomization, hooliganism and organized criminality? The idea that ethnicity is just an excuse in other words to perpetuate illegal and anti-state behaviour. There has been a long-standing tradition of banditry in the Balkan region; the prevalence of brigands operating in a style reminiscent of Robin Hood has found empathy within Balkan political culture. And with some modernisation, Gilberg notes, 'Yesterdays brigands and freedom fighters became the leaders of the established order.' (p. 119). In all of these regional states, organised gangs have emerged and as we have seen in recent media footage of the breakdown of law and order in Albania, this has lent to the flavour of anarchism and tribalistic behaviour. Gilberg confirms the suspicions of what many see happening in the post-communist era; that is the rise of alienation, depoliticization and the atomization of society. Many people have become marginalised and without a role in these societies where they feel dislocated and living in a state of permanent insecurity.

In sum he appears clearly pessimistic of the chances that Balkan history can be overcome. Even if history could be remedied, there are however other obstacles which are very real including 'cultural nationalism' and the disbanding of the old communist systems which allowed for the opportunity for people to act as 'free' agents. Moreover, Gilberg points to the very real importance of political leadership in tribalism, a factor that is taken up very strongly by A. Jeyeratnam Wilson's chapter on Sri Lanka.

In line with the theoretical case studies and preceding case studies, Denny Roy continues the argument that ethnicity represents a major political force, this time in China with the policies followed towards Tibet. Roy notes that China is a multi-ethnic state but one that is rarely examined in this light. And the Chinese problem in Tibet, he argues is one of 'Asia's most destructive and tragic ethnic conflicts.'

As with the chapter on the Balkans, Roy finds that the character of Tibetan ethnicity is different and in part unique and details the its development and the clash between Tibetan and Han groups showing the barriers between them. He points to the notion that Chinese occupation since 1959 can be equated to ethnic genocide, with 1.2 million Tibetans killed since the invasion in 1959. Genocide is not only a political tool: China has devised a policy of actively 'settling' Tibet with Han from core areas of China. It could also be argued that China sees it as a periphery and therefore exploitable from the perspective of extracting natural resources which are then transferred to enrich core areas of China.

Aspects of Tibetan ethnic hostility towards the Chinese can be seen in their various efforts at rebellion and the transferral of any form of political loyalty and legitimacy to the Dalai Lama and his government in exile. On the other hand the Chinese state clearly sees any manifestation of Tibetan ethnicity as a security threat. What is different about this case? To begin with Roy argues that it was not affected by the end of the cold war as were so many other cases and it had little if any connection with the revivalism of ethnic movements in other parts of the world. Perhaps the only effect of globalisation in the Tibetan scenario has been the massive influx of karaoke bars in the capital of Llhasa.

Tibetan ethnicity on the other hand reflects an attempt to stay alive, to preserve and maintain tradition in the face of cultural genocide. Roy also notes that tribalism is similar here however because it reflects modern political developments in two ways. It provides evidence that imperialism as a form of politics is redundant and spent and secondly it shows how the costs of ethnic domination have increased vis-a-vis the globalisation of liberal values of democracy and human rights. Around the world on a global scale, liberal democratization is making inroads even if it is just in forcing the issues (like East Timor in Indonesia, or slave labour in Burma) among many others. Dictatorships who violate human rights can no longer afford to sit comfortably with these problems because of the ascendancy of these values following the end of the cold war and the increased level of attention to these as a result of improved communications and an increasingly globalised media.

In Sri Lanka: Tribalism and Leadership in a Demotic state, A. Jeyaratnam Wilson continues in the vein suggested by Trond Gilberg when he demonstrates the potent leadership influence over the ethnic question. He provides a rich and detailed overview of the divisions in Sri Lanka through the medium of elites in the troubled state.

To some extent Wilson deals with the same kinds of problems that multi-ethnic states face in developing political institutions that can accommodate different ethnic minorities. As we have seen throughout the volume state building in multi-ethnic communities is a common theme. And he argues strongly that Sri Lanka has failed in this regard and this is one of the continuing sources of debilitation for the state from its post-colonial beginnings, the Sinhalese leadership expressed its preference for Sinhalese Buddhists to the exclusion of 'others' in its development of the Demotic state, a point touched upon by Nergis Canefe in her chapter on Turkey.

State building in these circumstances is a complex process, much more so than a political party seeking approval from the majority group. Instead of using Lijphart's model of inter-elite accommodation in consociationalism, Sri Lankan elites deliberately chose the demotic model in which competing parties appealed to the ethnic majority at the expense of the ethnic minority. By and large the result was large scale ethnic, armed insurrection and Wilson clearly believes this could have been avoided if the elites had chosen other more accommodating types of policy.

Alexander Johnston continues the general theme of the text in dealing with the 'new' tribalism in post cold war Africa, an area that many commentators see in reference to a 'pejorative' form of discourse on tribalism and ethnicity. Images of warring tribes, savagery, primitivism and barbarism have after all been part and parcel of imperial discourses and traditional colonial views of the 'Dark' Continent. And some of these perspectives would appear to have found dramatic confirmation if we are to believe the manifestations of state collapse and institutional decline in countries like Liberia, Rwanda, Somalia and even Zaire more recently.

Communalism and identity appear as driving forces in these conflicts, which are taking place in the most underdeveloped areas of the global economy. But Johnston has to qualify any assertions that politics and ethnicity 'here' is driven by tribal ambitions. We, as he notes, experience difficulties in generalising about Africa, the problem of historical perspective and the use of tribalism itself as part of the discourse. What stands out more than ever from our global and comparative perspective is the variety and difference in ethnic conflict we witness. The historical perspective is also very important as many of the chapters suggest; Johnston talks about the 'longue duree' (or the long term) as a means of assessing the impact and influence of this phenomenon. As he notes tribalism as a term has problematic and pejorative associations within the African continent, noting Vails comments for instance that 'If one disapproves of the phenomenon, it is 'tribalism'; if one is less judgemental, it is 'ethnicity.'

As an expert on contemporary conflict in Africa, Johnston has picked four case studies which aim to explore these terms and these are Liberia, Rwanda, Somalia and finally South Africa (and in specific Kwazulu-Natal). From the beginning case of Liberia, we note there is a similarity between Gilberg's version of tribalism as a form of anarchy and lawlessness and Johnston's descriptions of some of the more bizarre aspects of behaviour in the Liberian conflict including 'the youth of the combatants, their ritualistic behaviour, the role of drugs and popular culture, even cannibalism.' He deals with the explanations of human disaster here noting the ethnic aspects of the incoherence of the violence, its ritualistic forms and the role of modernisation in the literature of ethnic conflict here. Rwanda, in many ways represents the archetype of post cold war ethnic conflict: an area which has experienced extreme genocidal violence.

And again Johnston notes the global factors across the board which have contributed to its genocidal character. These include economic decline and the role of the IMF; pressure to create more democratic space by Western donors as well as neighbouring states, difficulties and prevarications by the UN over humanitarian intervention as well as the 'equivocal' role and status of international NGO's. Pointing to such factors Johnston can dismiss the mistaken and misplaced efforts at classifying Rwanda as a primordialist struggle. On the other hand, Somalia does not fit in neatly to the ethnic reviewers categories and appears as a difficult anomaly to perceived patterns. Somalia is different because its inhabitants share similar traditions, concepts and languages. Despite aspirations to nation-state status, we have witnessed in the early 1990's the breakdown of Somalia into warlordism, anarchic pillage and bankruptcy.

Finally, Johnston deals with South Africa, where he is based and a society which has known more than its fair share of political violence and ethnic conflict. This situation has been exacerbated in the post cold war period. Here he analyses the 'ambiguous' Zulu factor and the notion that 'perhaps nowhere else in the world does the term "tribalism" provoke such academic and political mistrust as it does in South Africa.' Given the political history of apartheid, this should not be surprising. The spotlight here is on Kwa-Zulu Natal, home of the Zulu's and the Inkatha Freedom Party (IFP), their political corollary. Since the mid 1980's the African National Congress

(ANC) and the IFP have been fighting a very bitter low level conflict over political and territorial control for Natal. Johnston specifically deals with the politics of this ethnic and power struggle and the role that tradition plays in it. And lastly in his conclusion he compares all of these cases with reference to the ethnic question in their specific conflicts.

In her chapter on Turkey, Nergis Canefe draws our attention further to how ethnicity is mobilized for political ends, and again specifically in the post cold war period scenario of Turkey. She notes the way in which tribalism has unique characteristics which attempt to reconstruct the past in an effort to imagine a different future. And she argues it represents a 'modern ideology that hinges upon utopianism'. Much of this teleological effort is similar to what we have seen in Gilberg's piece and Johnston's discussion of the phenomenon of 'new' tribalism. With its ideological populism here, the notion of the 'tribal' dwells upon a collective memory (of previously held territory) which seeks to justify it and sustain it in large measure. Every tribal or ethnic group in this sense must have an 'other' whether it is the Croats to the Serbs, the Xhosa to the Zulu's, or the Tutsi's to the Hutus and in this case the Alevi's to the Turks. Canefe shows how the Turkish extreme right have targeted religious minorities and in particular the heterodox Muslim Alevi community.

Behind an official facade of territorial and civic nationalism, Turkish ambitions hid a mask of ethnic consciousness and efforts to promote a demotic Turkish identity. Again we find similarities with Wilson's notion of the demotic Sri Lankan state. Canefe continues by looking at the links between the demotic idea and the Turkish, ultra-national right, and its various historical forms and development, again a reflection of the comparative and historical nature of the text. Nearly 20 million Alevi's live in Turkey, practising their unique traditional brand of Islamic faith and Canefe traces the way in which they have been historically targeted. In fact most Sunni fundamentalists believe that the Alevi's are inferior to both Sunni and Shii traditions. The latter groups have made vociferous claims that the former engage in defamatory religious ceremonies, incest and do not engage in fasting.

The Alevi's have been subject to harassment and even massacre from the extreme right throughout their history. In the end, tribal and ethnic projects for Canefe, derive from a strong sense of self justification and the need to establish and preserve an identity. It shares a reformulation of identity based on mythical historical events that are constantly subject to reinvention and revision. In this the author shows how utopian impulses of tribalism really foster ideals of 'revenge' and hatred rather than rejuvenation.

Ethnic unrest and communal strife have proved fairly resilient forms of conflict throughout developing and developed countries during the 20th century. Protestant Loyalists in Northern Ireland celebrate the victory of

King William of Orange over the Catholic King, James 11 at the battle of the Boyne in 1690 with parades and marches every twelfth of July. The answer to questions in the wake of artillery attacks during the Bosnian war of the 1990's typically started with reference to the year 925. Historical myths and memories of atrocities committed on either side are fuel for the ethnic fire. But some have argued that even within traditional nation-states, growing tribal sentiments are in fact a rearguard action, a form of comfort to the complications that modern, individual capitalism has wrought in the late 20th century as well as an attempt to free themselves from the domination of what are seen as foreign elites. In much of this volume we seek to learn what is 'political' about tribalism and how we can locate ethnicity within the realm of the political.

If the glue that binds multi-ethnic communities together is increasingly diluted, the bonds between members of similar ethnic groups, religious persuasions and cultural organisations will inevitably be exacerbated. Imagined communities may be inventions of one sort or another but in reality they often tend to have very real and deadly consequences.

NOTES

1 See Jacques Rupnik, 'Europe's New Frontiers: Remapping Europe' in *Daedalus* Vol. 123, No. 3, Summer 1994, p. 95.
2 See Michael Freeman Death Toll from the war in our midst' in the *Times Higher Educational Supplement* (5/3/93) p. 23.
3 See Morton H. Fried, *The Notion of the Tribe* (California: Cummings, 1975) p. 3. In this sense it was used to denote the Israelites.
4 For a useful account of the historical roots of the Rwandan conflict see Basil Davidson, 'On Rwanda' in the *London Review of Books* (18/8/94) p. 6.
5 See E. Colson, 'Contemporary tribes and the development of nationalism' in June Held (Ed.), *Essays on the Problem of Tribe* (Proceedings of the 1967 Annual Meeting), (Seattle: University of Washington Press, 1968), p. 203.
6 See Manning Nash (1989). *The Cauldron of Ethnicity in the Modern World* (Chicago: University of Chicago Press), p. 127.

Chapter Two

Theories of Ethnicity, Tribalism and Nationalism

Michael Freeman

THE RETURN OF THE PRIMITIVE?

The end of the Cold War produced an immediate and widespread belief that the United Nations would at last be able to make significant advances towards its aim of maintaining the international rule of law and that the diffusion of the principles of human rights, democracy and market economics would promote its goals of freedom and development. Few foresaw that this vision of a new world order would rapidly be threatened by the outbreak of several violent ethnic and nationalist conflicts. The revitalized universalist ideals of the UN appeared to be challenged by a new particularism.

The perception that the end of the Cold War released a pent-up torrent of ethnonationalist conflict was, however, to a significant degree illusory, for such conflict had been pervasive during the Cold-War period. Not only had the decolonization movements, which had been a prominent feature of world politics in the early decades after the Second World War, contained a strongly ethnonationalist character, but ethnic unrest had also been, in varying degrees, part of the politics of the first, second and third worlds.[1] Nonetheless, the collapse of Communist authoritarianism and the trend towards democratization created new opportunities and new motives for ethnonationalist mobilizations.

These developments have been very disturbing for observers of liberal democracy, for the political theory of liberal democracy is based on the liberty and equality of individual citizens, and has traditionally denied the political significance of ethnicity, confining it to the private sphere of society. The historical project of liberalism has been to emancipate the individual from traditional and authoritarian collectivities. The liberal-democratic state was to be the guarantor of the security of the individual. Liberalism has always been challenged by rival theories that rejected what they considered to be its excessive individualism and accorded more value to the solidaristic community. Insofar as actual liberal-democratic states and the capitalist economies associated with them have failed to provide many citizens with material well-being, a sense of community, and, in some cases, even physical safety, ethnonationalist ideologies promising all of these have attracted support.[2]

Ethnonationalism also threatens liberalism because it is infused with emotion and, it seems, often with fanaticism, whereas liberalism is committed to reason and toleration. The persistence of ethnonationalism has therefore called into question the Enlightenment belief in progress through the spread of reason. The Cold War, it has been suggested, constituted the hegemony of Enlightenment rationalism in its liberal and Marxist forms. The global penetration of Enlightenment rationalism, however, provoked an ethnonationalist reaction. The end of the Cold War has thus dispelled the illusion that this hegemony was ever as strong as it had appeared to be (Howard, 1995).[3] In this situation, it has also been argued, the international community has, by its practical ineffectiveness, encouraged the belief that power in the contemporary world comes out of the barrel of an ethnic gun (Posen, 1993: 33–4).

In response to the outbreak of new ethnonationalist wars and massacres, liberal scholars have replaced the short-lived talk of 'the new world order' with references to 'the new tribalism'.[4] In this discourse the term 'tribalism' is usually not defined and the reader is implicitly invited to accept its vaguely pejorative connotations. It has such connotations because it is derived from earlier discourses of evolution. Darwin himself believed that tribal peoples had a low morality because they had limited sympathies, and practised the virtues almost exclusively in relation to members of the same tribe, while they did not regard vices as crimes if they were practised on other tribes.[5] In the early post-colonial period, modernization theorists, influenced by functionalism, considered tribalism to be particularistic and ascriptive rather than universalistic and achievement-oriented, and therefore dysfunctional for the development of a modern society. They used the term 'tribalism' to denigrate loyalties to what were supposed to be more primitive collectivities, and dignified as 'nationalism' commitment to the modern nation-state.[6] A recent analysis of contemporary global politics follows this tradition by defining tribalism as the retreat by individuals, driven by fear and confusion, into ethnic communities.[7] However, this analysis offers no clear conceptual account of the relation between 'tribalism' and 'ethnicity'. The study of ethnicity and nationalism is notorious for its confused concepts, and the reintroduction of the term 'tribalism' has not contributed to their clarification (Connor, 1994, Chapter four, especially 107–8).

Underlying the lack of conceptual clarity in treating the relation between tribalism and ethnicity is a failure to make an empirical distinction between pre-modern tribes, which were commonly stateless societies, and modern ethnopolitical groups, which seek their goals in a world of states. Contemporary ethnonationalist conflicts are, therefore, not best understood simply as threats by primitive forces to a supposedly civilized world order. This interpretation is tempting because ethnonationalist combatants often commit gross and apparently frenzied violations of human rights. Yet the primitive/civilized distinction rests on a view of history, according to which once there was the primitive, the irrational, and the violent; then there was progress towards the civilized, the rational, and the orderly; a progress, however, that has been interrupted from time to time by reversions to primitive barbarism. This view is, however, flawed. Although early human groups may well have engaged in wars and massacres, they generally lacked the motives and means for protracted campaigns or extensive destruction. The first institutions to practise large-scale warfare were probably city-states with imperial ambitions. These states were based on the production of an economic surplus, social stratification, urbanization, religion, art, and writing. In a word, they were civilized.[8] Tribes may certainly be aggressive but states have generally been more destructive. Contemporary ethnonationalist conflicts are, therefore, not simply reversions to the primitive, since they take place within modern state arenas. Neither the concept of tribal hatreds nor that of the struggle between the primitive and the civilized is sufficient to explain these conflicts, because they have been structured by the 'civilizing' processes of state-building. [9]

THE NATION-STATE AND ITS LEGITIMACY

Distinctions between tribes, ethnic groups and nations have rarely been made systematically or precisely in social science. Smith argues that the confusion has arisen from the widespread belief of sociologists that there has been an evolutionary progression from small, primitive and solitary communities to large, complex and impersonal societies. Many writers, he says, have assumed that the development of technology, the growth of population and the elaboration of the division of labour would lead to the assimilation of earlier small communities into ever larger, more centralized and rationalized economic and political organizations. According to this theory, modernity would dissolve both tribalism and ethnic communities through the process of nation-building (Smith, 1986: 153).

Since both tribes and ethnic groups were destined to be absorbed by the modern nation, the distinction between them was theoretically unimportant (Connor, 1994: 32–4). When the persistence of ethnic politics became too strong to ignore, the first response of social scientists was to interpret it merely as conservative resistance to modernization. This interpretation ignores, in Smith's view, the ethnic character of the most developed states (Smith, 1986: 91, 207, 216; 1995: 101–2, 106). All nations, he argues, have an ethnic character, but not all ethnic groups are nations, for nations are, or aspire to be self-governing. This means that the distinction between tribes and ethnic groups, on the one hand, and nations, on the other, is contingent, for tribes and ethnic groups may come to demand self-government (Connor, 1994: 213–4). The blurred borderlines between these concepts are further confused by the fact that ethnic groups and nations seem to be both enduring and mutable. They can last for centuries, yet they can also come into being, change, and disappear quite rapidly (Smith, 1986: 17, 129, 169, 210–1).

The nation-state has become the principal unit of modern politics. Its name implies that the legitimacy of the state depends on the value ascribed to the national community, but it suppresses the fact that almost all societies are polyethnic. Because states are legitimated in part by reference to a particular ethnonationalist culture, polyethnicity is a basis for potential conflict. This potential is particularly disturbing for liberal democracies, which seek to ground their legitimacy in equality of citizenship and the protection of individual rights. Neither the idea of the nation-state nor that of liberal democracy, however, makes states immune from ethnonationalist challenge. *It is precisely the instability of the conceptual boundaries between ethnicity, nation and state that constitutes an inherent weakness in the structure of the contemporary political world.* (Smith, 1986: 224–5; 1995: 103–9). Yet there is considerable variability in the stability of nation-states. Theories of ethnonationalism, therefore, should account for the formation, persistence and change of ethnic groups, their political mobilization, and their propensity to stabilize or to subvert the state.

THEORIES

Ethnonationalism has attracted a number of familiar explanatory approaches by social scientists. Thus, we have structuralist, interpretive and rational-choice theories of ethnonationalist actions. It has also generated some distinctive theoretical debates, such as that between primordialists and instrumentalists. Smith has offered us the most comprehensive survey of these theories, but his own conclusions are by no means merely an eclectic synthesis. He insists on the *subjective* character of ethnonationalist identity, which depends on meanings, memories, myths, symbols, sentiments, values, attitudes and perceptions to mobilize people for ethnopolitical action. Structural explanations, he argues, are insensitive to these elements of identity, which can be captured only by an interpretive approach. Instrumentalism, which treats identity as situational rather than pervasive, cannot adequately account for the explosive and sometimes irrational nature of ethnonationalism (Smith, 1986: 7, 22, 46, 208, 211; 1995: 30, 39–40, 159). Hardin agrees with Smith that puzzling and disturbing ethnonationalist behaviour may be explained by the strange beliefs of the actors, but argues that these beliefs themselves require explanation. This may show that there is a hidden instrumental rationality to superficially irrational actions.[10] (Hardin, 1995: 145, 147, 160–1).

18

Whereas Smith sees ethnonationalist motivations as both enduring and contingent, and Hardin believes them often to be instrumental, primordialists consider ethnicity to be a fundamental feature of human nature that underlies and constrains the impact of its contingent, situational and instrumental manifestations. Thus the theory of ethnonationalism must clarify and articulate coherently the supposedly primordial, the persistent, the contingent and the instrumental elements of ethnopolitical action.

Primordialism

The concept of primordialism was introduced into social theory by Shils, who derived it from Tönnies' famous distinction between *Gesellschaft* and *Gemeinschaft*. *Gesellschaft* referred to societies based on the values of individualism and rationalism, such as those of the modern West. *Gemeinschaft* denoted communities characterized by strong and comprehensive solidarity. It was to be found in families, some other primary groups, villages, and tribal societies. Shils conceived of primordial attachments as those of the *Gemeinschaft*, which had a certain ineffable significance and consequently a coercive quality.[11]

Shils' conception of primordial ties was taken up by Geertz, who applied it to post-colonial societies. Geertz defined a primordial attachment as one that stemmed from the culturally 'given', from a sense of natural affinity rather than from social interaction. Among the primordial relations were those based on assumed kinship, as in tribes. The power of primordial 'givens', Geertz thought, was rooted in the non-rational foundations of the personality. Patterns of primordial identification and cleavage in new states were usually the product of centuries of gradual crystallization. Modern societies sought to raise the political above the level of the primordial. In modernizing societies, however, with weak traditions of civil politics, primordial ties tended persistently to form the basis of political legitimacy. Primordial politics consequently challenged the politics of modern nationalism.[12] Geertz's thesis was further developed by Harold Isaacs, who, in 1975, argued that the collapse of old power systems and the fragility of new ones had produced confusion and fear, leading to a global process of retribalization or neo-primordialism, in which people clung to the vestiges of a more stable past in a search for physical and emotional security.[13]

Primordialism, by emphasising the strength and non-rational character of certain social ties, explains the persistence of ethnic bonds and their power to override other motives, especially those based on economic calculation. It also explains the willingness of individual members of ethnic groups to sacrifice themselves for the collective good. However, primordialism has attracted a number of strong criticisms. Its claim that identities and attachments are natural, ancient, prior to social interaction and ineffable is said to have been refuted by sociological evidence. This shows that ethnic identities and attachments persist only as the result of continuing social interaction. They are subject to innovation, revision and revitalization. Primordialism is also insensitive to the structural and cultural differences among those societies in which ethnic revivals have occurred; it underemphasises the role of manipulation in ethnopolitical mobilization; and it ignores the fact that individuals risk their lives for collectivities that are not primordial, such as those based on class or ideology. Primordialism leaves ethnic sentiment mysterious, it is said, and therefore lacks explanatory power.[14]

In response to this critique, there has been an attempt to reformulate primordialism. According to the revised version, the most fundamental human group is normally the family. But humans do not belong only to their immediate biological family, but to a larger cultural collectivity, such as clan, tribe or nation. Their survival, safety and flourishing depend on family, community and territory. This is why community ties may seem sacred, ineffable and coercive. This is why individuals may be willing to sacrifice themselves for the good of the community. Kinship, real and presumed, is a pervasive pattern of human orientation. According to revised primordialism, ethnic sentiments are extensions of kinship sentiments (Van den Berghe, 1981: 15–6, 18).[15]

The dispute about primordialism can be resolved if we refuse to choose between two extreme positions. Geertz himself did not treat primordialism as static, but rather claimed that the replacement of the relatively remote colonial regime by the penetrative, mobilizing, modernizing post-colonial state *stimulated* primordial sentiments. In this view, ethnic revival is not explained by primordialism *tout court* but by the impact of the modernizing state on primordial ties. Thus, primordialism is not merely a conservative reaction to modernizing change but an instrument for taking advantage of it. Primordialism thereby becomes not opposition to, but part of the modernizing process. The distinction between the primordial and the instrumentalist conceptions of ethnicity is, therefore, sometimes over-drawn, for primordial identities can be used as instruments for the furtherance of various interests, and, while these identities can be manipulated, mobilized and changed, primordial ties provide the basis for these processes (Geertz, 1963: 120, 123; McKay, 1982: 405–7, 410). Ethnic groups, as Horowitz has pointed out, can be placed at various points along the birth-choice continuum. Most people, he maintains, are born into the ethnic group in which they will die, and ethnic groups consist mostly of those who have been born into them. However, individuals and groups can change their ethnic identity. Ethnic groups vary in the fluidity they are prepared to tolerate at their margins and their willingness to adapt their identity to changing conditions. Whether membership of ethnic groups is ascribed or achieved should be viewed in terms not of a dichotomy but of a continuum (Horowitz, 1985: 55–6).

Family values

The revised version of primordialism, therefore, treats ethnic groups and even nations as enlarged quasi-families. Horowitz maintains that, in many societies, it is difficult to say where the extended family ends and ethnicity begins (Horowitz, 1985: 60). Insofar as partiality in favour of family members is normal, and ethnic groups are like extended families, the psychological basis for ethnic discrimination is laid. Where the ethnic group constitutes a tribe or a nation, violence within the group is normally condemned while violence against outsiders is more likely to be tolerated or even praised. This process of identifying internal supporters and external enemies is said to relieve individual anxieties about identity and security. While the in-group culture provides both practical and metaphysical support, the out-group, with its alien culture, presents both a practical and metaphysical threat.[16] Where ethnic group members believe that kinship and ethnicity are indistinguishable, because, for example, they subscribe to a myth of the common ancestry of the ethnic group, the self and the group are mutually incorporated in each other, and thereby the distinction between self-interest and self-sacrifice for the group is blurred, if not wholly eliminated (Horowitz, 1985: 64; Smith, 1986: 24).

The conception of ethnicity as extended kinship has some plausibility, but it is contradicted by evidence that ethnic sentiments may come into being only in contingent situations (van der Dennen, 1987: 17). The theoretical basis for understanding the fluidity of ethnic sentiments is not only that kinship can take varied forms and relate in various ways to other commitments, but also that, even if ethnicity has a kinship basis, it has to be culturally elaborated (Smith, 1986: 21, 26). While a common culture can bind a group together and differentiate it from others, cultural elements are hard to fix, and it is thus difficult to close the frontiers of an ethnic group that is defined in terms of its shared culture. Ethnic cultures are often based on myths and memories, and these are readily manipulable (Smith, 1986). Ethnicity is also commonly tied to territory, but Horowitz has shown that changes in territorial boundaries can lead to significant changes in ethnic identities. Individuals may also regard each other as ethnic strangers in one place, but as ethnic kin in another where they may discover both common cultural commitments and common material interests in the face of competitors from radically different cultures. Horowitz argues that ethnic identity can be shifted upwards or downwards to more inclusive or narrower levels to meet situational exigencies. Ethnic and national groups can similarly fuse or split apart. Such processes may combine 'primordial' sentiments and strategic calculations (Horowitz, 1985: 66–70).

Sociobiology

The link that is commonly made between kinship and ethnicity has raised the question as to whether ethnicity can be explained by sociobiology. This takes us onto a terrain that is exceptionally controversial, both ideologically and scientifically. However, sociobiology promises an explanation that is both deep and general, and its claims must be both understood and evaluated.

Sociobiologists who have turned their attention to ethnicity have noted that ethnocentrism, xenophobia and group conflict are common among humans, and their motivation appears often to be irrational and even unconscious. These facts suggest that they may have a biological basis. Biology has a general theory to explain them: the theory of inclusive fitness. This theory says that genes will spread if their carriers act to increase, not only their own reproductive success, but also that of other individuals carrying the same genes. The theory holds that humans are genetically predisposed to ethnocentrism, because selection favours those groups whose members prefer their kin and who develop cultural (i.e., ethnic) markers to identify them.[17]

Sociobiologists attach considerable significance to the similarities in the survival strategies of human and other animals. For example, many non-human animals and human infants are attracted to the familiar and exhibit aversion to strangers (van der Dennen, 1987: 19–20). However, if there is a genetic basis for the fear of strangers, its explanatory power is probably quite weak. Fearful infants, for example, can learn complex patterns of response to strangers (van der Dennen, 1987: 20; Vine, 1987: 69; Flohr, 1987: 198; Meyer, 1987: 93). Sociobiology therefore rejects genetic determinism. It suggests that there is an evolutionary basis of ethnic behaviour, but admits that biological explanations must be supplemented by those of the social sciences (van den Berghe, 1986: 247; Reynolds, 1987: 213–4; Meyer, 1987: 88).

The most systematic attempt to combine sociobiology with social science to develop an integrated theory of ethnicity has been made by van den Berghe. In contrast to the interpretive sociologist, Smith, who emphasises the subjective nature of ethnicity, van den Berghe maintains that a science of ethnic behaviour cannot employ a wholly subjective definition of ethnicity, since ethnic subjects may define their ethnicity differently. He proposes instead that the proto-typical ethnic group is bounded socially by inbreeding and spatially by territory. His methodology is explicitly reductionist, materialist and individualist. He claims that its assumptions are similar to those of rational-choice theory. At the core of the ethnic group is the egoistic individual, who is predicted to behave as a selfish maximizer. The model neither assumes nor precludes rationality, free will, or consciousness. It conceives of ethnic behaviour as channelled into choices with outcomes that tend to be maximizing for individuals (van den Berghe, 1981: 18, 23–4; 1986: 248–9, 255, 259–60).

Van den Berghe's assumption of selfish maximization raises three problems. The first concerns the conception of the selfish individual. Evolutionary genetics requires that human individuals act in favour of their offspring and not of themselves. Van den Berghe calls this 'nepotistic selfishness' in contrast with selfishness *tout court* (van den Berghe, 1986: 260–1). His theory of ethnicity admits that sometimes nepotistic selfishness trumps egoistic selfishness, and at other time the reverse may be true. Thus, he lacks a consistent conception of selfish maximization (van den Berghe, 1981: 11, 37, 38–9, 254–8; Vine, 1987: 71).

Van den Berghe is even less consistent about what individuals are supposed to maximize. Sometimes he appeals to material interests, but at others he concedes that religious beliefs or social status can be powerful motivators.[18] (van den Berghe, 1986: 248; 1981: 259). These assumptions are not integrated with the thesis that individuals maximize fitness. Van den Berghe argues that over the long evolutionary haul cultural arrangements which enhance the reproductive success of their carriers have, by and large, been selected for (van den Berghe, 1981: 255; 1986: 257). This argument does not, however, conform to van den Berghe's reductionist individualism. The selection argument remains at the collective level of culture, and is reducible to the level of gene 'behaviour' and its consequences. Genes that favour nepotistic behaviour will enhance their own replication more effectively than genes favouring random co-operation (van den Berghe, 1981: 7–8). However, neither the argument from evolutionary selection nor that from gene behaviour provides explanations at the level of individual motivation.

The third problem is how van den Berghe can explain altruism with his assumption of egoism. Evolutionary genetics can explain altruistic behaviour by individuals if it can show that the proportion of altruism genes in the population is increased and that consequently natural selection will produce an increasing proportion of altruistic individuals in the future. The theory assumes that 'selfish' genes seek to reproduce themselves through kin selection. But it explains altruism only if selfish genes select altruistic kin. It is not clear why they should and there is therefore a gap in the explanation of altruism. The gap is partly filled by the concept of 'reciprocal altruism', which proposes that non-kin beneficiaries of altruistic acts reciprocate the altruism at a later time.[19] (Russell, 1987: 118, 123; Johnson et al., 1987: 157–8; Tönnesmann, 1987: 177). However, the theory still fails to explain how selfish genes produce individual choices and how such choices produce altruism. Van den Berghe's assumption of egoistic, quasi-rational choice does not solve this problem.

Another weakness of the sociobiological theory of ethnicity is that it predicts preference for kin whereas ethnic beliefs about kinship are often false. Van den Berghe responds by claiming that ethnic groups must be based on a credible conception of common descent, and such conceptions are credible only if they are partly true. Ethnicity is common descent, real or putative. When putative, it must be validated by common historical experience (van den Berghe, 1986: 255–6; 1981: 16). Van den Berghe must, however, explain why common experience is a sufficient substitute for real kinship and why large national groups lacking common historical experience can show solidarity in times of crisis (Reynolds, 1980: 311–2; Hardin, 1995: 48). It is doubtful whether he does this. Kin ties may have a biological base, but they can be culturally extended well beyond biological relationships. Biology thus explains very little ethnocentrism (Johnson et al., 1987: 159; Flohr, 1987: 199–200; Reynolds et al., 1987b: xix; Vine, 1987: 77; Russell, 1987: 130; van den Berghe, 1986: 258; Tönnesmann, 1987: 175; Reynolds, 1980: 308).

Van den Berghe claims that his theory is more general than rational-choice theories of ethnicity and that the latter are special cases of the former. He asserts, however, that ethnic attachments are primordial, biological, and non-rational (van den Berghe, 1986: 260–1; 1981: 35, 255). Clearly, rational-choice theories cannot be special cases of a theory which treats ethnicity as non-rational. Shaw and Wong seek to reconcile sociobiology and rational-choice theory by postulating that inclusive fitness is among the 'ultimate utilities that all individuals seek to maximize'. Their approach is more consistently individualistic than van den Berghe's, but it leaves unsolved the problem that individual egoism may sometimes be incompatible with ethnocentrism.[20]

Ethnicity, according to van den Berghe, is primordial, but ethnic behaviour is variable, because humans are intelligent, self-conscious organisms, capable of learning from their interactions with their environment, who often manipulate ethnic boundaries and engage in ethnic 'commuting', moving from ethnicity to ethnicity when it suits them. Culture has, therefore, some explanatory autonomy from genetic evolution (van den Berghe, 1981: 18–9, 21–2, 251–2, 254–6, 260–1; 1986: 258). The value of sociobiology in explaining ethnic behaviour is consequently limited.

Nevertheless, Van den Berghe claims that the biological basis of ethnic sentiments helps to explain their resistance to dissolution by the modern state. Ethnicity is a persistent basis of political legitimacy and has often proved to be a stronger bond than citizenship. The more unlike groups are, the more violent conflict between them will be (van den Berghe, 1981: 17, 27–8, 40, 57, 62, 75, 77, 257). However, both the motivation and the justifications given for collective violence are cultural, and often altruistic rather than selfish. Thus, cultural difference may explain violent conflict better than biological difference. Conflict may also be caused by competition for scarce resources. It is not clear that sociobiology can explain inter-group conflict better than rival theories that appeal to material interests without reference to biology. Sociobiology also distracts our attention from non-ethnic bases of solidarity and from intra-ethnic conflicts (van der Dennen, 1987: 38–9, 43; Irwin, 1987: 153; Reynolds, 1987: 213; Silverman, 1987: 114–6).

Sociobiology may help to explain the pervasiveness of ethnicity, but sociobiological tendencies are very general and cannot explain the details of human actions. Ethnocentrism is far from universal: co-ethnics fight each other; ethnic groups form alliances with those to whom they are not biologically related; and ethnic groups come into being and dissolve, sometimes in an instrumental manner. The admission by sociobiologists that the biological becomes social only when it is culturally elaborated places severe limits on the explanatory power of sociobiology, for it allows that its central concepts, such as 'kinship' and 'ethnicity', are socially constructed and have at best a variable relationship to biology (Reynolds, 1987: 214–5; van der Dennen, 1987: 16–7).

The Political Sociology of Ethnonationalism

Even if ethnic groups have a biological basis, then, they are culturally constituted. However, ethnicity is not simply a cultural basis for politics, for politics can decisively shape ethnicity. Elites can mobilize ethnic groups for political purposes, reshape their identities and even form new ethnic groups and nations. The construction of modern states has typically involved the bureaucratic incorporation and, to some extent, the cultural integration of diverse ethnic communities. The concepts of the sovereign, territorial state and of universal citizenship have been used to constitute the idea of the political nation. The penetrative and comprehensive reach of the modern state tends to produce a common life and a common culture (Smith, 1986).

States may, therefore, help to create nationalist sentiments, but nationalism may also be an ideology of state élites which is not accepted by all the people. The modern state is a powerful material force, but its legitimacy depends on its claim to represent a nation. The actual relations between states and nations are confused by modern terminology, which often treats the concepts of 'state' and 'nation' as interchangeable. This confusion has made it hard to conceptualize the challenge to so-called nation-states by ethnonationalist movements. The so-called 'international community', which is in fact an exclusive club of state élites, is extremely reluctant to recognize the political aspirations of nations when these are rejected by states. The consequence is widespread ethnonationalist violence and severe repression of ethnonationalist groups by states (Connor, 1994: 40–1, 90, 95, 196–7; Horowitz, 1985: 88; Smith, 1986: 150, 221, 225; Freeman, 1996).

In contrast to the primordialists, Smith emphasises the contingency of modern nationalism, while insisting also on crucial elements of ethnic continuity in its formation. In this view, nation-building is a continuing process, which may involve the destruction, incorporation, transformation or invention of putatively primordial groups. The fact that the modern nation-state does not replace, but is constituted by ethnic ties provides both the cultural and structural bases for ethnonationalist challenges, as incorporation into the modern state often involves real and/or perceived ethnic inequalities. Nationalist ideologies offer a degree of psychological security by telling stories of historical continuity and territorial unity, but these stories are particularistic, including some and excluding others (Smith, 1986: 17, 132–3, 149–51, 156, 166, 175, 212, 214; 1995: 40–1; 1995: 100–2; Connor, 1994: 36–7).

States adopting strong assimilationist policies may well provoke resistance from those who are unwilling to give up the identities, values and practical benefits that they may derive from group membership. The solidarity of relatively small and local particularistic communities can provide a psychological and material security which their members perceive as threatened by the impersonality of the modern state. Ethnic groups may also seek political power to affirm their own worth and to protect their cultural and material interests from distrusted ethnic strangers (Horowitz, 1985: 73, 185, 187–9, 567–8; McGarry and O'Leary, 1993: 20; Smith, 1986: 163–4).

The process of nation-building has been notoriously difficult in post-colonial states. After the departure of the colonial power new ethnic élites have commonly established hegemony over subordinate ethnic groups, thereby precipitating their resistance. The project of modernization has also stimulated the formation of new ethnic groups to mobilize excluded sections of the population in the struggle for power and practical benefits. Experiments in majoritarian electoral democracy have left ethnic minorities at the mercy of majorities. Since subordinated minorities have no electoral solution to their problems, they are tempted to resort to political violence. Thus modernization increases rather than reduces the attraction of ethnic membership. It is precisely to resist or to extract benefits from the modern state that ethnic organization is developed (Horowitz, 1985: 73, 77–8, 81–6, 101, 188, 537; van den Berghe, 1981: 257; Horsman and Marshall, 1994: 216, 235).

Horowitz, analyzing ethnic conflict in post-colonial societies, gives two reasons for scepticism about the once-influential plural-society theory, which holds that ethnic conflict is inherent in ethnically plural societies. Firstly, he argues that ethnic groups are not simply the source of ethnic conflict, but form and dissolve to meet practical needs, and both in anticipation and as a consequence of conflict. Secondly, institutions and leaders can have an important influence on the instigation or mitigation of conflict. Democracy *per se* does not guarantee ethnic peace, since multiparty democracies frequently split along ethnic lines, and thereby generate violent conflict. Trans-ethnic parties are often not viable, so that the best hope may lie with multi-ethnic coalitions. Institutional engineering may nevertheless fail, because either élites or their constituents are motivated by xenophobia and/or see group and/or personal advantage in conflict. Conflict-resolution strategies have little chance of success if the parties are motivated to fight, and settlements commonly are achieved only after war has taken a heavy toll (Horowitz, 1985).

Whereas Horowitz places more emphasis on self-affirmation than on economic motives in explaining ethnic conflict in post-colonial societies, Posen explains such conflicts in post-Communist societies by reference to the fear experienced by vulnerable groups in new states, and their incentive to strike first against potential enemies. The political uncertainty that attends the collapse of states produces psychic insecurity, cognitive distortion and xenophobia. Pre-emptive strikes, which seek quick victories but commonly lead to protracted wars, may, therefore, be either rational responses to potential threats or irrational responses to misperceived others. Ethnic conflict tends to be protracted because pre-emptive strikes provoke reprisals, leading to cycles of violence and suspicion that are hard to end. These cycles are very sensitive to contingent events, including the interventions of political élites, who may be able to mobilize, suppress or resolve the ensuing conflict (Posen, 1993).

In a world in which impersonal state bureaucracies and global markets predominate, ethnonationalism offers a combination of affective solidarity and political power. The liberal-democratic conception of civic nationalism, though still alive in its traditional homelands, is in question because of its apparent inability to deliver to many people either psychic or material satisfactions. The promised empowerment of citizens and accountability of governments are beginning to look implausible as important decisions are taken in remote places. The impact of technological and economic globalization is more complex than simplistic 'end-of-the-nation-state' prophesies allow, but it is re-ordering the world in such a way that many feel excluded and insecure. In this situation the so-called 'new tribalism' (which we have seen is not really new nor tribalism) appears to offer security and a measure of self-determination. As decision-making power moves away to trans-state or supra-state agencies, so sub-state ethnonationalist groups are encouraged to by-pass what they perceive to be their unresponsive nation-states and seek solutions either at higher levels, where the real power is thought to be located, and/or at more local levels, where autonomy seems possible. Globalism and 'tribalism' may, therefore, not only co-exist but mutually support each other (Horsman and Marshall, 1994: ix, 32–40, 76, 89–90, 100, 172, 177, 180, 206–7, 215, 218–20, 222–5, 228–32, 242, 247; Smith, 1995: 145–6; Connor, 1994: 128; McNeill, 1986: 77).

Rational choices

Ethnonationalism is characterized by strong emotions that can inspire self-sacrifice and destruction. It appears ill-suited to explanation by rational-choice theory, which is based on the premise that individuals rationally pursue their interests. Both the individualism and the rationalism of the theory are said by its critics to be called into question by ethnonationalism (Connor, 1994: 74; Hardin, 1995: 3; Hechter, 1995: 53).

Hechter acknowledges that nationalism generates such extreme forms of collective action that it is tempting to explain it by reference to primordial identities, values and sentiments. However, he argues, these concepts are difficult to operationalize and we are thus unable to identify the nature, causes and consequences of these phenomena with epistemological confidence. It is more rigorous to begin with the assumption that ethnonationalist action is rational, and then to treat its affective and irrational elements as deviations. Rational-choice theory is also superior to explanations that invoke emotions, Hechter says, because, whereas the causes of emotions are likely to be idiosyncratically distributed, the causes of instrumental action are likely to be widely shared. The common interests that supposedly underlie instrumental action might suggest structural explanations, for structural theories explain ethnonationalist action by reference to stratification systems and to the common interest of subordinate groups in collective action. The weakness of such explanations, however, is that stratification is much more common than collective action. Rational-choice theory can explain, as structural theories cannot, variations in the incidence and forms of ethnic collective action.[21] (Hechter, 1995: 53–7, 64–5; Hechter et al., 1982: 413–5, 420–1).

Hardin argues that individuals have an interest in joining ethnic groups which provide them with such goods as security, esteem, companionship, sense of purpose, economic opportunity, and a feeling of superiority or actual power over others. Group membership lowers the costs and increases the probability of leading a good life. Identification with and/or membership of an ethnic group is much of the time pleasurable and cheap. Individual members of such groups have an interest in the group's solidarity and power. These are, however, public goods, and rational individuals will bear their share of the collective action necessary to provide them only if free-riding is prevented by the production and distribution of private rewards and punishments. Ethnic groups may be a source of these incentives, but we must explain how such groups come into being. The solution to this problem is that political entrepreneurs have an interest in bearing the start-up costs of ethnic organization in return for expected private benefits to themselves. Collective ethnic action can also be motivated by organizations, originally established solely to provide private goods, that use their resources to allocate private rewards and punishments to prevent free-riding in pursuit of some public good. Conformity with group norms may therefore be rational and not primordial (Hardin, 1995: 16–7, 28, 37, 53–4, 70, 72, 77, 82–3, 89, 149–50, 156–8, 169; Hechter, 1986: 275; Hechter et al., 1982: 417, 420–4).

Rational individuals will participate in collective ethnic action, Hechter argues, only if they believe that such action is likely to be successful, that the group can monitor the contribution of all its members, that it is likely to reward them fairly for their contribution, and that the risk of harm to the individual is low. Organizations can play an important role in the promotion of collective action by controlling information relevant to making such estimates. The probability of ethnic collective action therefore varies positively with organizational resources, monitoring capacity, solidarity, control over information, a history of equitable distribution of benefits and adoption of non-violent tactics, and negatively with organizational size and the capacity and willingness of opponents, including the state, to punish prospective and actual participants (Hechter et al., 1982: 425–8).

Individuals may, therefore, have an interest in supporting ethnic groups, and ethnic groups may have an interest in gaining power over other groups. Thus, ethnic groups have the potential to conflict with other groups (Hardin, 1995: 56). Those groups that are likely to lose more than they will gain from such conflict may have an incentive to establish and support a state: a central political authority designed to regulate inter-group conflict. Since the state, in order to regulate inter-group conflict, must be more powerful than any group or alliance of groups, it may be perceived by some groups as a threat to their collective well-being. Thus the solution of the state to the problem of inter-group conflict may create a new problem of conflict between the state and oppositional groups. Since the state seeks to monopolize the control of violence, oppositional groups may develop and employ the capacity for violence in order to weaken the power of the state. It is, therefore, rational for individuals to support or participate in collective violence against the state if membership of a group is in their interest, if the group has an interest in using violence against the state, and the cost-benefit calculation of both individual and group is positive. This calculation will be affected by the perceived relative strength of state and group. The power of the state depends to a large extent on its freedom from fear of external or internal sanctions if it should use violence. Perceived weakness of the state increases the probability of oppositional violence, which in turn increases the probability of a violent state response (Hechter, 1995: 60–4).

According to the standard conception of instrumental rationality, action is rational as a means to an end. A well-known problem of rational-choice theory is that, if it acknowledges the actual diversity of human ends, it reintroduces the epistemological uncertainty and lack of rigour that it is designed to eliminate. Rational-choice theorists of ethnonationalism do not agree on the solution to this problem. Hechter assumes that individuals seek to maximize their wealth, power and prestige at the margin, because these are fungible goods that every instrumentally motivated individual can be expected to desire. He concedes, however, that these assumptions are insufficient to deduce *ex ante* propositions about the conditions under which ethnic or nationalist groups are likely to develop, and to engage in collective action (Hechter, 1995: 58–9). Hardin emphasises the psychological ease produced by cultural familiarity as a primary benefit of ethnic-group membership, and believes that this provides a reason for xenophobia, since strangers may make group members uneasy. Thus, rational individuals may be motivated to develop xenophobic sentiments and to engage in hostile forms of collective action that have often been thought to be inexplicable by rational-choice theory. Such individuals may also undertake very risky actions on behalf of groups, where such actions seem less costly than withdrawal from the group. Finally, it may be rational for an individual to be a member of a group, and rational for the group to maintain its solidarity, even though its norms of solidarity turn out to be self-destructive (Hardin, 1995: 52, 97, 100–2, 119, 148, 162).

Hechter's attempt to formulate a rigorous rational-choice theory of ethnonationalist collective action is not successful. He seeks to exclude values from his explanations on the ground of their epistemological uncertainty, but appears to reintroduce them by including cultural demands in his conception of instrumental action. He does not claim that individuals actually make the kind of conscious calculations specified by his theory, but only that patterns of collective action occur *as if* they had made these kinds of calculation. Yet he does claim to have identified the 'elementary mechanisms' of ethnic collective action. But, if he does not claim that individuals actually make rational calculations, it is not clear what these elementary mechanisms are supposed to be. He also concedes that instrumental analyses of nationalism 'have failed to meet the challenge of explaining nationalist violence' (Hechter, 1995: 64–5; Hechter et al., 1982: 419–20).

Hardin provides a more subtle account of the rationality of ethnic-group life by allowing psychic ease as an end of action. In doing so, he closes the gap between rational-choice and sociological explanations. Critics of rational-choice explanations of ethnicity continue to insist that plainly irrational factors, such as myths of common ancestry, motivate ethnic collective action (Connor, 1994: 145, 197, 199, 202–6). Hardin counters that it may be rational to subscribe to non-rational beliefs. Resolving this dispute requires a more precise conception of rationality and a more thorough empirical investigation of the motives for ethnic collective action.

CONCLUSION: NATIONALISM AND BEYOND

Primordialist theories of ethnicity and nationalism have been attractive because they appear to explain the strength and persistence of sentiments, which some influential sociological and political theories assumed would be eliminated by the forces of modernization. They are ill-suited, however, to explain the fluidity of ethnic and national attachments. Instrumentalism can show how ethnic identity can be shaped to serve practical needs. The political sociology of writers such as Smith and Connor not only emphasises the cultural dimension of ethnopolitics without subscribing to primordialism, but also relates the contingency of ethnonationalist identities to the political struggles of modernization. Hechter criticises both structural and cultural approaches for their inability to explain variations in ethnonationalist behaviour, but it is not clear that his rational-choice approach is more successful in this. Hardin differs from Hechter in attaching explanatory importance to psychological benefits such as emotional security, and, in doing so, reveals more than Hechter does of the 'elementary mechanisms' of ethnic group formation and action. The strength of Hardin's analysis is that he shows the hidden rationality of apparently irrational features of ethnic-group behaviour. Perhaps he does not fully meet Connor's objection that rational-choice theory cannot explain the emotional force of ethnonationalism. It is also important to emphasise that strategic action takes place in structured situations, so that structural analysis of ethnopolitics, though insufficient for a complete explanation, remains necessary.

Although no theory of ethnonationalist politics is wholly satisfactory, we now have a good understanding of how the two dominant Cold-War ideologies underestimated its importance. Marxist materialism was unable to comprehend the primordial strength of ethnonationalism and consequently its instrumental value. Liberal-democratic capitalism misperceived the way it had bolstered the appeal of citizenship with that of ethnic nationalism and the way that trans-national markets might undermine that appeal. Marxism has generally collapsed into various forms of ethnonationalism, whereas liberal-democratic capitalism has exhibited a mixture of triumphalism and unease in the face of particularistic challenges.

We live, Smith says, in a world of nations. Nationalism, he claims, is the only legitimating principle of politics that commands universal allegiance (Smith, 1986: 129). This is only partly true. Nation-states remain the primary political units of the contemporary world. However, state nationalism is under attack in many places by various forms of ethnic nationalism. Nation-states have a mixed record of success in establishing and maintaining internal order, delivering social justice and co-operating with each other in the interest of inter-state peace. Their legitimacy and consequently their stability are weakened by their inability to control global economic developments, and this in turn stimulates ethnonationalist responses. Despite their various weaknesses, the available theories of ethnonationalist politics explain forces that will have to be reckoned with in any attempt to construct a just and peaceful world order in the foreseeable future.

Smith is partly wrong, therefore, because nations are by no means the only important or legitimate actors in world politics. The previous neglect of ethnonationalism in social science and political theory has led to an over-reaction. Nationalism is now seen by some scholars as both pervasive and normatively desirable.[22] (Smith, 1995; Tamir, 1993; Miller, 1995). Yet all theorists of ethnonationalism recognize its dark side: its tendency to suppress individual freedom, to promote xenophobia, and to instigate ethnic cleansing, massacre and war. Political theory can no longer ignore the force of ethnonationalist politics. But it would be disastrous if it confused force with justice. Ethnonationalism is inward-looking, potentially oppressive and inherently discriminatory. However much it may meet the material and psychological needs of individual group members, it cannot regulate international relations in the interests of peace and justice. In the face of the ethnonationalist shock, universalism has lost confidence, both in practice and in theory. But nationalism is not enough. In a world of nations, of nation-states, of ethnonationalist challengers, of many and diverse non-ethnic solidarities, there is an urgent need to rethink Enlightenment cosmopolitanism in order to change the world, to the understanding of which theories of ethnonationalism have contributed so much.

NOTES

1 See A. Smith (1995) *Nations and Nationalism* (Cambridge: Polity Press), pp. 51–2.
2 See D. Horowitz (1985) *Ethnic Groups in Conflict* (Berkeley: University of California Press), pp. 87–8; A. Smith (1986) *The Ethnic Origins of Nature* (Oxford: Blackwell), pp. 163, 173, 176; 1995, 83; B. Posen, 'The Security Dilemma and Ethnic Conflict' in **Survival** 35(1) 27–41, 1993.
3 See M. Howard, 'Ethnic Conflict and International Security' in *Nations and Nationalism* 1(3): 285–95.
4 See T.M. Franck, 'Post modern tribalism and the right to secession' in C. Brolmann, R. Lefeber and M. Zieck (eds). (1993). *Peoples and Minorities in International Law* (Dordrecht: Martinus Nijhoff)), 3–27; M. Walzer, 'Notes on the New tribalism' in C. Bowen (ed) *Political Restructuring in Europe: Ethical Perspectives* (London: Routledge) Ch. 9; A. Casesse (1995) *Self-Determination of People's: A legal appraisal* (Cambridge: Cambridge University Press).
5 See C. Darwin (1871) *The Descent of Man in Relation to Sex* (London: Murray). 179, 182.
6 See P. Van den Berghe (1981) *The Ethnic Phenomenon* (New York: Praeger); W. Connor (1994) *Ethno-Nationalism: The Quest for Understanding* (Princeton: Princeton University Press).
7 See M. Horsman and A. Marshall (1994) *After the Nation-State: Citizens, Tribalism and the New World Disorder* (London: Harper-Collins).
8 See M. Mann (1986) *The Sources of Social Power Vol. 1, A History of Power from the beginning to AD 1760* (Cambridge: Cambridge University Press).
9 See M. Freeman, 'Death Toll from the war in our midst' in *The Times Higher Educational Supplement* (5/3/96): 23.
10 See R. Hardin (1995) *One for all: The Logic of Group Conflict* (Princeton: Princeton University Press).

11 See E. Shils, 'Primordial, Personal, Scared and Civil Ties: Some particular observations on the relationships of sociological research and theory' in *The British Journal of Sociology* (7) 130–45.

12 See C. Geertz, 'The integrative revolution: primordial sentiments and civil politics in the new states' in C. Geertz (ed). (1963) *Old Societies and New States: the quest for modernity in Asia and Africa* (London: The Free Press Of Glencoe), 105–57.

13 See H. Isaacs (1989) *Idols of the Tribe: Group Identity and Political Change* (Cambridge: Cambridge University Press).

14 See J. McKay, 'An exploratory synthesis of primordial and mobilzationist approaches to ethnic phenomena' in *Ethnic and Racial Studies* 5(4): 395–420; J.D. Eller and R.M. Coughlan, 'The Poverty of Primordialism; The demystification of ethnic attachments' in *Ethnic and Racial Studies* 16(2): 181–202.

15 Also see S. Grosby, 'The verdict of history: the unexpungeable tie of primordiality-a response to Eller and Coughlan' in *Ethnic and Racial Studies* 17(1) 164–71.

16 See J.M.G. Van der Dennen, Ethnocentrism in In-group/out Group Differentiation: A Review and Interpretation of the literature' in Reynolds et al. (1987a) 1–47; P. Meyer, 'Ethnocentrism in Human Social Behaviour: Some Biological Considerations' in Reynolds et al. (eds) (1987a), 94–111; B.W. Ike, 'Mans limited sympathy as a consequence of his evolution in small kin groups' in Reynolds et al. (eds) (1987a), 216–34.

17 See V. Reynolds, V. Falger and I. Vine (eds) (1987) *The Sociobiology of Ethnocentrism: Evolutionary Dimensions of Xenophobia, Discrimination, Racism and Nationalism* (London: Croom Helm).

18 See P.L. Van den Berghe, 'Ethnicity and the sociobiology debate' in J. Rex and D. mason (eds). *Theories of Race and Ethnic Relations* (Cambridge: Cambridge University Press): 246–63.

19 See R. Russell, 'Genetic similarity as a mediator of interpersonal relationships' in Reynolds et al. (eds) (1987), 118–30; Johnson et al. 'The Evocative Significance of kin terms in patriotic speech' in Reynolds et al. (eds) (1987), 157–74; W. Tonnesman, 'Group Identification and Political Socialization' in Reynolds et al. (eds) (1987), 175–89.

20 See P. Shaw and Y. Wong (1989) *Genetic Seeds of Warfare: Evolution, Nationalism and Patriotism* (Boston: Unwin Hyman); Reynolds et al. (1987), xvii–xviii; I. Silverman 'Inclusive Fitness and Ethnocentrism' in Reynolds et al. (eds) (1987).

21 See M. Hechter, 'Explaining nationalist violence' in *Nations and Nationalism* 1(1): 53–68, (1995); M.Hechter et al., 'A theory of ethnic collective action' in *International Migration Review* 16(2) 412–34 (1982).

22 See Y. Tamir (1993) *Liberal Nationalism* (Princeton: Princeton University Press); D. Miller (1995) *On Nationality* (Oxford: Clarendon Press).

Chapter Three

Minority Nationalism or Tribal Sentiments? The Case of Scotland, Quebec and Catalonia

Michael Keating

INTRODUCTION: NATIONS, ETHNICITIES AND STATES

The study of nationalism and nationalist movements has often tended to confound three ideas, those of the nation, the ethnic group and the state. Nationalism is presented as a project on the part of leaders of an ethnic group to establish their own state. My argument is that all three terms are problematic, they are only contingently and not necessarily linked, and that the meaning of all three is undergoing changes in the contemporary era. We are witnessing a reconfiguration of political and social space in which new forms of collective action and identity, rooted in but not determined by historical patterns, are challenging the basis of political order inherited from the nineteenth century model of the nation state. The resulting new movements represent a striving for new principles of collective action in the face of the disintegrative tendencies of the contemporary state and market. They may be benevolent, democratic and progressive, or represent a retreat into tribalism and the abandonment of the gains of the Enlightenment and of liberal democracy.

There is a long and well-rehearsed debate on the nature of ethnicity and its relationship to nationality. On one side are those who regard ethnic identities as an ascriptive characteristic and in fact some go further, to present it as primordial and unchangeable, at least in the short term. On the other side, are those who regard ethnic identity as a social construction, determined by the context and the needs of the time. So for example, the ethnic designation Hispanic has been invented in recent times to indicate Americans of South American origin; it makes no sense outside its specific spatial and temporal context. Bosnian Muslim became an ethnic identity some time in the mid twentieth century when it became necessary to demarcate the group from its expansionist neighbours (Ivanov, 1996). English, Scots, Irish and Welsh are regarded, for Canadian official purposes, as a single ethnic group. The evidence is in fact overwhelming that most ethnic identities are malleable, contextual and instrumental, used in order to advance specific claims or to resist others. However, ethnicity is defined, the relationship between it and nationality is equally contentious. Some scholars have used the terms ethnicity and nationality indistinguishably. Others insist on the ethnic origins of nations, arguing that there is always an ethnic core, which can be added to over time to construct nations and states (Smith, 1986). The discussion threatens, as so often, to degenerate into one about semantics. If one defines an ethnic group as one with national aspirations then the identity is tautologically exact. If one takes the two terms in the ordinary sense, then it is clear that they may coincide but usually do not. If the Celts are an ethnic group, they are not a nation but come together with other ethnic groups in the nations of Scotland, Wales, Ireland and arguably Brittany and Galicia. In the United States, a careful distinction is made between nationality and ethnicity, by use of the hyphenated identity, allowing one of the world's strongest and most deeply felt nationalisms to co-exist with ethnic distinctions. Connor (1978) recognizes that ethnicity is used to refer to several types of social grouping and strategy but seeks to resolve the question by confining it to those groups which are nations or potential nations. When he argues that there are few nation states in the world, he is more accurately saying that hardly any nations are ethnically homogeneous.

One way of resolving this problem is to recognize two types of national identity and therefore of nationalist project – the ethnic and the civic (Greenfeld, 1992; Smith 1992). The terms used often vary, but this is essentially the same distinction as between the continental or German and the liberal (Kohn, 1944; Snyder, 1954); the cultural and the political (De Blas, 1994); the voluntarist and the organicist (Renaut, 1991). They differ on the question of who constitutes the nation and on the basis for legitimacy of nationalist demands. One presents membership of the national community as given, or ascriptive; the other sees individuals voluntarily constituting themselves as a collectivity.

Civic nationalism is a collective enterprise based upon common values and institutions, and patterns of social interaction. The bearers of national identity are institutions, customs, historical memories and rational/secular values. Anyone can join the nation irrespective of birth or ethnic origins, though the cost of adaptation varies. There is no myth of common ancestry. Civic nationalism is based upon territorially defined community, not upon a social boundary among groups within a territory. This is not to say that any piece of real estate can form the basis for a nationalism. There needs to be a structured set of political and social interactions guided by common values and a sense of common identity. Nations in the civic vision are further distinguished from ethnic groups in being global societies, containing within them the full range of social institutions and mechanisms for social regulation. People within the nation do not need to share social customs, habits or ways of thinking; rather nationality is common to them in the way a table is to a group of diners (Parekh, 1994). Ethnic groups, by contrast, are partial societies, advancing the claims of one group within a broader context. So ethnic promotion and nationalism are not the same thing. It may be that one ethnic group takes the lead in nation building, the construction of a global society, but that is a stage beyond mere ethnic mobilization.

Some scholars have sought to exclude nationalist doctrine based on civic values and individual rights from the definition of nationalism, since these individual rights are typically cast in universal terms. Breuilly (1985, p. 60) takes the universal character of these declarations to disallow them as forms of nationalism: 'The nation was the sum of the citizens, whose rights were based upon their common humanity. France was simply the place in which these universal principles of humanity were being first proclaimed and realized.' Yet the point is surely that these rights need an institutional form to find their operational definition and expression. It is only in relation to the state or civil society that the ideals of liberty and equality have meaning. So these values, albeit couched in universal terms, do provide an underpinning for a form of nationalism. The same can be said of the United States, where the definition of 'American values' is couched in terms of universal rights and truths. Kedourie in his famous anti-nationalist polemic (1966, pp. 131–3) dismisses the liberal or Whig theory of nationalism as not truly nationalist, since liberal and Whig writers such as Mill and Acton allowed for the possibility of multinational states, indeed even welcomed them. This stems from a nineteenth century confusion of terminology. In modern terminology, Acton (1949) was saying that states can be multi-ethnic, containing a diversity of ascriptively defined groups and yet still form a national identity and civil society with common institutions if the population so will it; indeed he noted 'two views of nationality . . . connected in name only.'

It is necessary to insist on two points here. Firstly, ethnic and civic nationalism are ideal types, that is, abstractions against which to measure reality. They must not be taken as descriptions of any given movement. Secondly, the categories are normative and value-laden. This is not to say, as some critics assume, that civic nationalism is benign and tolerant and ethnic nationalism nasty. Civic nationalism can be violent and civic values may be narrow and intolerantly applied as in nineteenth century France. Any given movement may contain both civic and ethnic elements in its origins and use both types of appeal in its doctrine. Civic nationalism has potentially a broader appeal, since it does not exclude anyone within the society. On the other hand, it lacks the emotive edge of ethnic nationalism. So most nationalist movements make both types of claim depending on the circumstances and the audience. Leaders of nationalist movements rooted in ethnic particularism may use the language of civic nationalism in order to acquire international legitimacy or establish their liberal democratic credentials. Conversely, leaders of civic movements may seek to invent an ethnic identity as a mechanism for political mobilization; this happened in the early years of the Lombard League in Italy.

Even among those who accept that civic nationalism may be an attribute of the large states of western Europe, built by consolidation, there are many who insist that minority nationalism must by definition be ethnically based. In some cases, this represents the tautological position that minority nations are by definition ethnicities.[1] Others adopt a more normative position, seeing minority nations as somehow backward and large nation states as progressive. This attitude, which was common at the time of the minority nationalist revival of the 1960s, has re-emerged in the 1990s in observers such as Hobsbawm (1992). This appears to me to be no more than a prejudice fostered by metropolitan bias. In principle, there is no reason at all why small, stateless nations should be more ethnically-oriented and less civic than large ones which have attained statehood in the past. We can apply the typology of ethnic and civic nationalism to both.

Another commonly held view is that nationalism is necessarily aimed at the establishment of a state. If by this is meant the type of sovereign state which dominated world affairs from the mid nineteenth to the late twentieth centuries, then nationalism is a historically specific phenomenon and Hobsbawm (1990) is right to restrict it to the period c.1780–1990. Unfortunately, this excludes such expressions of nationalist doctrine and propaganda as the Declaration of Arbroath (1320) or Shakespeare's historical plays, as well as the vibrant minority nationalist movements of contemporary Europe. If we include these, then we must detach nationalism conceptually from the sovereign state and see it as a principle of collective self-determination which can be applied in a number of institutional settings of which the classic state is only one. Since the state itself is changing in form and functions, so must nationalist doctrine and strategy and we can see the re-emergence of minority nationalism as in part a response to these changes.

THE NATION STATE

The twentieth century nation state represents the coincidence in space of a number of principles of social, economic and political order. It provides the basis for identity. It has encompassed recognizable economic units, with an internal dynamic and recognizable external frontier. It is a policy making system, with a state apparatus and a capacity to mobilize society behind political goals. It contains within it a distinct civil society, with nationally defined groups, institutions and systems of interest articulation. In its liberal democratic version, it provides for representation, accountability of government, and legitimation. It has extensive functions in internal and external security, economic management, welfare provision, and culture. These are not a bundle of separate characteristics, but a mutually reinforcing set. National identity provides the rationale for social solidarity, which in turn underpins welfare states. The national arena provides a forum in which trade-offs can be made between economic competitiveness and social solidarity. National identity provides an overarching set of common interests, within which class, religious, regional and ethnic conflict can be managed through party competition, or systems of corporatist or consociational accommodation. In the contemporary state, however, these strands are being pulled apart. The state is challenged from above by international and supranational trends, from below by new territorial forces, and laterally by the advance of the market and of the self-regulating mechanisms of civil society. This poses questions about the traditional meaning of sovereignty (Camilleri and Falk, 1991).

External security in the North Atlantic region has long been collectivized under American leadership. Although internal security remains largely a state prerogative, it is becoming increasingly internationalized, with the opening of frontiers and the preoccupation with terrorism and drug smuggling. State economic management is eroded from above by globalization, integration of capital markets, free trade regimes and the rise of the multinational corporation (Schmidt, 1995). At the same time, there is a growing recognition that economic restructuring can be understood as a local and regional process, within the context of global forces (Stöhr, 1990; Dunford and Kafkalis, 1992). Laterally, the state's role in economic management is undermined by privatization and the advance of neo-liberal doctrine. Welfare provision remains a key feature of the nation state, but its ability to sustain the old social compromise is reduced by the demands of international economic competition. National cultures are under attack from global culture, or perhaps American cultural hegemony, while local and regional cultures and languages have in many cases experienced a revival; technological change has made state regulation of broadcasting a virtual impossibility. Institutionally, the west European state has transferred powers up to the European Union. Whether this represents the growth of a supranational entity or a mere pooling of sovereign powers the more effectively to exercise them (Milward, 1992) is not relevant to my main argument, which is that the state no longer exercises these functions autonomously. States have also decentralized institutionally, whether to local and regional governments as in Canada and many European states, or to the private sector as in the United Kingdom. As decision making systems have become ever more complex, policy making has retreated into networks spanning levels of government, the public and private sectors, and crossing national boundaries.

It would be a serious error to present this as totally new, or to contrast it with a mythical state of the classical era which was able to monopolize authority and internalize the policy process. These tendencies have always been present, but have been greatly magnified in the contemporary era and affect most seriously those states which in the past have sought to centralize and monopolize authority. In another sense, these trends represent a step back in history, to an era of overlapping authority, multiple identity and complexity, before the rise of the modern state (Majone, 1995). In many respects, they are positive, allowing for more flexible forms of organization and problem solving and removing the absolutes which have been at the basis of inter-state wars. Yet there is another side. By breaking the link between policy making, economic change and representation, they undermine the basis of modern democracy. The result is a disillusionment with democratic politics and a risk of the sort of social explosion seen in France in late 1995.

There are a number of intellectual and political reactions to the crisis of the interventionist welfare state and the postwar settlement. One is a retreat to a hyper-individualism typified by Margaret Thatcher's famous remark that there is no such thing as society. This is seen in the intellectual arena in the popularity of public choice[2] and rational choice forms of analysis; and in the political arena in the form of neo-liberalism. A second reaction takes the form of identity politics, which again denies the possibility of universal values or a public good and attributes interests to ascriptive identities. Ethnic and racial politics is one form of this, though certain forms of gender politics would also qualify. A third possibility is the construction of new forms of collective identity and action in both state and civil society which recognize the limitations imposed by current conditions as well as the plurality and complexity of contemporary identities themselves. One form of this is the new territorial politics, including some forms of minority nationalism.

Regarded in this positive sense, minority nationalism can be seen as the reforging of identities to suit the contemporary era but using, as always, historical materials to do this. It may have a strong democratic impulse, seeking to restore popular participation and accountability to the policy process. It may be guided by a search for new principles of social cohesion and for a way to insert the society in the global order on terms not entirely dictated from outside. Nationalism is not a mere instrumental doctrine; it has strong historical and emotive dimensions. Yet it can be seen as a mechanism for coping with a series of contemporary problems and tensions. One concerns the very workings of capitalism itself. Capitalism is not, *pace* most of its apologists, an individualistic system which works through acquisitive competition. As its most astute analysts have long noted, it depends on the existence of an individual or collective capitalist, who is motivated not by the hedonistic desire to consume but by a transcendent desire to accumulate and build. It also requires strong elements of social cooperation in the production of public goods, alongside competition in the market. Michel Albert (1991) has compared the Anglo-American model of stock market capitalism unfavourably with the more collective Rhineland model, which is more long term, more socially benevolent, and more efficient. Other authors have long argued on similar lines. Much attention has been paid to the rediscovery of 'industrial districts' and of civic cultures in which social cooperation is sustained by community norms, so as to solve collective action problems and enhance productive efficiency (Amin and Thrift, 1994; Putnam, 1993; Harrison, 1992). Collective identity is also needed to sustain social solidarity, especially in a restructuring economic order which allocates rewards increasingly unevenly. Yet if this solidarity is ethnically based, it fails to achieve social integration and instead may reinforce exclusion and allow members of the dominant group to monopolize the scarce employment opportunities. A more secure base is cultural identity, where the territorial culture is sufficiently open to assimilate incomers and members of minority groups. This is a delicate issue. A culture which has no common principles fails to provide the basis for solidarity and collective action or citizenship rights – this is the liberal criticism of multiculturalism (Bisoondath, 1994). On the other hand, a common culture defined too restrictively may exclude some members of the society and become a mere mark of ethnic differentiation. Minority nationalisms need to build new institutions. These may take the form of separate states. Free trade and the construction of international regimes like the European Union (EU) and the North American Free Trade Agreement (NAFTA) have lowered the barriers to independence for small nations (Young, 1992, 1995; Meadwell, 1993; Martin, 1995). Yet they have also raised the possibility, elusive though it still is, of new forms of national autonomy and self-determination beyond the traditional categories of federalism and separation. The reconfiguration of political space (Keating, 1992, 1995b) has created new forms of territorial politics and efforts to build new systems of action within the economy and civil society.

What I am seeking here is a new civic nationalism, detached from the exclusive connotations of the old nation state. Its competitors are hyper-individualism, state nationalism and ethnic differentiation. In an examination of the three minority nationalist movements of Quebec, Catalonia and Scotland, we can see how far these principles have advanced.

THE NEW POLITICS OF NATIONALISM

Quebec, Catalonia and Scotland provide three nationalist movements which are at once old and new. They are historic nations, with long histories; but their nationalist movements have been modernized and adapted with greater or lesser success to the needs of the late twentieth century. In official doctrine, all are civic rather than ethnic; are free trading rather than protectionist; do not aim at the creation of a classic nation state; and accept the idea of multiple rather than exclusive identity. In these

41

respects, they must be considered not as throwbacks to tribalism but as highly modern responses to the dilemmas of the contemporary era. These ideas find considerable echo in the local society, but putting them into practice is more difficult.

Nationalist doctrine

Nationalism in all three cases spans a rather wide range of views, from moderate home rulers to separatists, but there is a general agreement on putting the nationalist project in the context of international integration and free trade. This has the obvious advantage of lowering the barriers to independence and removing the old objection of disruption of trade patterns, but there is more. Continental integration and minority nationalism are seen as essentially complementary processes, eroding the old states and allowing for the emergence of new political forms. The Scottish National Party represents the most orthodox style of nationalism in the three cases. It has accepted membership of the European Union and is more strongly committed to it than either of the two main British parties, but it favours an intergovernmental rather than a supranational Europe, with Scotland among the states. The parties of the Scottish Constitutional Convention (Labour and Liberal Democrat) favour Home Rule within the UK, but with a strong European dimension. In Quebec, there is a similar division between the Parti Québécois (PQ), which favours a sovereign Quebec, and the Quebec Liberal Party, which wants more power within Canada. Yet both see Quebec as a special case within Canada and stress the need for a North American dimension to the constitutional settlement. The PQ's vision of sovereignty is highly attenuated. It includes provision not only for free trade with Canada, but for monetary union, free movement of people, joint citizenship and joint positions on international affairs (PQ, 1991, 1993). Under pressure from its nationalist allies in the *Bloc Québécois* and the *Parti Action Démocratique du Québec*, it modified its stance further in the referendum of 1995 proposing sovereignty along with economic and political partnership with Canada. The latter would include joint executive and parliamentary institutions. Catalonia has a long tradition of semi-sovereignty, dating from the period between Spanish unification and the abolition of its self-governing institutions in 1714. A commercial and trading nation, it was able to play in the Spanish political and economic arenas as well as the European and the Mediterranean ones. In the new Europe, it has resumed this tradition and its ruling party *Convergència i Unió* combines a strong assertion of nationalism with a lack of interest in separatism (CiU, 1992, 1994). The *Esquerra Republicana de Catalunya*, which gains around 8–9 per cent of the vote, has supported independence in recent years but this too is put in the context of a people's Europe. The Catalan Socialists favour a federal Spain with more powers for

42

Semi - sovereignty.

Catalonia. It would be a mistake to view this as a purely instrumental strategy. Catalan nationalism has a strong mystical element (Pujol, 1987, 1980; Hernández and Mercadé, 1981) but this operates in a modern context. This is indeed the case in all three examples. Nationalist ideology bridges the past and the future, the imagined community and the daily reality in an effort to cope with the dilemma of modernity.[3]

In all three cases, there is a strong popular support base for nationalism but minority support for separatism (Blais and Nadeau, 1992; Brand et. al., 1993, 1994, a, b; Font, 1988; Montero and Font, 1991; Montero and Torcal, 1991). For Scotland and Quebec, there are substantial time series data and these show growing support for nationalism and for independence, as this has been placed in the context of continental integration. When the question is put as independence in the classic sense, support falls away. Figure 3.1 shows support for constitutional options in Quebec since 1977 over a twenty year period. The hard option of independence consistently fares worst than the option of sovereignty, which in turn fares worse than the looser formulation of sovereignty association. Indeed, sovereignty-association has consistently gained majority support since the failure of the Meech Lake accord, which would have given Quebec a distinct status, in 1990. Figure 3.2 shows levels of support in Scotland since 1975.[4] There has always been majority support for constitutional change, but support for independence has grown steadily since the 1980s, especially since it has been placed in the European context. Table 3.1 gives a snapshot of Catalonia.

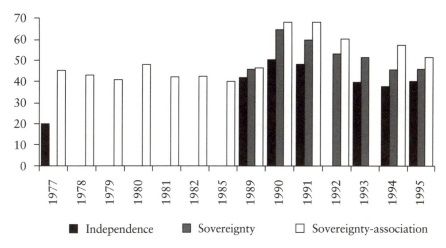

Figure 3.1: Support for sovereignty options, Quebec, 1977–95

Sources: CREATEC; Léger and Léger; Angus Reid; Maurice Pinard. Don't knows divided proportionately.

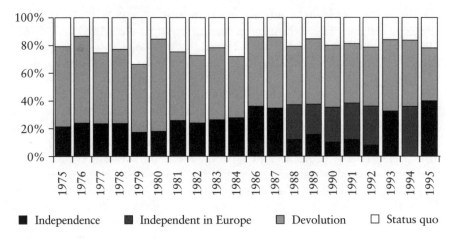

Independence   ■ Independent in Europe   ■ Devolution   □ Status quo

Figure 3.2: Support for constitutional options, Scotland, 1974–95
Source: MORI; System 3 Scotland; ICM Scotland.

Table 3.1: *Opinion on constitutional options, Catalonia, 1992.*

	Catalonia	Barcelona	Tarragona	Lleida	Girona
independence	10	9	14	15	17
more autonomy	41	40	41	45	46
present autonomy	33	35	30	27	24
less autonomy	1	1	1	0	0
abolish autonomous system	8	8	7	6	6

Source: Cambio 16, 16 March 1992.

All three nationalist movements consciously espouse a civic rather than an ethnic conception of the nation and have stated many times that anyone who lives and works in the nation is to be considered part of the nation. This is least problematic in Scotland, which has long been marked by cultural or 'ethnic' cleavages, between Highlanders and Lowlanders, Gaelic, Scots and English speakers, Irish and Scots, Protestants and Catholics. Modern Scottish identity is an amalgam of these elements, which recognizes the distinct features of each. It is rooted in institutions and commitment, rather than ancestry and ascription. In the early 1990s, two small fringe groups, Settler Watch and English Watch, targeted English in Scotland but made little impact.[5] In Quebec, the nationalist movement has made a transition since the 1950's from an ethnically-based movement of 'French Canadians' to a territorially based movement seeking to build a nation within Quebec (Balthazar, 1990; McRoberts, 1988). Official policy is to integrate immigrants into Quebec society through cultural assimilation. Here we can contrast two official statements about Quebec identity. The first is from the Tremblay commission of 1954, the second from the Bélanger-Campeau commission of 1992.

The French Canadians are almost all of the Catholic faith... The French Canadians are of French origin and culture ... the French Canadians are the only group whose religious and cultural particularism almost exactly coincide. Only French Canada, as a homogeneous group, presents the double differentiating factor of religion and culture (Tremblay, 1973: 6).a modern, multi-ethnic community, founded on shared common values, a normal language of communication, and participation in collective life (Bélanger-Campeau, 1992).

Sloppy editing

Yet ethnic nationalist elements remain and constantly embarrass mainstream nationalist leaders with their indiscretions. Perhaps the most notorious was uttered by Parti Québécois premier Jacques Parizeau on the night of the 1995 referendum, when he blamed the narrow defeat on 'money and the ethnic vote.' The outburst was significant and reflected one stream in Quebec nationalism; equally significant was the round condemnation from many other nationalists and Parizeau's prompt resignation. In Catalonia, nationalism has always had a strong civic dimension and since the 1960s this has been dominant. Nationalists repeatedly stress that anyone who lives in Catalonia and wishes to belong is Catalan.

Official policy is one thing, popular response perhaps another. Here we find some sharp contrasts. In Scotland, the former propensity of Catholics to avoid the SNP seems to have disappeared, marking an assimilation of descendants of Irish immigrants into Scottish identity. There has not been large-scale immigration into Scotland for many decades, but there are about 300,000 people of English birth. These show a rather high degree of assimilation into Scotland. Few complain about discrimination on ethnic grounds (Dickson, 1994) and few even identify themselves as English in Scotland. When asked about identity, most take refuge in the generic category of British, but as many consider themselves Scots as English. In the 1992 General Election, 9.6 per cent of them even voted for the SNP (against 23.3 per cent of Scots-born) (Dickson, 1994). So high is the rate of assimilation to Scottish identity of the children of English parents that no-one has even bothered to try and identify them. (System 3 Scotland, 20 July 1993 – see Figure 3.3).

Catalonia has had a very high rate of immigration since the 1960s. At the time of the transition to democracy, 40 per cent of the population had been born outwith the region and the figure has remained high. Yet there is a rather high degree of assimilation.

Quebec is another matter. No matter what the official nationalist doctrine, nationalism remains rooted in the Francophone community.

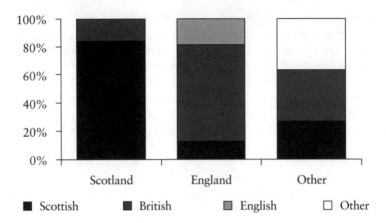

Figure 3.3: National identity by place of birth, Scotland 1993
Source: System 3 Scotland, 20 July 1993.

Support for the Parti Québécois and for sovereignty among Quebec's English speaking population is negligible. Equally important, it is also very low among the allophones, those whose native language is neither French nor English and who are the target of assimilationist nation-builders.

Although the issues of civic vs. ethnic nationalism and separatism vs. home rule are analytically distinct, there is a connection between them. Gaining support for the drastic step of independence, with the risks and costs which that entails, requires a huge mobilization capacity, which may only be available through crude ethnic appeals (Derrienec, 1994). This, however, may delegitimize the project both internally and externally. A more moderate programme focused on social institutions rather than ascriptive identity, and allowing multiple memberships of national entities, is potentially capable of wider mobilization, though less intense. The evidence shows that incomers and minorities in all three countries show wide support for more self-government. The difference arises in support for independence, which is almost entirely confined to the native-born.

Nation-building, culture and language

An important element in nation-building and collective identity is a common culture and language. These may function as markers of ethnic identity, distinguishing natives from others; or they may provide the basis for a common civic culture, by providing a vehicle for assimilation. A common culture may also have economic effects by fostering collective identity and thereby facilitating the production of public goods. Language is a key element of national identity in both Quebec and Catalonia and in

46

both cases language policy has been used as an instrument of nation building, serving less as an ethnic marker (Keating, 1996). For a long time Quebec governments sought to preserve the purity of the French ethnic community by insulating it from the anglophone economic community, and by discouraging immigrants from attending French schools. They tolerated an ethnic division of labour in which anglophones held the dominant economic power and francophones were concentrated in lower status occupations. The Quiet Revolution of the 1960s saw a change in strategy and a series of language laws was aimed at improving the position of the francophone community in the state and private sector. They gave exclusive official status to French and stipulated its use in business. In education, they sought to restrict access to English language schools and to force immigrants into the francophone ones, so expanding the French-speaking community and breaking down ethnic barriers. There is great controversy over the success of French-language education in assimilating the children of immigrants and the immigrant community as a whole has signally failed to rally behind the nationalist movement. Policy towards the native anglophone community has been very different. Despite the complaints of some anglophone anti-nationalists, there has been no real attempt at forced assimilation and they have been allowed to retain their own institutions, including schools, universities, and health and social services. This may be both tolerant and a political and constitutional necessity, but it shows the limits of nation-building through language. So some Quebec nationalist intellectuals have advocated abandoning the language laws after the attainment of sovereignty, with a view to building an inclusive nationalism which would embrace both communities, while recognizing the French majority. Efforts to relax the language laws, however, have consistently been defeated by the militants of the PQ.

Catalonia has followed a different path, deliberately avoiding a segregated two-language society in favour of bilingualism. Catalan is the official language of Catalonia but Castilian is recognized as the official language of the Spanish state. Education is to be through the medium of Catalan and, while the right of parents to have their children educated in Castilian is theoretically recognized, there is to be no segregation of schools or classes by language. All children are required to have a functional knowledge of both languages as a condition of school graduation. This policy is aimed at the assimilation of the large number of southern Spanish immigrants into the Catalan community and the avoidance of ethnic distinction. Since Catalan is a high status language, there is a strong incentive for lower-class immigrants to learn it and, especially to ensure that their children have a command of the language. Concentrations of non-Catalans exist in the older industrial areas and remain outside the mainstream culture, but steady assimilation is taking place across the generations. Polls show high levels of support even among immigrants for the policy of linguistic normalization (Keating, 1995); opposition is concentrated among the *españolista* sections of the middle class and the political hard right.

In Scotland, there is not a major language issue, since English predominates and the other two languages, Gaelic and Scots are limited in their range. Accent is sometimes used as a mark of distinction, but it is not a good one, since many Scots, even prominent nationalists, speak with English accents. Yet there are cultural markers. These are more subtle and have to do with identity and attitudes, which can be acquired. Support for Scottish sporting teams is one; complaining about London-based government is another. English people taking positions in Scottish public life usually go native, often with considerable enthusiasm. Culture in Scotland was for a long time depoliticized and the nationalist movement made little play of it. In the 1990s, there has been a strong cultural revival, breaking with the folkloresque parodies of Scotland[6] and addressing contemporary issues. This culture is not always nationalist but is distinctively national, and an integral part of the contemporary nation-building project.[7]

Civil Society and the State

In view of the weakening of the contemporary state, nation-building must proceed within civil society. A notable development in all three cases is the building of social and economic institutions within the national society, sometimes linked to those of the wider state society, sometimes not. In the realm of culture, leisure and voluntary social activism, just about every organization is distinct from that of the state society in all three cases and this trend has accentuated. For sports, the distinctiveness is particularly notable in Scotland. Professional organizations are often organized separately. In the economic realm there is less differentiation. Quebec trade unions are organized separately from their counterparts in the rest of Canada, though they participate in some joint organizations. In Scotland, the British trade unions operate, though their local branches affiliate to the Scottish Trades Union Congress, which is separate from its British counterpart and has played a more prominent part in public life since the 1980s. It has been a leading supporter of Scottish home rule within the United Kingdom. Trade unionism is weak in Catalonia (Andrés, 1991), and the separate Catalan trade unions are very minor actors. The main Spanish unions operate there in a somewhat distinctive mode, seeking to incorporate immigrant workers while inserting themselves into the Catalan world, for example by supporting decentralization and language normalization (Lope, 1992). Trade unions in all three cases are torn between the need to reach out to the local working class and the need to preserve unity of action at the state level. In the case of Quebec, this has led to support for sovereignty, combined with joint action with Canadian unions against North American free trade (Boucher, 1992; Dionne, 1991; Rouillard,

1989). In Catalonia and Scotland, it leads to support for home rule within the state. Employers' groups have also organized on the basis of the minority nations, though they have not been supportive of nationalism. They oppose anything which threatens to divide markets and, while nationalist support for free trade has assuaged some of their fears, they remain at most neutral, but more often opposed. Small business and lower middle classes, on the other hand, have been more supportive of nationalists goals. This has given a class dimension to the nationalist project, though it would be a major error to reduce the national issue to a class one. There is also growing evidence that business can accommodate itself to constitutional change, once it is assured that the market will not be divided and that it may even favour changes which improve government effectiveness and devolve decision making.

Civil society, however, cannot exist entirely on its own in the absence of state institutions and this growth has been paralleled by a decentralization of the state. In the case of Quebec this has taken the form of an expansion of the Quebec government's scope and competencies, so that it increasingly forms the reference point for Quebeckers. The fiscal crisis of the Canadian state will accelerate this process, whatever the constitutional provisions. In Catalonia, the restored Generalitat has gradually extended its competencies and sought to speak for Catalans in state politics as well as in Europe. In Scotland, the Conservative government has set its face against political devolution but has continued the process of administrative devolution in train since the 1960s, to the point that the Secretary of State for Scotland is now responsible for nearly all domestic policy in Scotland, with the notable exceptions of the tax and social security systems.

The construction of institutions within civil society, along with decentralization of the state, has internalized political debate within the three nations. Issues are increasingly appraised according to how they impact on Quebec, Catalonia or Scotland, and this in turn has aided the nation-building project.

The Economy

An important aspect of the nation-building project concerns the ability to manage the insertion of the national society into the global economic order. All three nations are heavily involved in trade, whether with the rest of the state or the world, as Figure 3.4 indicates. A policy of free trade is a logical consequence.

The move to support for free trade nonetheless represents a new form of nationalism, detaching it from economic protectionism (Meadwell, 1993; Martin, 1995). It also represents a shift in the historic nationalist mission in all three, but especially in Quebec and Catalonia and opens up a range of policy options and considerable scope for functional independence from the

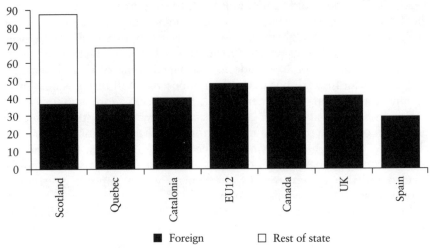

Figure 3.4: Trade as % of GDP
Quebec and Canada, 1984
Scotland, 1989
UK, 1989
EU, 1989
Spain, 1989
Catalonia, 1986

Sources: Scottish Office (1994); Eurostat (1994), Proulx and Cauchy (1992); Giraldez and Parellada (1990); Ministerio de Economía y Hacienda (1990); Cambra Oficial de Comerç, Industria i Navegació de Barcelona (1990); Generalitat de Catalunya (1992).

state. In the absence of tariff protection, promotion of the territorial economy depends on local ownership and the ability to mobilize resources and energies behind a development programme. Since the 1960s, Quebec has had such a project, sometimes dubbed 'Quebec Inc.', or 'market nationalism' (Courchene, 1986, 1990; Latouche, 1991; Arbour, 1993), a coalition of government and business actors committed to expanding Quebec ownership and Quebec's insertion into the North American economy. An early product was the expansion of Quebec ownership in industry. This was initially a project to increase Francophone control within Quebec but has led to the building of a series of large Quebec-based firms and the emergence of a new corporate elite, part of an integrated state-private sector business class. Figure 3.5 shows the growth of Francophone ownership. A lot of doubt has been expressed on whether Quebec Inc. can really survive North American Free Trade, with its competitive disciplines and Anglo-American style capitalism. Certainly, an independent Quebec would face much deeper scrutiny as to government support for industry, and would face the full weight of trading rules to which, as a sub-state entity, it is not subject.

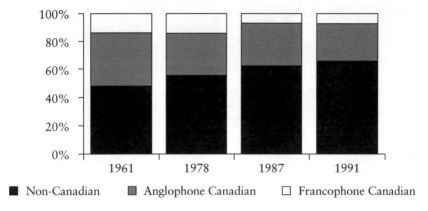

Figure 3.5: Ownership as percentage of employees, firms in Quebec
Sources: Conseil de la langue française (1992); Vaillancourt and Leblanc (1993).

In Scotland, by contrast, local ownership has receded, as Figure 3.6 indicates.[8]

There is a Scottish economic policy community and some commitment to cooperation among government, business and trade unions in the promotion of Scottish interests, but this is outweighed by partisan differences and the weakness of the Scottish indigenous sector.

We do not have equivalent figures for Catalonia but such evidence as exists suggests that the small and medium sized businesses which have been a strong feature of its economy face serious problems of modernization and competitiveness. Investment in large plants and technical

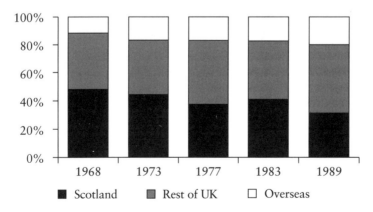

Figure 3.6: Ownership in Scottish manufacturing industry, 1968–89
Source: Ashcroft and Love (1993).

innovation come increasingly from multinational capital (Costa, 1990; Costas, 1990).

While Scotland and Catalonia face weaknesses in their indigenous industrial sectors, they can no longer look to their state governments for help as in the past. Internationalization and European regulations have limited the ability of state governments to manage their spatial economies or provide protection. Both were important in the past, tariff protection for Catalonia and regional aid for Scotland. This dependence on the national state is now replaced by a dependence on the international market and multinational capital. This has had a major effect on the political economy of nationalism, undermining the arguments of anti-nationalists who cleaved to the old state form.

The International Dimension

An important aspect of nation building is the projection of the nation in the global and continental area. An active external policy serves economic needs, in promoting trade and investment; it can secure support for language and cultural development; and it legitimizes nation building and helps consolidate it at home by placing the minority nation in the wider family of nation states. The external linkages of Quebec, Catalonia and Scotland have been intended to achieve these limited purposes, rather than to displace traditional forms of diplomacy and international power politics. Quebec's efforts go back to the Quiet Revolution of the 1960s and it has its own Ministry of International Affairs and an extensive network of offices abroad (Balthazar, 1991, 1992). Its efforts on the economic side are concentrated on the United States, while for cultural development and political support it looks to France and the francophone countries. It also has a presence in Latin America and Asia. For Catalonia, the main outlets are in Europe and the Mediterranean. The Catalan government has been a vocal supporter of a Europe of the Regions and, within the tight limits imposed by the intergovernmental system of policy making (Keating and Hooghe, 1996), plays the maximum role in the European Union. Scotland, lacking its own institutions of self-government, plays a much more limited role in the international arena, but its administrative institutions have made some efforts at separate promotion abroad. After battles with London departments, the Scottish Office and its agencies were able to mount a partially independent inward investment and tourism effort. Scottish representation in Europe has to pass largely through the Scottish Office and the office in Brussels of Scotland Europa has a very weak political role (Keating and Jones, 1995). The Scottish Constitutional Convention has proposed a stronger role for Scotland in the EU, including Scottish representation on delegations in the Council of Ministers and even invoking the Maastricht provision to allow the Scottish minister to lead them. Separatists in all three nations, of course, favour statehood with all its diplomatic prerogatives, but more moderate nationalists are content with the ability to project themselves in the international arena for specific aims. So globalization and continental integration, far from eroding minority nationalism, strongly encourages it (Parés and Tremblay, 1990; Mlinar, 1992).

CONCLUSION

We have traced the growth of minority nationalism as the state has been transformed and penetrated by supranational, subnational and private interests. This is a new form of nationalism, but rooted in historic traditions and identities. Nationalism has re-emerged as a vital principle of identity. It cannot be suppressed in the name of a supposed modernization but, as in central Europe, it can be diverted into beneficent or destructive channels (Michel, 1995). Support for separatism in all three cases is rather weak, but combined with a strong sense of national assertion. The modal point in public opinion in each case corresponds to the option of effective self-government in the context of a changed state and the respective continental free trade regime. It is tempting to point to contradictions in the evidence, summed up in the old saw that Québécois want an independent Quebec in a strong and united Canada. Many observers pointed to evidence during the 1995 Quebec referendum campaign that up to a third of YES supporters thought that Quebec would still send MPs to Ottawa and they would keep their Canadian passports. Similar findings are available from polls in Scotland and Catalonia. Opponents of minority nationalism are affronted by the practice of Québécois, Catalans and Scots of playing in different political arenas at the same time, pressing for autonomy at home while retaining a presence in state politics and venturing into the international arena. It may be, however, that it is not the electors who are wrong, but the categories used by political scientists and constitutional lawyers, who insist on an outdated notion of sovereignty and on the uniformity and homogeneity of the nation state.

In all three cases, the civic conception of the nation continues to compete with the ethnic, but the former has been gaining ground. It is dominant in Scotland, largely dominant in Catalonia and stronger in Quebec, though here there continues to exist a sharp ethnic distinction based on language. This modernized nationalism represents, not a lapse into tribalism or identity politics, but a search for collective identity and a capacity for collective action in a complex world. As well as carrying support in the society as a whole, a civic nationalism also carries greater external legitimacy. Another striking finding is that citizens in these three cases refuse to adopt exclusive identities but recognize that they belong in multiple spheres and groups; different identities can be mobilized for different purposes. Again, those scholars who wish to force data into their own procrustean categories might choose to see this as evidence of contradictions. Others might see it as a realistic adaptation to contemporary reality and the need to operate within distinct spheres of action if we are to retain the capacity for collective action. The success of nation-building is testified by the fact that, increasingly, citizens regard their Québécois, Catalan or Scots identity as primary, while recognizing the reality of the others. This is not because the three societies are becoming different as measured by economic or social indicators. On the contrary, in these respects they have become more like their host nations,[9] illustrating de Tocqueville's paradox of convergence (Dion, 1991). It is that the local society has become the reference point for judgements on social, economic and political issues and the local institutions are the ones accorded primary legitimacy. They have thus become global societies, not partial societies as are ethnic groups.

The final question must be whether a 'third way' between separatism and belonging as an undifferentiated part of the host state, is possible. One answer is that this is already happening. This paper has traced the increased differentiation of the three territorial societies, and their governing arrangements as well as their civil societies are already very distinct. On the other hand, there is great unwillingness within the wider host states to recognize this and provide for variable geometry constitutional arrangements. This may be because they are themselves searching for a new national identity to match the contemporary world. Two global societies may find it harder to co-exist in the same space than two ethnic groups (Langlois, 1991a,b). Unless such a formula can be found, however, the minority nations may be forced down the separatist road in the course of which there is indeed a danger of a relapse into tribalism. In that case, they might have to be listened to.[10]

REFERENCES

Acton, Lord (1949), *Essays in Freedom and Power* (Boston: Beacon Press).

Aguilar, S. (1987), 'L'impresariat i les seves organitzacions', in J.M. Rotger ed), *Visió de Catalunya. El canvi i la reconstrucció nacional des de la perspectiva sociològica* (Barcelona: Diputació de Barcelona).

Albert, M. (1991), *Capitalisme contre capitalisme* (Paris: Seuil).

A. Amin and N. Thrift (eds) (1994), *Globalization, Institutions, and Regional Development in Europe,* (Oxford: Oxford University Press).

Andrés Orizo, F. and Sanchez Fernández, A. (1991), *El sistema de valors dels catalans. Catalunya dins l'enquesta europea de valors dels anys 1990* (Barcelona: Institut Català d'Estudis Mediterranis).

Arenas, J. 'La situació sociolingüística de l'escola primària a Catalunya', in *Estudis i propostes per a la difusió de l'us social de la llengua catalana,* volem 2 (Barcelona: Generalitat de Catalunya).

Arbour, P. (1993), *Québec Inc. and the Temptation of State Capitalism* (Montreal: Robert Davies).

Ashcroft, B. and Love, J. (1993), *Takeovers, Mergers and the Regional Economy* (Edinburgh: Edinburgh University Press).

Ashcroft, B. and Love, J. (1994), 'New Firm Formation in the British Counties and Regions of Scotland', *Scottish Economic Bulletin*, 49, pp. 13–22.

Assemblé Nationale (1992a), Commission d'étude des questions afférentes à l'accession du Québec à la souveraineté, *Projet de Rapport.*(Québec: Assemblé Nationale).

Balthazar, L. (1990), *Bilan du nationalisme au Québec* (Montreal: l'Hexagone).

Balthazar, L. (1991), 'Conscience nationale et contexte internationale', in L. Balthazar, G. Laforest and V. Lemieux, *Le Québec et la restructuration du Canada, 1980–1992* (Saint-Laurent: Septentrion).

Balthazar, L. (1992), 'L'émancipation internationale d'un Etat fédéré (1960–1990)', in Rocher, F. ed), *Bilan québécois du fédéralisme canadien* (Montreal: vlb).

Bélanger-Campeau (1991), *Rapport de la commission sur l'avenir politique et constitutionnel du Québec,* co-chairs, M. Bélanger and J. Campeau (Québec: author).

Bissoondath, N. (1994), *Selling Illusions. The Cult of Multiculturalism in Canada* (Toronto: Penguin).

Blais, A. and Nadeau, R. (1992), 'To Be or Not to Be Sovereignist: Quebeckers' Perennial Dilemma', *Canadian Public Policy*, XVIII:1, pp. 89–103.

Blas Guerrero, A. de (1994), *Nacionalismos y naciones en Europa* (Madrid: Alianza).

Boucher, J. (1992), 'Les syndicats: de la lutte pour la reconnaissance à la concertation conflictuelle', in G. Daigle and G. Rocher (eds), *Le Québec en Jeu* (Montreal: Presses de l'Université de Montréal).

Brand, J., Mitchell, J. and Surridge, P. (1993), 'Identity and the vote. Class and nationality in Scotland', D. Denver ed), *British Elections and Parties Yearbook, 1993* (New York; Harvester Wheatsheaf), pp. 143–57.

Brand, J., Mitchell, J. and Surridge, P. (1994), 'Social Constituency and Ideological Profile: Scottish Nationalism in the 1990s', *Political Studies*, 42.4, pp. 616–29.

Brand, J., Mitchell, J. and Surridge, P. (1994b), 'Can Labour win with Scottish help?', in A. Heath, R. Jowell and J. Curtice (eds), *Labour's Last Chance: the 1992 Election and Beyond* (London: Dartmouth).

Breuilly, J., Nationalism and the State (Manchester University Press, 1985).

Cambra Oficial de Comerç, Industria i Navegació de Barcelona (1990), *Cataluña, Exporta, Cataluña Importa,* .

Camilleri, J. and J. Falk, *End of Sovereignty? The Politics of a Shrinking and Fragmenting World* (Edward Elgar, 1991).

Centro de Investigaciones Sociológicas, *Conocimiento y uso de las lenguas en España* (Madrid: CIS, 1994).

Connor, W. (1978), 'A Nation is a Nation, is a State, is an Ethnic group, is a . . .', *Ethnic and Racial Studies*, 1, pp. 377–400.

Connor, W. (1994), 'From Tribe to Nation?', reprinted in W. Connor, *Ethnonationalism. The Quest for Understanding* (Princeton: Princeton University Press).

Conseil de la langue française (1992), *Indicateurs de la situation linguistique au Québec* (Quebec: Publications du Québec).

Convergència Democràtica de Catalunya (1992), *Construir la Catalunya del 2000. IX Gongrés* (Barcelona: author).

Convergència i Unió (1994), *Amb força a Europa. Programa electoral, Eleccions al parlamento europeu* (Barcelona: CiU).

Costa, M.T. (1990), 'La organización industrial en el territorio. Descentralización productiva y economías externas', in M. Parellada ed), *Estructura económica de Cataluña* (Madrid: Espasa Calpe).

Costas, A. (1990), 'El marco de la política económica autónoma', in M. Parellada ed), *Estructura económica de Cataluña* (Madrid: Espasa Calpe).
Courchene, T. (1986), 'Market Nationalism', *Policy Options*, 7, pp. 7–12.
Courchene, T. (1990), *Québec Inc. Foreign Takeovers, Competition/Merger Policy and Universal Banking* (Kingston: School of Policy Studies, Queen's University).
Derrienic, J-P. (1995), *Nationalisme et démocratie. Réflections sur les illusions des indépendantistes québécois* (Québec: Boréal).
Dickson, M. (1994), 'Should Auld Acquaintance be Forgot? A Comparison of the Scots and English in Scotland', *Scottish Affairs*, 7, pp. 112–34.
Dion, S. (1991), 'Le nationalisme dans la convergence culturelle. Le Québec contemporain et le paradoxe de Tocqueville', in R. Hudon and R. Pelletier (eds), *L'engagement intellectuel. Mélanges en l'honneur de Léon Dion* (Sainte-Foy: Presses de l'Université de Laval).
Dionne, B. (1991), *Le Syndicalisme au Québec* (Montreal: Boréal).
Eurostat (1994), *Basic Statistics of the Community* (Luxembourg: Office of Publications of the European Communities).
M. Dunford and G. Kafkalis (eds) (1992), *Cities and Regions in the New Europe* (London: Belhaven).
Font, J. (1988), 'Som dos milions: Els abstencionistes a les eleccions al Parlament de Catalunya de 1988, in Equip de Sociologia Electoral (Universitat Autónoma de Barcelona), *L'electorat català a les eleccions autonòmiques de 1988: opinions, actituds i comportaments* (Barcelona: Fundació Jaume Bofill).
Generalitat de Catalunya (1992), Departament d'Industria i Energia, *Quadernos de Competivitat, La Internalització*.
Giraldez, E. and Parellada (1990), 'Los flujos con el exterior', in M. Parellada ed), *Estructura económica de Cataluña* (Madrid: Espasa-Calpe).
Greenfeld, L. (1992), *Nationalism. Five Roads to Modernity* (Cambridge: Harvard University Press).
Harrison, B. (1992), 'Industrial Districts: Old Wine in New Bottles?', *Regional Studies*, 26.5: 469–83.
Hernández, F. and Mercadé, F. (1981), *La Ideología Nacional Catalana* (Barcelona: Anagrama).
Hobsbawm, E. (1990), *Nations and Nationalism since 1780* (Cambridge: Cambridge University Press).
Hobsbawm, E. (1992), 'Nationalism. Whose fault-line is it anyway?', *Anthropology Today*, February 1992.
Institut d'Estadistica de Catalunya (1993), *Cens de població 1991. Vol. 8 Cens lingüístic. Dades comarcals i municipals* (Barcelona: Generalitat de Catalunya).
Ivanov, A. (1996), *Minorities in the Balkans, Euro-Atlantic Security Studies*, Vol. 1 (Peter Lang).
Keating, M. (1992), 'Regional Autonomy in the Changing State Order: A Framework of Analysis', *Regional Politics and Policy*, 2.3.
Keating, M. (1995), *Nations against the State. The New Politics of Nationalism in Quebec, Catalonia and Scotland* (London: Macmillan).
Keating, M. (1995b), Les régions constituent-elles un niveau de gouvernement en Europe?', Colloque, *Les Régions en Europe*, Rennes, September 1995.
Keating, M. (1996), 'Nationalism, nation-building and language policy in Quebec and Catalonia', in H.G. Haupt, M. Müller and S. Woolf eds), *Regional and National Identities in Europe in the Nineteenth and Twentieth Centuries* (Dordrecht: Martinus Nijhoff).

Keating, M. and Hooghe, L. (1996), 'By-Passing the Nation-State? Regions and the EU Policy Process', in J.J. Richardson (ed), *Policy Making in the European Union* (London: Routledge).

Keating, M. and Jones, B. (1995), 'The nations and regions of the UK in the European Community', in B. Jones and M. Keating eds), *The European Union and the Regions* (Oxford: Clarendon).

Kedourie, E. (1966), *Nationalism*, 3rd ed. (London: Hutchinson).

Kohn, H. (1944), *The Idea of Nationalism. A Study in its Origins and Background* (New York: Macmillan).

Langlois, S. (1991a), 'Le choc des deux sociétés globales', in L. Balthazar, G. Laforest and V. Lemieux, *Le Québec et la restructuration du Canada, 1980–1992* (Saint-Laurent: Septentrion).

Langlois, S. (1991b), 'Une société distincte à reconnaître et une identité collective à consolider', Commission sur l'avenir politique et constitutionel du Québec (Bélanger-Campeau Commission), *Document de travail*, 4, pp. 569–95 (Quebec: Commission).

Latouche, D. (1991), 'La stratégie québécoise dans le nouvel ordre économique et politique internationale', Commission sur l'avenir politique et constitutionnel du Québec, *Document de travail* numéro 4 (Quebec: Commission).

McCrone, D. (1992a), *Understanding Scotland. The Sociology of a Stateless Nation* (London: Routlege).

McRoberts, K. (1988), *Quebec. Social Change and Political Crisis*, 3rd edn. (Toronto: McClelland and Stewart).

Majone, G. (1995), 'Unity in Diversity, Competition with Cooperation: Europe's Past as its Future' (Florence: European University Institute, mimeo).

Martin, P. (1995), 'When Nationalism Meets Continentalism. The Politics of Free Trade in Quebec', *Journal of Regional and Federal Studies*, 5.1.

Meadwell, H. (1993), 'The Politics of Nationalism in Quebec', *World Politics*, 45.2, pp. 203–41.

Michel, B. (1995), *Nations et nationalismes en Europe centrale* (Paris: Aubier).

Mill, J.S. (1972), *Utilitarianism, On Liberty and Considerations on Representative Government* (London: Dent).

Milward, A.S. (1992), *The European Rescue of the Nation State* (London: Routledge. Berkeley: University of California Press).

Ministerio de Economía y Hacienda (1990) *Informe de Comercio Exterior* (Madrid, author)..

Mlinar, Z. (1992), *Globalization and Territorial Identities* (Aldershot: Avebury).

Montero, J.R. and Font, J. (1991), 'El voto dual: lealtad y transferencia de votos en las elecciones autonómicas', in Equip de Sociologia Electoral (Universitat Autónoma de Barcelona), *L'electorat català a les eleccions autonòmiques de 1988: opinions, actituds i comportaments* (Barcelona: Fundació Jaume Bofill).

Montero, J.R. and Torcal, M. (1991), 'La opinión pública ante el estado de las autonomías: un visión panorámica', *Informe Pi i Sunyer sobre las Comunidades Autónomas 1990* (Barcelona: Civitas).

Parekh, B. (1994), 'Discourses on National Identity', *Political Studies*, 42.3, pp. 492–504.

Parés i Maicas, M. and Tremblay, G. (eds) (1990), *Catalunya, Quebec. Autonomia i Mundialització* (Barcelona: Generalitat de Catalunya).

Parti Québécois (1991), *Programme* (Quebec: author).

Parti Québécois (1993a), *Le Québec dans un monde nouveau* (Montreal: vlb).

PSC (Partit dels Socialists de Catalunya) (1992), *Programa de Govern. Eleccions al Parlament de Catalunya, 1992* (Barcelona: PSC).

Proulx, P.P. and Cauchy, G. (1992), 'Un examen des échanges commerciaux du Québec aves les autres provinces canadiennes, les Etats-Unis et le reste du monde', for Bélanger-Campeau *Commission sur l'avenir politique et constitutionel du Québec*.

Pujol, J. (1976), *Una política per Catalunya* (Barcelona: Nova Terra).

Pujol, J. (1980), *Construir Catalunya* (Barcelona: Portic).

Putnam, R. (1993), *Making Democracy Work. Civic Traditions in Modern Italy* (Princeton: Princeton University Press).

Renaut, A. (1991), 'Logiques de la nation', in G. Delannoi and P-A. Taguieff eds), *Théories du Nationalisme* (Paris: Kimé).

Rosonvallon, P. (1992), 'L'état au tournant', in R. Lenoir and J. Lesourne eds), *Où va l'état?* (Paris: Le Monde Editions).

Rouillard, J. (1989b), *Histoire de Syndicalisme au Québec* (Montreal: Boréal).

Schmidt, V. (1995), 'The New World Order Inc. The Rise of Business and the Decline of the Nation State', *Daedalus*.

Scottish Office (1994), *Scottish Input-Output Tables for 1989* (Edinburgh: HMSO).

Smith, A. (1986), *The Ethnic Origins of Nations* (Oxford: Blackwell).

Smith, A. (1991), *National Identity* (London: Penguin).

Snyder, L. (1954), *The Meaning of Nationalism* (New Brunswick: Rutgers University Press).

Stöhr, W. (1990), *Global Challenge and Local Response. Initiatives for local economic regeneration in Europe*. London: Mansell.

Touraine, A. (1992a), *Critique de la modernité* (Paris: Fayard).

Touraine, A. (1992b), 'L'Etat et la question nationale', in R. Lenoir and J. Lesourne eds), *Où va l'état?* (Paris: Le Monde Editions).

Tremblay, A. (1973), *Report of the Royal Commission of Inquiry on Constitutional Problems*, edited by David Kwavnick (Toronto: McClelland and Stewart).

Young, R.A. (1992), 'Does Globalization Make an Independent Quebec More Viable?', in A.R. Riggs and T. Velk (eds), *Federalism in Peril. National Unity, Individualism, Free Markets, and the Emerging Global Economy* (Vancouver: Fraser Institute).

Young, R.A. (1995), *The Secession of Quebec and the Future of Canada* (Montreal: McGill-Queen's University Press).

NOTES

1 In this case, ethnicity ceases to be an explanatory factor or attribute of the national identity. In other words if minority nationalist identity is ethnic identity then ethnicity cannot be the independent variable which causes nationalist identity.

2 Some exponents of public choice will be infuriated at being bracketed with Thatcher. Yet, however ingenious their mechanisms for deriving social utility functions which might justify the welfare state, they do start from the same point, the detached, self maximising, rational individual.

3 This is the problem that a society based entirely on the present has no basis for values; on based purely on the past cannot adapt to the present and the future. See Touraine (1992a).

4 Matters are more simple in Scotland than in Quebec. In Scotland, the three main options have been status quo, home rule and independence. In the 1970's, the home rule category was divided into two, corresponding to devolution on the lines of the Labour Government's proposals, and federalism. Later these categories were collapsed but the independence category was divided into

two:independence in the European Union; and independence outwith the EU. Sometimes this distinction is not made, but the European context is assumed since no major party in Scotland is now against membership. In Quebec the question is frequently changed at the PQ has modified its policy and vocabulary. I have presented roughly equivalent categories here but the data are indicative rather than definitive. In Catalonia, there are very few polls on the constitutional issue. For a longer explanation, see Keating (1995).

5   Settler Watch turned out to be led by a German born woman, who was expelled from the SNP.

6   'Tartanry', a romanticized and bowdlerized version of Highland culture; and the kailyard, sentimental and pawky representation of a small town Scotland unsullied by the evils of modernity and class conflict.

7   Two examples illustrate this point. Tutti Frutti, a 1980's television show about the hilarious adventures of an aging rock band, pitched in the Scottish off key mode, caused bewilderment in England. The 1994 Booker prize novel, James Kelman's How late it was, how late, about the mishaps of a petty criminal at the hands of the state apparatus, deeply offended some of the jury, who could see nothing but bad language, Glasgow dialect and a disrespectful attitude to the welfare bureaucracy.

8   It should be noted that the data in Figures 5 and 6 cannot be compared, since they measure different contexts. What is of interest is the development over time indicated in each case.

9   For example, on just about every social and economic indicator, Scotland is now the median British region. On why Scotland does not have to be different to exist, see Mcrone (1992). Modern Quebec nationalism arrived with the decline in the old, isolationist Catholic culture. catalan nationalism has prospered with Catalonia's integration in Europe and the decline of religion and old social institutions.

10 This is the perennial problem for the Scots. Their very moderation and tolerance leads them not to be taken seriously. The British Conservatives have refused them any constitutional concession, while pressing ahead for devolution in Northern Ireland.

Chapter Four

Ethnic Conflict in the Balkans: Comparing ex-Yugoslavia, Romania and Albania

Trond Gilberg

INTRODUCTION

While there has been a vast array of theories and concepts forwarded to explain tribal phenomenon, there are certain commonalities which serve to underpin this analysis. I argue that regardless of whatever view one adopts, ethnonationalism is nationalism based primarily on ethnicity, while ethnochauvinism denotes a condition in which an organized ethnic group derives its internal legitimacy by aggressive behaviour towards groups and individuals that fall outside the ethnic marker.

These conceptual differences are of considerable importance for an analysis of current political phenomena in the Balkans. Here, ethnic groups have lived intermingled with each other for centuries; hence, regionalism as an exclusive notion (separating one region from another) is not possible, because ethnic and linguistic heterogeneity prevails. True regionalism is only possible if there is a movement of population groups from one region to another, thus producing ethnically and linguistically 'pure' regions. It can be argued that this is precisely the process now underway in ex-Yugoslavia.[1] Conceptually, this adds up to a causal chain of behaviour which reads ethnonationalism-ethnochauvinism-ethnic cleansing-'pure' regionalism, or the ultimate nation-state, which is based on the confluence of the nation, the state, and a definable territory, based on one ethnic group.[2]

This still does not help bridge the gap between tribalism and nationalism as concepts, however; it merely establishes some connection between the tribe, the state, the nation, and current political trends. If one assumes that tribes naturally developed into nations which then produced their own states, current events in the Balkans can only be explained by the notion that the inherent inclusiveness and exclusiveness of the tribes involved made it impossible to keep the larger unit, the state, together once a unifying symbol (such as a 'founding father' or an overwhelming external threat has disappeared (e.g. Yugoslavia); alternatively, it can be argued that a dominant 'tribe' in a 'multi-tribal' setting has 'hijacked' the state for the purposes of utilizing this structure to discriminate against others in ways that we normally attribute to tribes. This, in my opinion, is what has happened in the other Balkan states (Romania, Bulgaria, and Albania) after the demise of communism. And it is in this vein that the analysis will proceed.

Moreover, there are the Gypsies (or Roma), who have always constituted a set of groups apart from the societal order in much of the Balkans. The Roma live in a clan system, which in many ways resemble tribes as defined here. They are universally despised, and all the states of the region have enacted discriminatory laws against them. Even so, they do represent an element that falls outside the usual definition of 'nation', and nationalists of various stripes utilize them as scapegoats in their unending quest for someone to blame in the process of establishing ethnic, religious, and political boundaries. No examination of 'tribalism' would be sufficient without some investigation of this group.

WHY NOW?

The current interest in ethnicity is based on the fact that in recent years the incidence of such behaviour has seemingly increased in frequency as well as intensity. This notion is based on faulty historical knowledge; much of eastern Europe (and certainly the Balkans) has experienced waves of such behaviour before, both before and after the emergence of modern states in the region. Those who are well versed in the history of antiquity may well argue that the tribes of ancient Greece set the model for various forms of ethnic cleansing through the brutality of their warfare. Still, it is legitimate to ask why at this time, tribalism (as defined) seems to be particularly virulent, at least for the twentieth century.

As usual, there are several reasons. First of all, there is now the opportunity for tribalistic behaviour, since the old, oppressive political order has given way to a new, more open, but still chaotic system which is still sorely lacking in the tolerance exhibited by so called civil societies. This is particularly relevant in the Balkans, where there never has been a tradition of pluralistic democracy to begin with, and the dislocations of the post-communist era is not likely to produce one in such a short period of time. Secondly, historical antecedents have proven much more resilient than the forced societal change of the communist period; thus, the old order is resurfacing, and with a vengeance. This old order was very long on ethnochauvinism but very short on tolerance. Furthermore, it can be argued (correctly, I think) that the communist leaders of the region themselves adopted important elements of this nationalism in their frantic quest for a minimum of legitimacy; in the process, they represented historical continuity rather than change, thus reinforcing old traditions and hatreds.[3]

A third factor of great importance is the fact that there are now individual leaders in the region who are willing to utilize tribalistic slogans and policies to bolster their power. If we believe, with Gellner,[4] that nationalism is manufactured (as is, presumably, tribalism), the prevalence of men like Milosevich, Karadzic, and Mladic in Yugoslavia and Bosnia, and a Funar in Romania (to name but a few) is an important ingredient in the recent importance of various extremist behaviour patterns, tribalism among them. And finally, it is true now as it has always been that those places that pride themselves on having achieved 'civil society' will not risk lives and large expenses to try to foster it elsewhere. Thus, the tribalists have an open field of historical antecedents, cultural traits, and popular myths on which to build their dangerous doctrines. In this field, ethnicity occupies a central part.

ETHNICITY AS THE ESSENCE OF BALKAN NATIONALISM AND TRIBALISM

It has often been remarked that ethnicity is central to individual and group behaviour in the Balkans. On this point we are aided by a very large literature, and it is unnecessary to elaborate much on it. Ethnicity is not merely an expression of certain physical or genetic features; it stands also for religious adherence, cultural traits, and expected behaviour patterns. Thus, most Croats are Catholics, and most Serbs are Orthodox. Croats think they are hardworking, thrifty, culturally refined, 'European'; they consider the Serbs wild, uncultured, 'Asiatic'.[5] In other words, you are not a Serb because you exhibit these characteristics but rather these characteristics stem from your being a Serb. Ethnicity becomes the 'independent variable' which carries with it the other markers that help delineate one group from another and also establish a perceived hierarchy of groups, in which one's own is naturally on top, and others are both inferior and vile.[6]

This last point is very important, because it virtually precludes the development of civil society. With civil society I mean not just the existence of subgroup autonomy (you can have that in a society where groups exist in virtual ghettos, with little communication with each other); I am also referring to a state of affairs where groups coexist in mutual acceptance and respect- a society with civility. Only in such a society can the nation successfully incorporate and accommodate tribes, in the sense that the political and socio-economic leadership has succeeded in establishing a sense of commonality that goes beyond the tribe or subgroup while at the same time allowing for the tribes' existence inside the larger unit, the nation. In the Balkans, by and large, the political leadership of the last one hundred and fifty years failed to accomplish this, even as they established the political structures of democracy. This failure to produce an overriding notion that would supersede limited, ethnic notions of the polity, lies at the heart of the current trouble in the Balkans.[7]

The period of communist rule in this region turned out to be merely a lengthy interlude in the history of the area, and its legacies, while important, did not override more longstanding legacies, as discussed above. Specifically, communist rule did not produce nation-building- the crucial stage in which tribes (or other groups) accepted an overriding political order, with all its implications for culture, institution-building, decision-making and implementation, and functional pluralism. During the first two decades of communist rule, nationalism was denounced, and real or alleged perpetrators thereof were severely punished. After all, nationalism was the very antithesis of 'International' Marxism, and its presence in Eastern Europe would certainly have reduced Soviet control in the region. And when the communist leaders themselves turned to nationalism in order to bolster their flagging legitimacy, it was, ipso facto, the tribalist kind that prevailed, pitting ethnic groups against each other (e.g. Yugoslavia) or establishing discriminatory domination of one group over the others (e.g. Romania, Bulgaria). In retrospect, it is hard to see how it could have been otherwise, because the very nature of communist rule precluded the development of civil society as defined here; without civil society, overarching nationalism is difficult to establish, as argued above. In the event, the national communists of the Balkans adopted the myths and prejudices of ethnochauvinism, thereby appealing to the most deep-seated feelings of the masses constituting the largest ethnic group. In Gellner's terminology, national communism appealed to the low culture, disregarding the high. Under these circumstances, communist rule exacerbated the problem rather than solving it.[8]

The communist appeal to mass prejudices was made all the more likely since most of the technocratic elite was disillusioned with the existing order and hankered after a more open society in which its members could have a greater impact in the political system. These tendencies were widely perceived as a threat by the party apparatchik and the fellow travellers of the cultural and artistic elite; these latter elements therefore tended to make an alliance, in which literature, theatre, the cinema, and other areas of culture became the handmaiden of party propaganda, extolling ethnochauvinistic and tribalistic ideals in a form of 'proletkult' that presumably, appealed to the 'workers and peasants'. This is one of the main reasons why the Balkan scene after the demise of communism as a system of rule was quickly filled up with so called 'intellectuals' whose messages inflamed ethnochauvinism and tribalism, while denigrating civility and diversity.

While national communism often exacerbated ethnic relations, the system did provide a modicum of order and societal peace. This was so, I would suggest, because the communists wanted to maintain a monopoly on the use of force or the threat thereof; it was not necessarily because of a commitment to civility per se. Even so, tight control over violence (and the institutionalization of it, resulting in a regime monopoly of it) did eliminate the possibility of intergroup skirmishes and pogrom-like clashes. Intergroup animosity simmered just below the surface. When the communist monopoly on coercion was broken, and a freer political climate emerged (freer in the sense of removing regime controls), latent conflict burst into the open, with tragic consequences in Yugoslavia, but also with significant occurrences elsewhere in the Balkans, as will be seen below.

BALKAN LEGACIES: THE ATTITUDINAL DIMENSION

The Balkans constitute a region with an unusually rich heritage of tribalist myth as well as political leaders willing and able to use them for their own purposes. The most important of these myths are the following:

The notion of a glorious past that must be recaptured

An important part of the political culture in contemporary Romania, Bulgaria, Albania-, and ex-Yugoslavia is the notion of a glorious past that was somehow 'hijacked' by 'others', thus preventing the 'nation' from reaching its full potential and its rightful place in the world. As discussed above, the absence of civil society in these countries ensures that the perception of this problem, as well as the proposed solution to it, would remain essentially in the purview of the largest (and thus politically dominant) ethnic group, i.e. the Rumanians in Romania, Bulgarians in Bulgaria, and Albanians in Albania. In Yugoslavia, with its erstwhile federal structure and a political organization based on ethnicity, multiple myths developed, with disastrous results.[9]

The glories of the past are reflected in the identification of certain historical periods and events which presumably reflected the true stature of the nation or tribe. Thus, the Rumanians have discussed the archaeological finds in many areas of the country which indicate very early settlement by humans and a quite advanced culture before their neighbours reached such a stage. During the Ceausescu era, the regime and its sycophantic scholars, writers, and artists propagated the notion that the Dacians, who inhabited the territory of contemporary Romania before the arrival of the Romans, represented a higher culture than the imperial newcomers; this, of course, places indigenous Romanian culture above one of the two cultural superpowers' of European antiquity. Similarly, Romanian historiography has assiduously promoted the concept of fabulous achievements under the medieval kings Michael the Brave and Stephen the Great, even Vlad Tepes, the Impaler, who is seen as a 'provider of law and order', while all of the aforementioned leaders are depicted as saviours of Christianity in the struggle with Islam. Recent iconography includes Marshall Antonescu and the leaders of the Iron Guard and the League of the Archangel Michael. The main achievements of the latter leaders and groups were pogroms of the vilest sort and ideologies based on extreme intolerance of others.[10]

The concept of national glory reflected in this form of historiography has several characteristics. First of all, it is claimed on behalf of the Rumanians, and nobody else; in fact, it is claimed in contradistinction to other groups. Secondly, it is directed against others; the glory of the Rumanians stems to a considerable extent from their actions against Muslims, Jews, Hungarians. Thirdly, the 'others' actively sought to deprive the Rumanians of their rightful place and were temporarily successful; lost glory, territory, or heritage must now be reclaimed. This is unfulfilled nationalism, and because its claimant is only one of the groups residing on Romanian soil, it becomes frustrated tribalism.[11]

Similar mythologies can be found elsewhere in the region. Much has been written about the use of such concepts in the quest for 'Greater Serbia' (which includes the glorification of a lost battle, the battle of Kosovo Pole, in 1389).[12] The Bulgarians likewise eulogize the medieval period of Dushan and other leaders, while the Albanians remind the world that they were the original inhabitants of the region (Illyrians) while everybody else is, in reality, an intruder.[13] And, by the same token, other ethnic groups maintain their own perceptions of history, thereby enhancing group cohesion while sharply delineating themselves from others. This is particularly important for the Croats and Slovenes, who revel in their 'European' and 'Western' heritage, derived from their erstwhile inclusion in the Austro-Hungarian Empire and the European Kulturkreis.[14] It is a curious case indeed when nationalism and tribalism derive part of their distinction because of former subjugation to imperial power; the point here is the notion that the Habsburgs were more 'progressive' and 'modern' than their counterparts in Istanbul. Thus, the imperial heritage becomes another facet of tribal bragging rights.[15]

The orchestration of symbols for mass consumption is a relatively new phenomenon. The Romanian peasantry who fought the Turks in medieval times, or the foot soldiers of the lost Serbian cause at Kosovo Pole were illiterates who had been pressed into service. It is doubtful that they had much of an idea of the collective cause for which they were dying; perhaps in an elemental sense they understood the difference between 'their' god and 'ours', and thought that this was worth standing for. More complicated ideas of national honour or 'national interest' were probably beyond their ken. Since those remote days, however, several generations of political and religious leaders have succeeded in establishing these events and myths in the public consciousness, and playwrights, poets, and schoolteachers have followed suit in this quest. The movement of national liberation in the Balkans in the nineteenth century was spearheaded by elements of the clergy, thus adding a strong religious element to it. This clearly enhanced the fervour of the movement beyond the mythmaking of other nationalists. Now, those who were 'in' could claim the support of God for their group, while those who were 'out' had committed a truly tribal sin by rejecting the correct path (or having been excluded from it by God himself). The message from the pulpit was clearly effective because it reached a large audience of the least educated, the poorest, the most downtrodden, and the most gullible- the peasants. Later, as education spread among the population, the messages of ethnonationalism and chauvinism could be transmitted through this medium as well. Thus, the beginning of nationalism in the Balkans was, in reality, a form of tribalism. In Western Europe, by contrast, the entrepreneurial middle class became the chief purveyor of nationalism. This class understood the notion of 'civil society', at least in part. On this basis, the tone and tenor of nationalism there was quite different. Furthermore, the development of state structures and administrative procedures allowed for the furtherance of the 'political' nation, which accepted some diversity among groups and individuals. In Eastern Europe, and especially the Balkans, nationalism was 'cultural', as discussed above, and the development of state and administrative forms reflected this phenomenon. In short: Cultural nations lend themselves to tribalism, whereas political nations do not.[16]

The idea that others deprived the group of its rightful glory

Like all ideologies, Balkan ethnonationalism provides powerful symbols, pressures, and institutions devoted to establishing inclusiveness, but it is also particularly prone to emphasize the vicious and perfidious nature of 'others', who are seen as having deprived the group of its glory and its rightful place in history and in the concert of nations. Group failures are not the result of one's own mistakes but rather lie at the door of scapegoats. This mindset reduces the willingness of each group to examine its conduct, thus removing incentives for corrective mechanisms and behaviour as well as systematic reform of the political and cultural processes and structures of the group itself. Barring the existence of restraining forms and attitudes, this mindset will ultimately result in war, but before that stage is reached, it produces discriminatory behaviour of various kinds. And if war comes, it is particularly vicious, with more than the usual share of rape, murder, and hostage taking, because the issue is not simply victory on the battlefield but also destruction of the very core of the 'out' group. In the contemporary Balkans, it has produced the Bosnian war; outside of this area, it has produced anti-Semitism everywhere, as well as severe discrimination against the Roma; furthermore, anti-Hungarian behaviour in Romania, anti-Turkish policies and attitudes in Bulgaria, and persecution of Greeks in Albania are hallmarks of such 'tribalistic' mindsets.[17]

The crimes and discriminatory behaviour perpetrated in the name of the nation are not perceived as such by the perpetrators; rather, such behaviour is a form of 'avenging' past grievances, real or imagined. In the entire region of the Balkans, this tendency is further aggravated by the fact that the most important minorities in each state have strong supporters and their 'own' state just beyond the borders, as witnessed by the Hungarians in Romania, Turks in Bulgaria, and Greeks in Albania. This produces irredentism and countertribalism. Tribalism elevated to official nationalism breeds counter-tribalism, particularly if the groups now suffering discrimination by the self-proclaimed defenders of the nation had once occupied a dominant position. Thus, the Hungarians in Romania passionately nurtured their own form of ethnochauvinism based upon the historical fact that they used to control part of contemporary Romania for a considerable period of time in relatively recent memory. During the communist era this form of countertribalism could also pose as anticommunism, insofar as the dominant and oppressing tribe of communists was essentially (and increasingly) Romanian in ethnic terms. This was at least in part an artifact of time and circumstance, however; once communist rule was gone, the Hungarians in Romania proved reluctant to accept the notions of 'civil society' and turned out to be as dogmatic in their quest for political autonomy as their Romanian counterparts were in denying it. This is indeed what happens when tribalism substitutes for nationalism in the political sense, and parochial concerns preclude real nation-building. And the experiences of post-communist Romania in this regard do not augur well for the future development of pluralistic democracy or 'civil society' in that unfortunate country.[18]

As indicated above, the demise of communism did not spell the end of ethnochauvinism in Romania; it rather re-enforced it. This was so because the new leadership of the country was really a continuation, in body and spirit, of certain elements of the old order, so that a continuation of policy could also be expected. More important, however, was the fact that the new leaders now had to operate in a competitive political order, and in these circumstances, parties, interest groups, and movements had to deal with prevailing attitudes and values in the mass public. By 1990, the ethnochauvinistic policies of the Ceaucescus had clearly deepened resentment between the various ethnic groups in the country, but most of the national myths of the Rumanians had already been internalized and nurtured by the masses; these now claimed their due in the form of public opinion which drove chauvinism further. Even those elements in the political elites who would have liked to start the process of ethnic reconciliation and the development of 'civil society' values could not effectively do so and remain serious contenders. Thus, the ethnochauvinism of the 'high' culture of political elites may have started the process, but by the beginning of the post-communist era, the attitudes of the 'low' culture drove political discourse and produced a fertile field for chauvinists of all kinds (more will be said about these individuals later).[19]

During the five years that have now passed since the demise of the Ceausescu regime, ethnochauvinism has increased rather than decreased. At the same time, political discourse has been reduced to personal attacks and the crudest form of ethnic slander, and street mobs frequently provide the most forceful 'input' into the political system, while the regular parties and interest groups of the country feel constrained to express themselves in similar language, lest they lose mass support. The following developments are particularly illustrative of this trend:

a. Extremist parties, which advocate discriminatory policies against minorities while demanding a foreign policy devoid of 'Western' and 'dilettantish' influences, have become major political players, which represent crucial support mechanisms for the current government and, to some extent also for the president, Ion Iliescu;

b. In some areas, notably Transylvania, these parties have had considerable electoral success and have taken power in certain communities, e.g. the city of Cluj;

c. A number of political parties and movements, including strong elements of the ruling coalition and the established opposition, have campaigned actively for the restoration of Marshall Ion Antonescu to his 'rightful' place in Romanian iconography (despite the well-known fact that Antonescu's military dictatorship was marked by extreme persecution of Jews, Hungarians, and Roma);

d. Clearly discriminatory ordinances have been passed against minorities in areas under the control of extremist parties, thus producing a hardening of political attitudes among these minorities, notably the Hungarians of Transylvania;

e. Any attempt at moderate policies in inter-group relations is met by vicious personal attacks by extremist leaders and tacitly supported by many in the so called 'mainstream' parties;

f. A law on education, after much debate, rejected the expanded autonomy demanded by the Hungarians in this field; the debate on this issue produced some of the most vicious rhetoric ever seen in Romania (a tall order, indeed); the rejection of wider autonomy was supported by a very wide spectrum of the Romanian political scene, including most of the so called 'democratic opposition'.[20]

Add to this the widespread lawlessness which darkens much of Romanian daily life, as well as the high level of governmental corruption and the continued importance of a number of security agencies which habitually flaunt notions of law and order, and it is clear that Romania is very far indeed from the notions of 'civil society' to which the regime is, presumably, dedicated. Officially, there is democracy. In the day-to-day political process, a form of tribalism (as defined in this chapter) reigns. It is most accurate, therefore, to characterize contemporary Romania as a Scheindemokratie.[21]

Bulgaria and Albania: The Clash of Cultural Zones

Romania is clearly the place where extreme ethnochauvinism has been most prevalent in the post-communist era, but there are strong elements of it elsewhere in the Balkans as well. In Bulgaria and Albania, this kind of political phenomenon takes the form of clashes between groups that belong in different cultural zones; the struggle is therefore more verbal than physical, and extremist groups have not yet managed to capture political parties or, for that matter, the government itself. But the influence of political values and attitudes based on ethnicity, religion, and historical background is all-pervasive; such values dominate political discourse, and they are clearly deeply held by most of the population. They stem from the age-old tradition of cultural borderlands- areas which are located on the frontiers of two dominant cultures, with representatives of both zones coexisting on the same territory. These cultural zones are represented by Islam, Ottoman 'Orientalism', political autocracy, and traditional economic and social systems, on the one hand, and Orthodox Christianity, Greek-Hellenistic notions of politics and society, and a somewhat more advanced economic and social order, on the other. In Albania, the former tradition is dominant, while the Greek minority represents the second; in Bulgaria, the roles are reversed.

The notion of 'cultural zones' has a long and honourable tradition in history, anthropology, and social science. Basically, it holds that throughout history, identifiable political, social, economic, and cultural patterns predominate in certain areas, while a different mix of conditions prevail elsewhere. The mix is the result of a complex interaction of major events, broad trends in various areas of human endeavour, conscious decisions by elites, and pure happenstance. Major events such as the Renaissance, the Reformation, the development of alternative trade routes, the emergence of an entrepreneurial middle class, and the creation of a system of philosophy that emphasized the individual rather than the collectivity were fundamental events, as was the Enlightenment. Some political leaders made conscious decisions about the cultural zone to which they wished to belong, and they set about making policies that would ensure such a development. Their success or failure depended upon their capability of penetration, that is, the extent to which they could successfully implement their policies in the mass public and thereby ensure the requisite alteration of mass attitudes and values. Other leaders were content to choose certain specific conditions and characteristics for themselves, while making little effort to penetrate the masses for the purposes of societal transformation. Thus, we find royal courts where the language was French, while the masses of the population spoke the local vernacular and had little in common with the rulers. Similarly, geographic location proved to be crucial in the economic development of certain areas, which were favourably situated along new trade routes, while others, which had once been dominant in economic intercourse, became a stagnant backwater. The development of technology had similar effects. Finally, the spread of religion depended very much on the missionary zeal of certain monks and other transmitters of the word, as well as the decisions by kings and emperors to adopt one or another of these religions. Missionary zeal often went hand in hand with military conquest; thus proselytizing religions often reached the mass level, while other religions, notably Islam, made sharp distinctions between believers and infidels, and made few efforts to effect mass conversions. All of these factors produced cultural zones. In the Balkans, these zones intersected for a very long time. In Albania and Bulgaria, they continue to intersect, because both countries border on major representatives of the 'other' zone-Albania on Greece, the birthplace of 'Western' political and social forms, Bulgaria on Turkey, the last representative of conquering Islam. Albania and Bulgaria are cultural borderlands, and their populations are acutely aware of this fact.[22]

It is important to realize that at the end of the twentieth century, the concept of 'cultural zones' and the attendant hierarchy of cultures that it represents constitute political myths, not established fact. Thus, Bulgaria is not a shining example of 'Western' democracy, and Turkey is no longer the decadent harem society of the Porte. Furthermore, Greece is, in many ways, the contemporary 'sick man' of Europe in terms of economic development, and its political system can be of little inspiration to most of us. Albania is not necessarily a bastion of Islamic faith, especially after forty years of relentless proselytizing for atheistic Marxism in the form of Hoxhaism. But this hardly matters as long as the myths are believed by the masses and utilized by the political elites for their own purposes. If this is the case, 'zone' mythologies become prevalent in the political discourse, and they become political realities which produce behaviour on the part of the masses and elites alike. This is what has happened in Albania and Bulgaria since 1990.

Cultural zone mentality is coupled with strong nationalism in both countries. Albania represented an extreme case of national communism for decades; in fact, the ideology and policies of Enver Hoxha and his successors became exclusivist to the point where Tirana proclaimed all others as heretics and sinners against Marxism and proceeded to establish themselves as the defenders of the true faith. In foreign and economic policy, the Albanian leaders practiced extreme autarky based on paranoia, as seen today in the form of the hundreds of thousands of pillboxes that dot the land as a mute testimony to national readiness to fight all comers, regardless of the source of the incursion. Hoxha's proclamation of complete

71

success on behalf of atheism was in itself a monument to faith and paranoia. And, as the decades marched on, Hoxha, too, began to justify his policies and his power in terms of Albanian history and the great heroes of the past, especially Skanderbeg. The message thus was quite similar to that of Nicolae Ceausescu in Romania, and it was heavily influenced by Albanian nationalism. That nationalism was, in turn, typically Balkan; it hailed the efforts by the Albanian nation to stay alive in the midst of rapacious enemies and, after the conversion of most of the population to Islam, as an outpost fighting to preserve the faith and the teachings of Muhammed. As stated above, Hoxha rejected Islam, but he, too, saw himself as an outpost of orthodoxy, this time on behalf of Karl Marx, and the message of exclusivity was very much the same as it had been for the religious defenders of old.[23]

Since the demise of communist power, questions of ethnicity, religion, and national origin have dominated the politics of Albania. During the last few years, a number of Greeks have been put on trial, accused of spying for Greece; there have been a number of instances when discriminatory policies have been undertaken in terms of confiscation of property, and Greeks have been apprehended under the guise of prosecuting members of the communist party. There is clearly widespread discrimination at the mass level, with occasional reports of violence perpetrated upon members of the Greek community.[24] But the most important manifestation of ethnochauvinism in Albanian politics is to be found in the general political discourse, which is replete with the symbols and myths of national glory, discussed in more general terms above. This is disturbing, but it does not yet amount to tribalism, Romanian style.[25]

One of the most clear-cut examples of official discrimination against the Greek minority was the refusal by all political parties in the Albanian parliament to allow an organization representing ethnic Greeks to run in elections in 1992. Other issues that have inflamed political discourse include the question of the leadership of the Albanian Orthodox church, the problem of Serb policy towards (or against) the ethnic Albanians in Kosovo as well as the atrocities perpetrated by the Serbs in Bosnia, primarily against Muslims; furthermore, the government in Athens has charged the Albanians with ethnic discrimination against Greeks in the southern part of the country (which is, significantly enough, called 'Northern Epirus' in Greece). From Tirana's point of view, the strong ties between Greece and Serbia, coupled with the clearly anti-Muslim attitudes represented in this relationship, constitute a major foreign policy problem for Tirana, especially since they signify an age-old alliance of Orthodox Christians against Muslims. The fact that Albania maintains excellent relations with Turkey adds to the cauldron of international relations in the Balkans. Turkey, in turn, has been sponsoring the cause of Albania in rather aggressive terms in both bilateral and multilateral fora, producing some apprehension in the foreign ministries of the other Balkan states. Thus, history repeats itself in this troubled region, and it does so along lines which are clearly identifiable as cultural zones and the breakpoints between them.

All of this is troublesome, but it does not amount to tribalism as defined, nor does it approach the levels of ethnochauvinism found in contemporary Romania. This is further underlined by the fact that recently formed parties on the extreme right in Albania have failed to gain much support, in contradistinction to the Romanian case. Albanian politics primarily reflects ethnic animosity of the general kind found everywhere in the Balkans.[26]

Bulgaria, too, has produced its share of ethnochauvinism, but in this case, the worst excesses were clearly perpetrated during the communist regime, and specifically in the waning years of that era. During the second half of the 1980's, the Bulgarian communists desperately tried to bolster their legitimacy by conducting a discriminatory policy against the sizable Turkish minority in the country. Turks were forced to change their names so that they reflected a Slavic origin; unofficial quotas were established and enforced for Turkish enrollment in institutions of higher learning; there was active discrimination in employment; educational opportunities in the Turkish language were significantly curtailed; and there was widespread confiscation of economic assets. Turkish language publications were shut down. The rhetoric of the regime became significantly more strident in its proclamation of the typical myths of national glory, foreign discrimination and dastardly behaviour, focusing on the crimes perpetrated by the Ottomans during the long centuries of misrule by the Porte. The culmination of this campaign was the expulsion of several hundred thousand Turks from Bulgaria into Turkey in the summer and early fall of 1989. In this campaign, which turned quite violent, Bulgarian army units allegedly used artillery to bombard Turkish villages into submission.[27]

The dramatic events of 1989 represented a desperate attempt by a deeply unpopular regime to gain support by appealing to old prejudices in the mass public of ethnic Bulgarians. There is considerable evidence that in this, at least, the communist leadership was relatively successful, but it was not nearly enough to shore up a system which was tottering for other, more fundamental, reasons. The communists eventually fell in Bulgaria as elsewhere in the region, and they have been resurrected in a way subsequently, as they have elsewhere. Ethnonationalism and chauvinism have remained as a factor of great importance in Bulgarian politics, indicating the staying power of this old issue and the possibilities which exist for its exploitation in relatively open and competitive political systems.

The importance of ethnonationalism and chauvinism in the twilight years of communist power was not only as a ploy for regime enhancement; it represented a turn towards much older values and prejudices in a society which had lost all meaning for most people. During the 1980's, there was a strong religious revival in Bulgaria (much the same can be said for the rest of Eastern Europe as well), and this revival had a fundamentalist bent, mixed with mysticism and the glorification of old values. One of the most bizarre (and most interesting) of these movements was 'transcendentalism', which became particularly important in Bulgaria, due to its sponsorship by Lyudmila Zhivkova, the daughter of the communist dictator Todor Zhivkova. The adherents of 'transcendentalism' numbered in the tens of thousands, including many high ranking communist leaders. This eventually engendered a major political scandal, because it clearly undermined the authority of a regime officially dedicated to atheistic Marxism, but the purges that ensued failed to root out the problem. There was support for the movement in the mass public as well, even though the message of the 'transcendentalists' was too complicated and convoluted to really appeal to the average worker and peasant. The man in the street and the field instead held onto religious and ethnic prejudices and sought solace in the mythology of a glorious past. At the time, these values and myths had the added attraction of seemingly rejecting an unpopular regime; one could be anti-minority, anti-Turkish, and anti-communist at the same time. But this did not make the average man and woman a democrat in the Western sense of the word, and this, in turn, ensured that the establishment of the forms and procedures of pluralistic democracy did not produce a civil society or truly competitive politics. Once again, history has proved itself more durable than formalism, and optimism about the inevitable sweep of democracy has taken a setback to the facts of political culture, which in the case of Bulgaria (as well as the rest of the Balkans) has only the barest minimum of the necessary ingredients for democracy. Time may develop these elements further; the success or failure of that process will depend, in no small manner, upon the relations between the Bulgarians, on the one hand, and the ethnic minorities (especially the Turks) on the other.[28]

While the development of pluralism in Bulgaria leaves much to be desired from the point of view of Western reformers and model-builders, the politics of Sofia are not subsumed under extreme ethnochauvinism, which tends to be the case in Romania. Despite the fact that nationalistic and even chauvinistic rhetoric was frequently used in political discourse in Bulgaria after 1989, it did not promote the development of mass extremism. The extremist groups that did spring up in this period were quite unsuccessful in attracting a large following. Eventually, the barriers that were erected against organizations with primarily Turkish membership were also removed. By 1992 a political party whose membership and leadership were primarily made up of Bulgarian Turks had become a crucial player on the national political scene, and during the following three years this party actually served as a crucial coalition partner or informal support mechanism for the main government coalition. In fact, the party became the linchpin and the kingmaker in the last two governments. Ethnochauvinism at the elite level has succumbed to political expediency and the need to stay alive in a fragmented political system.[29]

Clearly, attitudes and values normally associated with ethnochauvinism still exist at the mass level, and there are still organizations that cater to such elements, but the lack of response by the political elites has made such groups into fringe elements. As a result, relations between Bulgaria and Turkey have also improved to a level unknown in recent history.[30]

The analyst is confronted with the need to explain the difference between Bulgaria and Romania on this issue. In both countries, ethnochauvinism has long traditions. Both of these systems reflected such attitudes during the communist era. Thus, the current differences must reflect policy variations in elite approaches at this time. Here, the differences are major indeed. As discussed above, ethnochauvinism is a very important aspect of the value system professed by all major political actors in Romania, albeit to different degrees. This has isolated the main political organizations of the Hungarians and other minorities; they cannot play a constructive role at the national level because the other parties will not allow them to do so. By contrast, extremism in Bulgaria has become largely a fringe phenomenon, and this has made it possible for parties and groups dominated by ethnic Turks to play a pivotal and system-supportive role in the current political order. Given the fact that Turkish-dominated organizations are needed by both major formations in the Parliament in order to establish a workable majority, chauvinistic rhetoric and policy must be toned down or eliminated. Mass prejudices, undoubtedly present, will not be nurtured under such circumstances. They may not wither and die, but they certainly will not grow and prosper.

Tribalism as International Politics: The Case of ex-Yugoslavia

The cruel war in Bosnia has received so much attention that it is unnecessary to dwell upon it here. At the same time, this case represents a laboratory exercise in tribalism as official policy by all of the combatants, with the Serbs as the most blatant perpetrators, but with the Croats, and to some extent, the Muslims relatively close behind. The world has now grown accustomed to the gory manifestations of ethnic cleansing, in which rape has become a form of warfare, and the forcible murder and expulsion of tens of thousands of individuals have become the norm. By the time the convulsions of this part of the Balkans are over, the quest of nations seeking to occupy 'their own' territory in an exclusivist manner may have been fulfilled, and probably also the notion that a nation with its own territory is entitled to utilize the state machinery for its own purposes, with no regard for any 'others' that may be around. There will be no diversity, no tolerance, and therefore no civil society and no democracy. Ex-Yugoslavia will most likely become the first European example of tribalism triumphant in both domestic and foreign policy.

As mentioned above, a superficial look at Yugoslavia in the 1970's would have made that country an unlikely candidate for triumphant tribalism. A more thorough examination would have revealed the great potential for just such a development. The various ethnic groups in the federation had well-established myths and prejudices. They had experienced actual persecution by 'others' during World War II, particularly in the form of atrocities committed by Serbs and Croats against each other. As the 1980's wore on, leaders emerged in all of the constituent republics who were committed to utilizing ethnochauvinism for their own purposes. These leaders were aided and abetted by scholars, artists, writers, even members of the technical and managerial intelligentsia, who perceived personal and group advantages in the perpetration and indeed intensification of mythmaking. And due to the decentralization of Yugoslavia and the considerable devolution of power on the constituent republics, particularly after the death of Tito, each major group also had national resources, including arms, so that they could engage in ethnic and religious wars with each other. Herein lies one of the main reasons why ethochauvinism turned to armed conflict in this country. And once that conflict was underway, the old hatreds could be verified through action – action of the bloodiest and most despicable kind.

The second major reason for armed conflict was the fact that the main combatants were relatively well matched in terms of size and economic potential. Thus, no group could single-handedly hijack the state, as was the case in Romania. Given the momentum of verbal and then physical conflict, no political leader could afford to preach moderation (which, by and large, had been done in Bulgaria and Albania). The dominance of one group over another could only be determined on the battlefield. Tribalism armed and organized ruled the day. The rest is well known from the mass media and a growing descriptive literature on the subject.[31]

Tribes in possession of modern weaponry and destructive technology can only be restrained by counterforce. This was eventually established in a rough way on the battlefield and lastly by a multinational peacekeeping force. But organized and armed tribalism is unlikely to give up its quest for exclusive domination, and this makes it highly unlikely that the countries of ex-Yugoslavia can approach anything like 'civil society' in the foreseeable future.

An Alternative View: Tribalism as Atomization, Hooliganism, and Organized Criminality.

The analyst of tribalism in the Balkans is most likely drawn to ethnochauvinism as the most prominent manifestation of it, for reasons which have been discussed in detail above. There is another way of looking at this problem, however; this would be to focus on atomization, alienation, hooliganism, and organized criminality. The formation of gangs, replete with elaborate membership rituals and identifiable markers as well as clearly established hierarchies and boundary lines, can be likened to the development of tribes. This kind of phenomenon is now quite prevalent in an unstable area such as the Balkans.[32]

There are long-standing traditions of tribalism as banditry in the Balkans. During the long centuries of Ottoman occupation, roaming bands of brigands, sallying forth from their mountain hideaways, were a regular feature of the Balkan landscape. These brigands robbed landlords and other representatives of the political and socio-economic elites and thus functioned as Robin Hoods while at the same time harassing an establishment which had been installed by the Turks; this was often perceived as freedom fighting. Thus, some of the early heroes of Balkan folklore were brigands, who clearly operated in a tribalistic fashion vis-a-vis the political order.[33]

With a political culture that accepted (indeed at times strongly supported) activity that was essentially illegal, it stands to reason that criminal activity reached a high level, Furthermore, alienation from the political order was profound, even though it was not necessarily based on individual withdrawal and resentment but rather the entire village community. The political parochialism that resulted has persisted to this day, producing a culture of profound cynicism, in which there are few values that can produce the overarching commitment needed to build a 'civil society'.[34]

Independence changed some of this, but not the basic values which had developed. Yesterday's brigands and freedom fighters became the leaders of the established order. With this development, criminal behaviour moved to the seat of power and took the form of widespread corruption, a feature which has remained an important element of Balkan politics ever since. Even the communist era failed to dislodge such behaviour patterns; indeed, the communist regimes in the Balkans were every bit as corrupt as their predecessors and rather more so than their northern neighbours. As it has been said, the criminals had captured the state and made extrasystem behaviour the official code. This was particularly the case in Romania, as discussed in some detail above.

As the communist regimes of the region stagnated, alienation of both groups and individuals deepened, and this had become a serious political liability by the end of the 1980's; indeed, it was probably the most important factor in the rapid downfall of the structures of power.

In all of the Balkan states organized criminal gangs emerged, often organized along the lines of the Mafia. Extremist groups such as skinheads and neo-Nazis roamed the streets, and simple hooliganism and vandalism became a factor of daily life. Smuggling became a lucrative business, particularly in Albania, where gangs helped keep a lifeline open to embargoed Serbia, with enormous profits as a result. There was also smuggling in Romania and Bulgaria. Prostitution and drug abuse flourished in all of the post-communist Balkan states, and protection rackets became a feature of ordinary business practices. Many of the organized gangs and Mafia-style organizations indeed resembled tribes. In ex-Yugoslavia, criminal elements became part of the established order in Serbia and Croatia, and in Bosnia, there have been similar developments lately. Serbia must receive the dubious honour of ranking on top in this list of tribalistic power.

For the analyst, systematic study of this phenomenon is hampered by the obvious lack of reliable information. This is so because criminal activity is by definition hidden from view; furthermore, unreliable statistics have always been a problem in the Balkans, and the undermanned and undertrained staff of the various information-gathering agencies are clearly unequal to the task of providing the necessary raw material for analysis. But perhaps the greatest handicap arises from the fact that organized crime in the Balkans has its tentacles all the way to the top of the political order (and, in some cases, have their 'own' ministries installed in the respective governments.) These authorities cannot be relied upon to produce the information needed.

Corruption and other illegal activity should be distinguished from violent behaviour on the part of individuals and gangs. It is possible to have widespread corruption and still maintain a form of 'civil society', insofar as basic rules of subgroup autonomy and tolerance for others are maintained. Criminals in such systems rather value the predictability of a functioning system, and they are not likely to violate its basic features, as long as their business interests are safeguarded. It is otherwise with widespread violence perpetrated by gangs and individuals. Violence by definition breaks the rules fundamental to 'civil society'. In fact, a high level of such lawlessness becomes a weapon in the struggle between ethnic groups and other actors who use ethnochauvinism as a justification for their activities. Such physical violence is present in varying degrees everywhere in the Balkans. It has reached horrifying epitome in ex-Yugoslavia, with Romania emerging in second place. In Bulgaria and Albania such violence has been reduced considerably from the early years of the post-communist era.

Alienation, depoliticization, and atomization are clearly on the rise in the Balkan states, as indeed is the case in the rest of post-communist Eastern Europe. The euphoria of the immediate aftermath of communist rule has given way to widespread pauperization and a pervasive insecurity among large segments of the population who feel that they have been cast adrift, without jobs, houses, or other aspects of the social safety net taken for granted in more stable societies. Millions of people now constitute a declasse element, and millions more have emerged as an underclass of drifters and marginal people, who have few prospects for personal improvement in the short or even intermediate run. Health statistics show a disturbing trend towards greater mortality, lower life expectancy, and re-emergence of 'illnesses of poverty', which had presumably been eradicated earlier. Clearly, these tendencies (and their attendant results) have created a large population segment that is 'mobilizable' for gangs and other groups we can call tribes. They are also mobilizable for ethnic chauvinists, and they constitute the hard core of these groups, especially in Romania and ex-Yugoslavia. On the other hand, this large scale societal dislocation has not produced revolution and the kind of wanton destruction that permeates part of the 'tribalist' continent of Africa at the moment. It should be pointed out, however, that the leaders of certain Balkan parties and movements are well aware of the support group that exists in this population, and they are able to mobilize it (or at least part of it) on relatively short notice. Then, latent tribalism becomes active tribalism, with disastrous results, as discussed.

Future political developments in the Balkans will depend greatly on the direction each state takes in relation to the marginalized population on its territory. Economic expansion will reduce this stratum and give at least some of its members a stake in the existing society. The larger this reintegrated group becomes, the better the prospects for 'civil society'. Conversely, the larger the marginalized groups, (and the deeper their debilitation), the greater the likelihood of latent tribalism becoming activated. On this will hinge stability or instability, and ultimately war and peace, in this troubled region.

CONCLUSION I: TRIBALISM, CIVIL SOCIETY, AND THE FUTURE

The post-communist political systems of the Balkans suffer from serious deficiencies which will not be easily overcome. As discussed above, those deficiencies are products of history, the prevailing culture, and expediency on the part of elites, be they political, economic, or social. The scope and magnitude of these problems give the analyst reason to be pessimistic about future political developments for the short or even the intermediate run. Particularly doubtful are the prospects for the development of pluralistic democracy and civil society. That is true even if one takes the long view of history, which argues that it took Western Europe, too, many decades to develop political systems of legal transparency, established procedures for decision-making, generally accepted rules for the recycling of political elites, and a sense of political and administrative efficacy in the general population. The process of developing ethnic and religious tolerance and a sense of nationhood among the many groups with narrow loyalties to parochial values and outlooks was also a long one. While all of these arguments are correct, they may not be fully relevant for the Balkans today, because the circumstances of Romania. Bulgaria, Albania, and ex-Yugoslavia are quite different from those that prevailed in France, Great Britain, Scandinavia, or the Low Countries one hundred years ago, say, when pluralistic political systems began to emerge there. Thus, even if some of the main deficiencies of Balkan history can be overcome, other factors now present in the region represent formidable obstacles on the path to 'civil society'.

CULTURAL NATIONALISM RESISTS PLURALISM

It has been argued that nations which exist before the establishment of political and administrative structures to rule them become 'cultural' nations; they define membership in terms of race, ethnicity, religion, language, or other non-negotiable characteristics, and they tend to look upon political structures as mere codification of these commonalities, to the exclusion of those who do not possess them. 'Political' nationalism, by contrast, is: produced by elites who have certain goals and objectives in mind, chief of which is the notion of breaking down existing group loyalties and rebuilding them around a broader concept, that of the 'nation', whose characteristics are defined by the nation-building elites for their own purposes. The political nation is likely to produce a culture that accepts racial, ethnic, linguistic, and religious differences as tolerable because they are secondary to the overriding commonality of the 'nation'.

Tribalism as it appears is more likely to be more prevalent in cultural nations than in their political counterparts. In the former case, tribalism can seize control of the machinery of the state, thus in effect defining the characteristics of the 'nation' in its own image. Furthermore, the very process of nation-building becomes nothing more than tribal expansion, in which the leaders of the dominant tribe expand their exclusivist characteristics and goals to 'others' or, alternatively, destroy them or expel them. In the case of political nations as defined, tribalism is largely irrelevant in terms of power, but it is tolerated as something that exists at the subnational level, without any real threat to the political order that has been constructed. The Balkan states were formed in cultural nations; now, groups which we can call 'tribes' have captured the state mechanisms and utilize the institutions of formal democracy to make their tribalistic goals into national goals. As discussed, this tendency is most pronounced in ex-Yugoslavia, followed by Romania; Bulgaria and Albania have less of this tendency.

POLITICS IN THE BALKANS IS SEEN AS A ZERO-SUM GAME

For large numbers of people, the removal of the communist order produced systems which gave them an opportunity to act relatively freely inside the new order. Their goals, aspirations, prejudices, and hates could now be given political form. The immediate effect of this was the emergence of all kinds of movements and parties that utilized freedom of expression and aggregation to argue these hates and dislikes openly, and indeed to compete for the privilege of capturing power and thus implementing their discriminatory views in the form of public policy. This attitude is further enhanced by the fact that people in the Balkans have always looked upon politics as a zero-sum game that had to be won at all cost, lest the 'others' use the system to the grave detriment of 'us'. Such political cultures tend to give rise to tribalistic behaviour as defined in this chapter. It is arguable that the adoption of democratic forms and procedures virtually overnight in such systems is not beneficial for the development of 'civil society', and that some kind of enlightened authoritarianism', which could foster adminis-trative efficacy, would be more beneficial. Then again it is questionable that such authoritarianism can be found and maintained in political cultures that are divided by ethnic and religious attachments which are held with great fervour, with little experience in interpersonal or intergroup tolerance. In such systems, authoritarian rulers most likely would hijack the state on behalf of their own group, with results already known from parts of the Balkans. Zero-sum game political cultures simply lend themselves to tribalism as a mass phenomenon, which will then become mainstream politics. By the same token, variable-sum cultures, with their emphasis on compromise and accommodation, will tend to confine tribalism to the fringes of the political order. There is a world of difference between these two scenarios. Unfortunately, the Balkan states fall mostly in the first category.

LEADERSHIP AND POLITICAL MOBILIZATION ARE CRUCIAL IN THE DEVELOPMENT OF TRIBALISM

The experiences of the Balkans since the demise of communist systems clearly show the importance of political leadership in the development of tribalism. In Yugoslavia, the ethnic and religious animosities that erupted in the 1990's had always been present, but they were intermittently latent and active, depending on the impetus provided by individual leaders and their groups. Thus, in the period between the two world wars, Serbian nationalism and chauvinism dominated the country. In the Titoist period, the stature of 'the father of modern Yugoslavia' prevented serious disturbances, at least until his power was in relative decline. By contrast, the deliberate use of ethnochauvinism by Tito's successors, primarily in Serbia (but also to some extent in the other republics) helped inflame the mass public, which in turn fed these rekindled passions back to the leadership in a Teufelskreis of escalation, with the tragic results now known to all. In Romania, the ethnochauvinism of the Ceaucescu's helped pave the way for Gheorghe

Funar and Adrian Paunescu, to name but two of the most rabid chauvinists now in operation. Ion Iliescu, the President of the Republic and thus the most powerful politician in the country, has been reluctant to take decisive steps against the likes of Funar and Paunescu and has been partly dependent upon their support in Parliament; one of the reasons for the President's weak stance on ethnic chauvinism is the likelihood that, deep down, he sympathizes with them. And, as a former high level bureaucrat in the communist system Iliescu cannot be expected to believe in the 'Western' notion of 'civil society'; in fact, he has provided us with his own definition of the good society which has strong overtones of collectivism and authoritarianism. With a different leadership, Romanian extremism would most likely have a different hue, but then, would a different leadership be produced by this kind of political culture ? And, furthermore, a more 'pluralistic' leadership which would battle ethnochauvinism could expect serious problems at the ballot box, given the mass attachment to authoritarian values now clearly present in much of the mass public. Such are the ways of democratic forms in chauvinistic cultures.

CONCLUSION II: TRIBALISM, ETHNOCHAUVINISM, NATIONALISM: WHAT IS IN A CONCEPT?

As is clear from the preceding discussion, the analysis of tribalism in the Balkans is heavily influenced by concepts such as ethnochauvinism, ethnonationalism, ethnic separatism, even extremism. It is widely held (and correctly so, I think), that one cannot understand contemporary Balkan politics without reference to ethnicity, religion, and the national myths of grandeur and of nefarious 'others' who try to demean one's own nation. Tribalism as it is usually perceived in the literature is mostly present in the way in which this Balkan ethnonationalism expresses itself in the brutality with which 'others' are treated, in the zero-sum approach to the political process, and in the relentless quest to fuse nation, state, religion, and territory. If we assume (as do most analysts of this question) that political development means a move towards a 'civil society', established forms and procedures in political deliberation, decision-making, and implementation, as well as a variable-sum approach to the game of politics, the Balkan systems represent a more 'primitive' stage in which passion and prejudice rule, where intolerance supersedes tolerance, and where fundamental 'truths' are more important than compromise (indeed, compromise is despised as 'selling out' the core interests and values of the group). At the same time, horsetrading and extra-systemic behaviour abound, because politics is still a game of great personal influence and prejudice as well as unbounded cynicism, unfettered by real rules of civility or any common goals and aspirations that go beyond the markers of the 'we' group, as discussed above. Thus, large groups behave like tribes, but they do not behave like nations that have transcended the tribal stage. This gives the notion of Balkan tribalism a special meaning.

'Tribes' are also said to exist in modern societies, where individuals and groups, alienated from the 'superstate' of the contemporary era, focus their political attention on smaller units for their attachment. This form of 'tribalism', seen at times in the post-industrial West, is a form of rejection of both the 'state' and various forms of socio-economic characteristics of the 'post-modern' society. In the Balkans, at the end of our tumultuous century, it is self-styled nations that behave like tribes, utilizing the machinery of the state to implement their particularistic goals and aspirations. Perhaps we can call these political entities 'nation-tribes'. Their activities are particularly pernicious because they operate at a relatively high level of technology, certainly in the field of coercive capability. Their control of the state machinery and armed forces thus lends unprecedented destructive power to tribalism. By contrast, tribes in the early developmental stages of humankind had limited numbers, primitive technology, and only small areas under contest. In 'political' nations at a high level of development, most political participants compete for power according to rules and procedures that are broadly accepted by all; 'tribes' in this context become fringe movements, and the power of the state can be brought to bear against them, if need be, since the forces of relative consensus still control the state machinery and the elements of legitimate coercion. Thus, the most important manifestations of tribal power are located at the intermediate levels of development. In Europe, that is where the states of the Balkans are located today. It will be a rather long and difficult haul to move to the next stage. Since the concepts 'tribe' and 'nation' are thus fused to some extent at this stage (and under these specific circumstances), the concept of 'tribalism' as a discrete and explanatory variable will need to be modified for the analysis of the contemporary era.

NOTES

1 See for example, V.P. Gagnon, Jr., 'Serbia's Road to war' in Larry Diamond and marc F. Platter (eds) (1994). *Nationalism, Ethnic Conflict, and Democracy* (Baltimore, MD: The John Hopkins University Press), pp. 117–32.
2 See also Janusz Bugajski, 'The Fate of Minorities in Eastern Europe' in *ibid.*, pp. 102–17.
3 I have discussed this in some detail in my *Nationalism and Communism in Romania* (Boulder, CO; Westview Press, 1990) esp. Ch. 3, pp. 39–57.
4 See Gellner, *Nations and Nationalism* esp. introduction.
5 Ramet and Adamovich, *Beyond Yugoslavia* esp. Ramet, 'Introduction: The Roots of Discord and the language of War' (pp. 1–13).
6 For an excellent analysis of the Romanian variant, see Michael Shafir, 'Romania' in the *Politics Of Intolerance*, pp. 87–94.
7 A good overview of Balkan history is Robert Lee Wolff (1974). *The Balkans in our Time* (Cambridge, MA: Harvard University Press).

8 On national communism, see Peter Zwick (1983). *National Communism* (Boulder, CO: Westview Press) esp. Ch. 1 (pp. 1–15).

9 Ivo Banac,'The Dissolution of Yugoslav Historiography', in Ramet and Adamovich, *Beyond Yugoslavia*, Ch. 2, p. 39–67.

10 See, for example, Aurica Simion (1979). *Preliminarii Politico-Diplomatice ale Insurectiei Romane din August 1944* (Political and Diplomatic Preliminaries to the Romanian Insurrection of August 1994) (Cluj-Napoca: Editure Dacia); further, Paul Everac (1992) Reactionarul (The Reactionary), (Bucharest, Romania: Editura Romanul). Everac was director of Rumanian television until January 1994.

11 Michael Shafir is excellent on this; see his 'Extreme Nationalist Brinkmanship in Romania', in *RFE/RL Research Report*, Vol. 2, No. 21, 21 May, 1993.

12 This is now a theme routinely pronounced by Serbian intellectuals; see for example the 1994 Congress of Serbian intellectuals in Belgrade, as discussed in *Borba* (belgrade) and analyzed by Stan Marketich in 'Serbian intellectuals promote the concept of Greater Serbia', in *RFE/RL Research Report*, Vol. 3, No. 23, 10 June, 1994.

13 A thorough discussion of this is Bernard Toennes (1980). *Sonderfall Albanien* (Munich, Germany: R. Oldenbourg Verlag) esp. part 1, Ch. 1. (pp. 35–59).

14 Dijana Plestina, 'Democracy and Nationalism in Croatia: the first three years' in Ramet and Adamovich, *Beyond Yugoslavia* Ch. 6 (pp. 123–55).

15 *Ibid.*,

16 See, for example, Larry Diamond and Marc F. Plattner, 'Introduction' in Diamond and Plattner, *Nationalism, Ethnic Conflict and Democracy*, pp. ix–xxix.

17 I have relied on a considerable literature in this summary. For a recent discussion, see 'Southeastern Europe' in *The Politics of Intolerance*, pp. 72–104. (Robert Austin on Albania, Kjell Englelbrekt, Bulgaria; Patrick Moore on Croatia; Macedonia, by Duncan M. Perry; Romania by Michael Shafir; Stan Marketich on Serbia and Slovenia).

18 See, for example, Tom Gallagher, 'Ethnic tension in Cluj', *RFE/RL Research Report*, Vol. 2, No. 9, 26 February 1993.

19 In the elections to the Parliament in 1992, parties that would normally be termed 'extreme right' obtained roughly 155 of the seats(fairly equal in both chambers), but more significantly, the larger parties by and large argued along lines similar to the extremists in matters pertaining to ethnic relations (albeit in a less flamboyant fashion). The electoral results can be found in Rompres (1993). Partide Police 1993 (Political Parties 1993), Annex 4, pp. 185–91.

20 For an example of the extreme personal attacks now common in Romanian political discourse, see Adrian Paunescu, a well known right wing political leader, criticizing President Ikon Iliescu for visiting the opening of the Holocaust museum in Washington, in *Totusi Iubirea* (Bucharest journal), No. 16, 23–30 April 1993.

21 I have summarised a great deal of literature here. For a superb discussion of the intellectual and ideological foundations of these movements, see Michael Shafir, 'The Mind of Romania's Radical Right' (Unpublished paper delivered at a conference on the radical right in Eastern Europe, held at the University of Seattle, WA, March 1996).

22 This is certainly so in the field of ethnic relations, See for example, discussion of Iliescu's weak democratic credentials in the Bucharest weekly *Zig Zag* No. 25, 28 August–3 September 1990.

23 One important volume that discusses this and other related concepts is John A. Armstrong's *Nations before Nationalism* (Chapel Hill, N.C.: University of North carolina Press).

24 A very large literature can be drawn upon to illustrate this point. See for example, John A. Garrity and peter Gay (eds) (1972). *The Columbia History of the World* (New York, N.Y. Harper and Row Publishers), esp. Ch. 22, 23, 24 (pp. 253–89); Ch. 52 (pp. 604–19); and Ch. 59 (pp. 681–92).

25 Toennes, *Sonderfall Albanien* Part 1, Ch. 2 (pp. 59–84) and Part 1, Ch. VI (pp. 199–249).

26 Such activities were reported in *Neue Zuercher Zeitung* (Zurich), 8 July 1993.

27 E.g., Hugh Poulton (1991). *The Balkans: Minorities and States in Conflict* (London: Minority Rights Group), esp. pp.190–7.

28 See Robert Austin, 'Albania' in *The Politics of Intolerance* pp. 72–4.

29 One of the many books on this is Robert D. Kaplan (1994). *Balkan Ghosts* (New York, N.Y.: Vintage Books), esp. pp. 193–220 and 226–84.

30 On the religious revival in Bulgaria, see *ibid*, pp. 221–40.

31 The best research on the Balkans after the fall of communism is clearly carried out by Radio Free Europe and its successor OMRI. On Bulgaria see Kjell Engelbrekt, 'Bulgaria's Political Stalemate', in *RFE/RL Research Report*, Vol. 3, No. 25, 24 June 1994, p. 2025.

32 *Ibid.*

33 The best recent book on this is ramet and Adamovich (eds), *Beyond Yugoslavia*, e.g., Dennison Rusinow, 'The Avoidable Catastrophe' (Ch. 1, pp. 13–39).

34 E.G., Wolff, *The Balkans in Our Time*, Ch. 4 (pp. 50–69). See also Mary Edith Durham (1928). *Some Tribal Origins, Laws and Customs of the Balkans* (London: Allen and Unwin).

Chapter Five

Ethnic Conflict in China: The Case of Tibet

Denny Roy

Much like the former Soviet Union, China is a multi-ethnic empire with a government that strives to be totalitarian. Just as the collapse of the Soviet Union unleashed a torrent of tribalistic sentiment, we may someday find that the breakdown of Beijing's central control yields similar results in the territory now administered by the Chinese Communist Party. In the meantime, however, Chinese-controlled Tibet already qualifies as one of Asia's most destructive and tragic ethnic conflicts.

The story of Tibet is well known, but not necessarily in the context of tribalism. Nonetheless, Tibet is an appropriate case-study under the definition I employ: 'tribalism' exists, in my view, when people identify with a sub-state group, defined by a common culture and/or ethnicity, and invest their political loyalty in this group rather than in the reigning state government.

In this sense, Tibetans (i.e. ethnic Tibetans who live in Tibet) certainly display tribalism; to a certain extent, so do the Han Chinese who live in Tibet. This chapter will substantiate these points, assess this case in terms of the principal questions this book investigates, and analyze the implications for the People's Republic of China and the regime's larger goals. We will find, I hope, that the origins and character of Tibetan tribalism are unique, putting the phenomenon of tribalism in a different perspective than do many of the other cases examined in this book.

THE TIBETAN-HAN CLASH

As many analysts have noted, China's is a relatively inclusive civilization (in contrast with, for example, those of Japan or Korea). Peoples of a variety of ethnicities may be accepted as 'Chinese' provided they adopt basic aspects of Chinese culture, such as speaking the Chinese language, eating Chinese food and practicing Chinese social and political customs. There are of course geographic limits to 'Chineseness.' In ancient history, Chinese elites categorized their known world through a set of concentric circles radiating outward from the Chinese heartland (demarcated roughly by the Great

Wall in the north, the Yangzi River in the west, and the East and South China Seas). Countries in the outermost circles were thought to be peopled by barbarians who were hopelessly incapable of appreciating Chinese culture. Sinicization was possible, however, for those in the near circles, where Tibet was located. Tibetans thus fell into China's traditional sphere of influence, and Chinese over the centuries grew accustomed to thinking of Tibet as part of the Chinese empire. More recently, the Communist Party regime has realized Tibet's economic, strategic, and domestic political value (more on this below); these have convinced the leadership to make a determined effort to resist what they see as an attempt by their enemies to change the status quo. The tribal clash in Tibet is thus best understood as a result rather than a cause of Chinese efforts to dominate Tibet.

The borders of Tibet roughly follow the edges of the 2.5 million square kilometer Tibetan Plateau. Buddhism entered Tibet in the seventh century and eventually overwhelmed the pre-existing Tibetan folk religion of Bon, although Tibetan Buddhism has incorporated some features of Bon. As the state religion, Tibetan Buddhism brought religion and politics together; since 1642, Dalai Lamas have served as both head of state and chief religious ruler. Furthermore, Buddhist teachings heavily influenced every aspect of Tibetan life, from government to family relationships to lifestyle.

Other than the infusion of Buddhism, Tibet until recent times had little contact with the outside world, isolated by the rugged mountains bounding it and by the height of the plateau it occupies. During most of the first half of this century, virtually no Chinese had lived there. This changed, however, with the Chinese Communist revolution. Troops of the People's Liberation Army invaded in 1950, overwhelmed Tibet's small army, and placed the area under CCP administration as the Tibet Autonomous Region (TAR), commonly known in Mandarin Chinese as Xizang. When Chinese Communist Party troops moved against Tibet, it had the key attributes of statehood outlined by international law: well-defined and inhabited territory, a functioning government, and the capacity to conduct diplomacy. Nevertheless, the United Nations ignored Tibet's pleas for protection, and no major foreign government has recognized Tibet as an independent state.

Over 90 per cent of the inhabitants of China proper belong to the Han ethnic group. The civilizational clash in Tibet, therefore, is primarily between recently-arrived Han administrators, soldiers and settlers and native Tibetans.

While many Han have developed an appreciation for the Tibetan people and their culture, Han generally view Tibetans as primitive, uncouth barbarians. At best, Chinese treatment has been condescending. One foreign observer notes, 'Television, radio and newspaper media all pour out a constant message of how the Tibetans are backward 'little brothers,' and China the 'big brother' [has] come to help them. Tibetan Buddhism, art, architecture, music and so forth are all presented as quaint yet obsolete.

Everything from afternoon soap operas to roadside billboards echoes this same theme.'[1] The uglier side of this Han sense of the inferiority of Tibetans has manifested itself in the staggering brutality Chinese authorities have inflicted upon Tibetan dissidents, or even upon law-abiding Tibetans who found themselves in exploitative circumstances. Mary Craig, for example, relates the story of Lhakpa Chungdak, a rural Tibetan girl who joined the PLA at age 15 after being promised she would be trained as a doctor. Instead, she was made a 'servant' to various male officers, a virtual sex slave, repeatedly drugged and raped.[2]

The clash between Tibetans and the Han invaders is exacerbated by significant cultural dissimilarities. The unique geography of Tibet, a harsh, underpopulated land, has had important cultural implications. Traditionally, half the population have been nomads who made the raising of livestock their livelihood. This background instilled a sense of autonomy and rugged individualism. The Chinese offended these sensibilities when they required Khampa horsemen to give up their rifles in 1955, an act that triggered a major rebellion. Tibetans were similarly disturbed by the Maoist policy of forced collectivization, in which privately-owned land, tools and livestock became the property of communes administered by CCP commissars.

In another example of the contradiction in Han and Tibetan lifestyles, the Chinese forced local farmers to change traditional agricultural practices, insisting that wheat be grown instead of barley, which is more suitable to Tibet's climate, and that a crop be produced every season, breaking the Tibetan tradition of leaving the land fallow on alternate seasons to allow regeneration of the soil. The results were predictably poor, leading to large-scale starvation, hitherto virtually unknown in Tibet.

Religion is one of the major cultural barriers between Tibetans and Han. Chinese Communist Party ideology accepts the Marxist view of religion as the 'opiate of the masses.' The regime has interpreted Tibetan Buddhism as a prime example of this dictum. Lamas are accused of having used their religion for centuries as a means of repressing the masses and enriching themselves off the labor of others. From the Party's standpoint, Tibetan Buddhism is feudal, counter-revolutionary, and fit for nothing but eradication. For much of the PRC's history, Chinese authorities in Tibet have systematically worked to destroy the local religion, although the pervasive entrepreneurism of the Deng Xiaoping era has tempered this campaign by alerting Party officials to the revenue-generating possibilities of foreign tourism.

For the Tibetans, the atheistic Communist Chinese worldview seems to focus totally on material progress, on satiating the selfish urge for comfort in this life, when the point of Buddhism is to learn to extinguish one's carnal cravings as a way of preparing for the next life. As a Tibetan monk from the Drepung monastery explained, 'As the Chinese reject the existence of future lives, that is one difficult point. If freedom is only to eat and drink, it doesn't have much significance. That can be done by any animal such as a dog or a cat who only worry about food or drink. . . . To be human has deeper meaning.'[3]

The primary source of Han-Tibetan friction, of course, is the fearsome mistreatment of Tibetans by the Chinese Communist administration. The Dalai Lama laments that his people have 'not only been shot, but also beaten to death, crucified, burned alive, drowned, vivisected, starved, strangled, hanged, scalded, buried alive, disembowelled, and beheaded,'[4] and his claims are heavily corroborated by scholars, journalists and human rights monitoring organizations.[5] There have been numerous reports of dissidents, including monks and nuns, arrested en masse, tortured and often killed during detention; excessive force used by PLA troops against demonstrators; especially shocking atrocities, encompassing a variety of cruel tortures, during the infamous Cultural Revolution; forcible abortions performed on Tibetan women found pregnant with a second child, even though overpopulation is not a problem in the region; and even young Tibetan children arrested, beaten and tortured with electric shocks.[6] As in China proper, the Chinese authorities in Tibet organized 'struggle sessions,' public hearings in which local landowners, clergymen and others the regime considered 'counter-revolutionary' were denounced, humiliated and beaten, with the audience encouraged to participate. Egged on by Chinese officials, mobs murdered and cruelly abused untold numbers of people, often on the flimsiest of pretexts.

The Tibetan government-in-exile has estimated that the Chinese occupation has killed 1.2 million Tibetans, nearly 20 per cent of the Tibetan population.

Besides these all-too-common abuses of civil and political rights, Tibetans and outside observers also accuse the Chinese government of various forms of exploitation of Tibet and its people. Tibetans have been forced to donate blood. Han occupiers have looted thousands of precious works of local art. Tibetan dissidents accuse the Chinese administration of severely damaging Tibet's ecology through unrestrained pollution, uncontrolled extraction of timber and other natural resources for shipment back to China proper, and offering parts of the land as dump sites for the hazardous wastes of foreign countries.

A common perception among Tibetans is that Chinese officials posted to Tibet are carpetbaggers who use their privileges to gather up the region's riches and transport them back to China proper. Dorje Tsephel says of CCP officials: 'The Chinese claim they've come to help the Tibetans, but all they do is rob us and take all our natural wealth to China. When they arrive, they come with empty bags, but they go away with two or three truckloads of possessions. A posting to Tibet is a guarantee that they will make their fortune.'[7] During the demonstrations of 1988, a poster appeared depicting a fat Chinese official and his possessions, which were so heavy they were being lifted by a crane, over the caption, 'Thin on arrival, fat on departure.'[8] Hu Yaobang, then considered the most likely successor to Deng, visited Tibet on a fact-finding mission in 1980 and reportedly concluded of the Chinese occupation, 'This is plain colonialism.'[9] Unfortunately, Hu's views proved unrepresentative of the powers that be in Beijing.

The Chinese have attempted by various means to destroy Tibetan culture. The most visible methods have been to close down places of worship, forbid or limit religious practices, and harass practitioners of Tibetan Buddhism. The Tibetan exile leadership says the Chinese government has destroyed over 6,000 monasteries and temples. A more subtle means has been secularization and Sinicization of Tibet's formerly religious-oriented schools. In the education system administered by the Chinese government, Tibetan culture and language are belittled, while Chinese culture and history are extolled. Both Tibetan-language and Mandarin schools exist, but the former are manifestly inferior in facilities, educational materials and quality of instruction. According to a Briton who lectured at the University of Tibet in Lhasa, 'The system is definitely discriminatory. It is certainly not easy for Tibetans to get into Chinese sections, and if they do they have to give up Tibetan.' Some of the brighter and more promising Tibetan youth are taken to China for schooling, sometimes against the wishes of their parents. In May 1991, Chinese authorities in Tibet reduced the price of liquor by one-half, a move many observers charged was designed to further debilitate the Tibetan community.

If the long-term goal of PRC officials is to destroy Tibetan culture, they have also sought to hijack it in the short-term, a practice consistent with the CCP regime's treatment of other religions in the People's Republic. The recent row over the Panchen Lama succession is a case in point. The Panchen Lama is second only to the Dalai Lama in the ecclesiastical hierarchy of Tibetan Buddhism. The 10th Panchen Lama died in 1989. According to Tibetan Buddhist doctrine, the soul of the departed Panchen Lama migrates to the body of a boy born soon thereafter. The Dalai Lama named Gedhun Choekyi Nyima, then age 6, as the 11th incarnation of the Panchen Lama in May 1995. Beijing protested that the Dalai Lama had violated the usual protocol for this procedure, which by tradition includes consultation with the Chinese government. The following November, Chinese government officials presided over the selection of another 6-year-old Gyaincain Norbu, as the Beijing-approved Panchen Lama. Not surprisingly, many Tibetans saw the Chinese ceremony as a farce. 'This is very amazing since [the Chinese communists] don't believe in religion in the first place,' one wryly noted.[10]

While plenty of the damage the Han have done to Tibetan society has been direct and intentional, some of it has been indirect and perhaps unintentional. An example is the effect of Han colonization on the employment prospects of the natives. Once they enter the workforce,

Tibetans, especially those who went through the Tibetan-language stream, find fewer and lower-paying jobs in their homeland than do the Han settlers. Another foreign educator and former resident of Lhasa observes, 'All menial tasks are performed by Tibetans – they are undoubtedly second-class citizens in their own country. You will never find a Chinese doing the following jobs: toilet cleaning, street sweeping, gate keeping, road mending, electrician, plumber or carpenter.'[11]

With the local economy increasingly controlled by and oriented toward higher-earning Chinese settlers, most Tibetans are finding themselves effectively locked into a lower socioeconomic stratum. As a Tibetan farmer complains, 'seeds and fertilizers, which we have to buy from the Chinese shops, are so expensive that in the end it is not enough to give a family even one meal a day. We have to buy everything in the shops run by the Chinese: things for the land, the clothes I am wearing, even my shoelaces. The Chinese charge us very high prices, but we have no option.'[12]

At the conclusion of one struggle session soon after the Chinese takeover of Tibet, the conducting Chinese official asked the audience for comments. The feelings of many Tibetans were summarized by one defiant old man who said,

> Since I am poor, I have nothing to lose; since I am old, death will come for me soon anyway. I have this to say to you Chinese: ever since you entered our land, we have been barely able to tolerate your behavior. Now you try to force some new-fangled 'democratic reforms' on us, that all of us think are ridiculous and nothing but a mule-load of conceit. What do you mean you will give us land, when all the land you can see around has been ours since the beginning of time? . . . If anyone is oppressing us, it is you. Who has given you the right to force your way into our country and foist your irrational ideas on us? We are Tibetans, you are Chinese. Go away to your homes, go back to your own people. We have no need of you here.

The old man was arrested the next day and soon himself became the victim of a severe beating at a struggle session.[13]

MANIFESTATIONS OF TIBETAN TRIBALISM

To be sure, some Tibetans have benefitted from Chinese rule, using Chinese education as a springboard to better jobs than they would otherwise find. And the regime is never at a loss to produce Tibetan spokespersons who endorse the Party line. Nevertheless, three phenomena attest to the prevalence of tribalism in Tibet.

First, most Tibetans feel hostility toward the Han Chinese, even though this is discouraged by the Dalai Lama. Generalized, ethnically-based animosity is a characteristic of a tribalistic mentality. Some murders of Han by Tibetans are clearly politically motivated, and politics is probably a factor in many others. Lobsang Nyima, who lived in Lhasa in the 1980s, recalls, 'Lhasa was flooded with Chinese, and there was nothing left of the old city except the tumbledown Barkor area. The Tibetans were being treated as though they were animals or ignorant savages and they resented it bitterly.'[14]

Ribhur Tulku, a *Rinpoche* (highly-honored monk) who was frequently and severely beaten by Chinese authorities and later went into exile, says of the Chinese, 'Of course I hate them. After living through such a harrowing time, how could I fail to hate them? Compassion is not at issue here. They destroyed our culture and our civilization. There is nowhere they can hide from our hatred. Compassion for them is out of the question.'[15]

Tashi Namgyal, General Secretary of the Tibetan youth Congress: 'Let's be quite frank. We can't say: since the Dalai Lama doesn't hate the Chinese, we won't either. We simply cannot. On the contrary, we hate the Chinese. They invaded our country. . . . If we kill Chinese, no one should accuse us of being terrorists; no Chinese who comes to Tibet is innocent.'[16]

A second manifestation of Tibetan tribalism is continuous rebellion against the authorities of the occupying Chinese government. Several major flare-ups have occurred since the 1950s, each put down by the PLA with terror and naked force. The persistence of demonstrations and resistance in the face of these brutal shows of force is remarkable, and indicates a massive reservoir of discontent and desperation. Tibetan Pema Saldon recalls that 'People were totally disenchanted with the regime. Everyone wanted freedom and the return of the Dalai Lama. Those demos were not organized, they just happened spontaneously, and everyone joined in, from small children throwing pebbles to old people breaking up paving stones and handing them to those who were strong enough to throw them. It was an absolutely universal rejection of the regime.'[17]

A foreign visitor who witnessed the uprising of 1988 writes, 'I saw with my own eyes how the whole Tibetan sector, as many as many 10,000 people, rose up against the Chinese. It was as though years of pent-up frustration suddenly came to the surface.' And this despite the fact that 'it seemed so hopeless. There were the tin-hatted Chinese soldiers, thousands of them, with tear gas and machine guns, and all the Tibetans could do was throw stones.'[18] This widespread rage indicates the locals consider Chinese rule in Tibet wholly illegitimate. In terms of the definition of 'tribalism' I am employing, the state's central government does not enjoy the political loyalty of the local community (to say the least!).

In most instances, that loyalty goes to Dharamsala, the seat of the Dalai Lama's government-in-exile across the border in India, instead of Beijing, which is the final manifestation of Tibetan tribalism. Even during the darkest days of repression in Tibet (the Deng regime has been more lenient than the Mao regime), traditional veneration of the Dalai Lama continued, even his photograph being valued as a religious icon. Several visits by representatives of the Dalai Lama's shadow government have elicited great outpourings of public support, much to the chagrin of the CCP authorities. In 1979, for example, the Dalai Lama got permission from Beijing to send a delegation from Dharamsala into Tibet on a fact-finding mission. Soon after the group's vehicles crossed the border, the local people

> gathered in huge numbers to convey to the 16 emissaries of their lama-king their tokens of love and their expressions of despair. Thirty years of brutal Chinese oppression had failed to shake their profound faith. Secretly they produced their prayer-wheels from their hiding places, brought out *khatas*, wept and touched the visitors. It was a demonstration of allegiance such as no-one had dreamed of.[19]

Lobsang Samten, one of the delegates and brother of the Dalai Lama, recalls,

> Everywhere people were shouting, throwing scarves, apples and flowers. They broke the windows of all the cars. They climbed on the roofs and pushed inside, stretching out their hands to touch us. The Chinese were screaming, 'Don't go out! They'll kill you!' All of the Tibetans were weeping, calling, 'How is the Dalai Lama? How is His Holiness?' We yelled back, 'He's fine. How are you?' Then, when we saw how poor they were, it was so sad, we all started crying too.[20]

The authors of these accounts, to be sure, are sympathetic to the Dalai Lama's cause. Nevertheless, most independent observers would also agree that Tibetans would prefer indigenous leadership over rule by Beijing.

As noted earlier, many of the Han in Tibet also exhibit tribalism. Visitors to Lhasa are often surprised to find that besides the Potala Palace, the monasteries and the small Tibetan quarter, the city resembles a typical Chinese town – Chinese architecture, Chinese-style decoration, Chinese shops and restaurants, Chinese products, and Chinese proprietors. In addition, there is the segregation of Han and Tibetan schools and neighbourhoods, the lack of interest among Han residents in learning Tibetan language and customs, and the attempted destruction of Tibetan culture.[21] All these suggest a desire among the Chinese residents of Tibet to stay safely within the confines of their own tribe – to associate with their own, to transplant and maintain their own way of life in a foreign land, and to avoid adopting the local lifestyle.

BEIJING'S VIEW:

Tibetan Tribalism as a Security Threat

Tibetan tribalism and its immediate consequences, animosity between Tibetans and Han and the Tibetan separatist movement, have important ramifications for Chinese national security.

Tibet is a strategic asset to the PRC. With its harsh climate and difficult terrain, it is an excellent buffer between China and rival India. By possessing Tibet themselves, the Chinese preclude the existence of a small bordering state that would surely attract the blandishments of China's enemies, and might even serve as a site for foreign military bases (including, perhaps, launch sites for nuclear missiles). Its natural resources and even its vast stretches of wasteland (which can generate revenue by serving as hazardous-waste dumps for wealthy foreign countries) make Tibet a potential economic asset, although the central government has spent large amounts of money developing and policing the region.

While Beijing has incurred high political costs in its efforts to hang onto Tibet, losing Tibet would be a disaster for the CCP. The Party leadership tends to view the separatist pressures in the various parts of China (as the regime interprets 'China') as interrelated; thus, giving concessions to the Tibetans would invariably encourage the 'separatists' in Xinjiang, Inner Mongolia, Manchuria and on Taiwan.

Furthermore, the Party leadership has backed itself into a corner by insisting that Tibet is a 'sovereignty' issue, in the same sense as the recovery of Taiwan. As one officially-sanctioned Chinese scholar writes, 'If China's sovereignty is seriously harmed – e.g., if certain countries support Taiwanese or Tibetan independence and try to separate Taiwan or Tibet from the PRC – China has no choice but to adopt all necessary means to protect its sacred sovereignty and will spare no blood and life in doing so.'[22] Having taken this approach, the leadership could not assent to Tibetan independence without opening itself to the criticism from the Chinese public and from rival domestic political factions that it had given away 'sovereign' Chinese territory, much like the corrupt and feeble Qing Dynasty regime had done during China's 'century of shame.'

From Beijing's point of view, therefore, Tibetan tribalism is a security problem. It is a national security problem, as granting Tibet independence would immediately reduce the PRC's territory by some 13 per cent, while ceding this chunk of land, population and resources to the control of China's potential adversaries. It is also a regime security problem, as the loss of Tibet would be a major political defeat for the ruling Party faction, and the ongoing difficulties in a Chinese-occupied Tibet indicate ineffective government.

The ideal solution for the CCP would have been a graceful assimilation of Tibet into the PRC, with the local population accepting if not welcoming Chinese rule. The persistence of Tibetan resistance, even against ruthless and overwhelming force, has clearly destroyed this possibility. Beijing has therefore developed alternate approaches to deal with the Tibetan problem. One is the promulgation of an alternative discourse on Tibet, a version that portrays the regime in a favorable light and its enemies in a negative light, and that puts liberal critics on the defensive.

According to the official line, Tibet before the Chinese Communist occupation was an 'extremely decadent feudal society,' one 'darker and more cruel than the serf societies of the European Middle Ages.'[23] Most Tibetans were impoverished serfs, while a small minority of religious elites owned nearly the entire wealth of the country and enjoyed a sumptuous lifestyle.

(In response, Tibetan Dhondup Chodon has written in her book *Life in the Red Flag People's Commune*,

> I belong to what the Chinese now term as serfs of Tibet.... There were six of us in the family.... My home was a double-storeyed building with a walled compound. On the ground floor we used to keep our animals. We had four yaks, 27 sheep and goats, two donkeys and a land holding of four-and-a-half khel (.37 hectares).... We never had any difficulty earning our livelihood. There was not a single beggar in our area.[24]

The Westerners who now express concern for the plight of Tibetans are clearly hypocrites, says Beijing, because Westerners committed imperialist aggression against Tibet around the turn of the century. It is true that a British army commanded by Francis Younghusband did force its way into Tibet in 1904, badly mauling the small, backward Tibetan army. This British expedition, however, was interested only in establishing trade. Having secured a commercial treaty, the British soldiers withdrew, leaving the Tibetan civilian population and their religion unmolested.

Nevertheless, Beijing claims that the PLA's intervention in 1950 rescued Tibet from 'British and American imperialist influence,'[25] although there were only a handful of Westerners living there during the first half of the century. The Communist Party also claims that its reforms rescued ordinary Tibetans from the poverty and injustice imposed by the feudal system; 'under the leadership of the Communist Party of China, the masses of serfs have been liberated and have gained personal freedom,' says regime-approved 'Living Buddha' Donggar Losang Chilai, and 'the living standard of Tibetans has greatly improved.'[26]

How, then, does Beijing explain the frequent anti-government demonstrations and heavy PLA military presence in Tibet's major cities? The vestiges of the old feudal class are responsible for the trouble. They hope that by separating Tibet from China, they can reinstitute the exploitative old order and regain their privileges. In addition, powerful foreign enemies who want to see China divided and weak are happy to support these 'reactionary' holdovers.

Thus, anyone who supports Tibetan independence must fall into one of three categories: frustrated would-be feudal lords; hegemonists who want to subjugate China and the rest of Asia; and well-meaning but ignorant dupes swayed by the human rights rhetoric of Western liberals.

It has been established that the CIA trained several hundred Tibetan exiles in a remote camp in the mountains of Colorado in the early 1960s, intending to use them as the nuclei of anti-Chinese guerrilla groups in Tibet. But while the U.S. government may stand accused of attempting to exploit pre-existing separatist sentiment in Tibet, foreign agitation can hardly be credited with creating such sentiment. Ronald Schwartz notes that the principal organizers of protest in Tibet since 1987 have been young monks and nuns from the countryside; 'their attraction to Western democratic ideas,' he argues, 'and the enthusiasm with which they applied these ideas creatively to their own situation, cannot be explained through contact or influence from outside.'[27]

Another Chinese approach to solving the Tibetan problem has been to populate the area with Han. The case for an independent Tibet becomes far less compelling if Tibetans are a minority in a mostly Chinese province, and governing it will be easier as more of its citizens accept the central government's legitimacy (as Han in Tibet generally do). Indeed, all things considered, this may be Beijing's hope for quelling Tibetan separatism. Accordingly, the CCP has encouraged Han from China proper, be they professional or unskilled workers, permanent relocators or employees on temporary contracts, to settle in Tibet. Since both the land and people of Tibet are repulsive to most Chinese, the central government has provided attractive financial incentives, including two to four times the usual salary, additional hardship pay for the high altitude, free furniture and guaranteed housing, extra vacation time, and increased pensions. The result has dramatically altered the region's demography. Besides dominating economic and cultural life, Han residing in Tibet now outnumber the native Tibetans by over a million.[28] This development further decreases the chances that Tibetan civilization will survive Chinese occupation.

CONCLUSIONS

The struggle between the Tibetans and the Han can be understood as a battle of ideas and assumptions, of which tangible political and social phenomena such as human rights abuses, demonstrations, the destruction of Tibetan culture, and Chinese immigration are manifestations. The essential issue is the identity of the Tibetans: do they understand themselves as having become Chinese (in the cultural and political sense)? Identity is a social construct determined through discussion and consensus. The theory of constitutive rhetoric comprehends this process. In a classic study, Maurice Charland describes how French Canadians have redefined themselves as a distinct people, the 'Quebecois,' who should seek independence from Canada.[29] More recently, Gary Purse has applied the same analysis to the American Revolution, arguing that the rhetoric of separatists rearticulated the colonists as Americans rather than British subjects and thereby legitimized, and even demanded, armed rebellion against British rule.[30]

Similarly, the Han Chinese government has effectually attempted through several means to re-define the Tibetans as Chinese. The abstract exercise has concrete consequences: if the Tibetans accept that they are Chinese, the notion of Tibetan independence will dry up; otherwise, maintaining its hold over a restive Tibet will continue to drain Beijing's resources and undercut its international prestige.

Based on the discussion throughout this chapter, we may isolate three key aspects of this Chinese effort. The first is the denigration of Tibetan history. If the Tibetans can be made less proud their history, they will cling to it less tenaciously. The second is the replacement of Tibetan culture with Chinese culture. Like history, culture is an important way the Tibetans might distinguish themselves from the Han; once these are eroded away, the basis for a separate identity is also weakened. Finally, the Chinese attempt to vilify campaigners for Tibetan independence. These activists are portrayed as frustrated would-be tyrants or the dupes of foreign imperialists. The upshot is that noble, patriotic Tibetans are not found in this camp, but rather support unity with the People's Republic of China.

The Chinese have not won this battle of ideas. As was the case with British colonists in America and with French Canadians in 1969, the Tibetans have chosen to view themselves as a separate nation.

What can be said about Tibet from a global perspective on tribalism? Unlike some other cases, Tibetan tribalism today does not appear to be related to the end of the Cold War. Nor is it closely connected to or inspired by the re-emergence of tribalism in other regions, such as Europe.

The origins of Tibetan tribalism are different from those of the tribalisms of the Balkans or the Middle East. Tibetans and Chinese have not lived together for centuries, with dormant or suppressed animosities recently whipped up by recent global political trends. Rather, Tibetan tribalism is primarily the expression of an ancient and highly distinctive civilization's desire to survive in the face of attempted cultural genocide. It is a continuation of the struggle against the Chinese Communist Party begun in 1950.

Tribalism is usually considered a negative impulse, a primitive, irrational, even silly attitude unbecoming cultured and modern societies, and one that destroys peace. This negative characterization does not seem to befit the Tibetans. If there was ever a case where tribalism was justified, it is Tibet.

Nevertheless, despite these differences, tribalism in Tibet displays many of the same features as tribalism in other parts of the world: ethnically-based prejudice and hatred, intolerance, self-segregation, and a determination that political power can only be entrusted to members of one's own 'tribe.'

Furthermore, the Tibetan case is consistent with 'modern' political developments in two ways. First, it provides further evidence that the era of the empire, the oversized state composed at least partly of nationalities held within the state's boundaries by force, is over. Second, it illustrates how the costs of compulsion have risen in the postwar period due to improved communications, increased economic and cultural contact, and especially the ascendance of liberal values such as democracy, self-determination and human rights. (The liberal discourse has become so dominant that even authoritarian states have been forced, reluctantly, to accept the ground rules – i.e., 'We, too, have human rights and democracy, it's just that our versions are different than the West's.') The rebellion in Tibet would continue regardless of what happened in the outside world, but because Chinese policy in Tibet has violated the dominant international norms, Beijing is being forced to pay a greater political price in its relations with the international community than it might have a century or two ago, when brutal colonialism was more acceptable.

Finally, we have also seen that Tibetan tribalism affects China's foreign relations, increasing China's sense of national insecurity and inviting foreign criticism of the CCP regime. This aspect of the Tibetan case supports one of the general findings of this book: tribalism contributes to inter-state conflict.

What is likely to become of Tibetan tribalism in the future? Through ruthlessness, craftiness, and the sheer weight of population and economic power, the Chinese are gradually consolidating their control of Tibet. The upper echelon of Tibetans is Sinicized and assimilated, while the rest are becoming further marginalized economically and politically. The attitudes associated with economic development and modernization (now sweeping through China) tend to break down traditions, and will begin to turn the hearts of younger generations of Tibetan away from the religion and lifestyle of their parents. If the status quo continues, Tibet faces the eventual prospect of practical extinction as a distinct society, with separatism and ethnic pride gradually giving way to the despair, self-loathing and submissiveness typifying a conquered people. Tibetan tribalism, as well, would diminish.

A case could of course be made that the PRC would benefit on balance by yielding the administration of Tibet to the Dalai Lama, withdrawing the PLA, and offering instead extensive economic agreements and a mutual security treaty. Beijing would thus retain many of the economic benefits of its association with Tibet (pathetically underdeveloped, Tibet would have no choice but to offer Chinese traders and investors good deals), while minimizing the possibility of a new security threat emerging in Tibet and ridding itself of the economic drain of maintaining up to 200,000 PLA troops there. Tibetans could then rule themselves under the auspices of a government that has become far more democratic during its years in exile than the system in which ancient Tibetans lived. Tibetan tribalism would be transformed into Tibetan nationalism.

While this would be desirable from the point of view of the Tibetans, it is unfortunately not a realistic possibility while the People's Republic remains under its present system of government. The barriers to democratization in the PRC are presently so large that this eventuality can safely be ruled out for the foreseeable future. Much more likely is the institution of some form of federalism early in the next century. This might result in greater autonomy for China's provinces. Even in this case, however, the benefits Tibetans would actually realize might be insignificant, given that Han already make up the majority of inhabitants of Xizang and that the proportion of Tibetans continues to shrink every year.

Tibetan tribalism is virtually synonymous with Tibetan resistance to China's dictatorship and cultural genocide. While the Chinese government longs for the extinction of Tibetan tribalism, the rest of us may, and perhaps should, view it in a different light.

NOTES

1 Glenn H. Mullin, 'Impression of Tibet Today,' *Tibet Bulletin*, Vol. 21, No. 2 (March–April 1990), p. 25.
2 Mary Craig, *Tears of blood: A Cry for Tibet* (London: Harper Collins, 1992), pp. 247–51.
3 Ronald Schwartz, 'Democracy, Tibetan Independence, and Protest Under Chinese Rule,' *The Tibet Journal*, Vol. 17, No. 2 (Summer 1992), pp. 15–6.
4 Tenzin Gyatso, *My Land and My People* (New York: Portala Press, 1983), p. 222.
5 See, for example, Amnesty International, *People's Republic of China: Repression in Tibet 1987–1992*, ASA 17/19/92 (May 1992).
6 'A Child Prisoner Tells His Experience,' *Tibetan Bulletin*, May–June 1990, p. 14.
7 Craig, p. 241.
8 Donnet, p. 124.
9 *Emancipation Monthly* (Hong Kong), No. 115, December 1987; Donnet, p. 97.
10 Reuter news dispatch, 'Tibetan Exiles denounce China's Panchen Lama move,' November 29, 1995, http://www.deltatech.com/china/p1/html.
11 'The ABCs of Discrimination in Tibet,' Tibetan Bulletin, January–February 1992, pp. 10–11.
12 Vanya Kewly, *Tibet: Behind the Ice Curtain* (London: Collins/Grafton, 1990), p. 253.
13 Jamyang Norbu, *Horseman in the Snow: The Story of Aten, an Old Khampa Warrior* (Dharamsala, India: Dharamsala Press, [n.y.]), pp. 102–3.
14 Craig, p. 241.
15 Donnet, p. 80.
16 Donnet, p. 186.
17 Craig, p. 266.
18 Craig, p. 272.
19 Heinrich Harrer, *Return to Tibet* (London: Weidenfeld & Nicholson, 1984), p. 47.

20 John F. Avedon, *In Exile from the Land of Snows* (London: Michael Joseph, 1984), p. 333.
21 Rong Ma, 'Han and Tibetan Residential Patterns in Lhasa,' *China Quarterly*, [n.v.], No. 128, 1991, pp. 834–5.
22 Qimao Chen, 'New Approaches in China's Foreign Policy,' *Asian Survey*, Vol. 33, No. 3 (March 1993), p. 249.
23 'Tibetans Enjoy All Human Rights,' *Beijng Review*, April 13–9, 1992, p. 15; 'Tibetans on Human Rights in Tibet,' *Beijing Review*, October 5–11, 1992, p. 4.
24 Quoted in *The Office of Tibet* (London), 'Traditional society and democratic framework for future Tibet,' December 6, 1996, http://gnew.gn.apc.org/tibetlondon/white4.html.
25 1950 Xinhua News Agency report, quoted in Allen S. Whiting, *The Chinese Calculus of Deterrence* (Ann Arbor, MI: University of Michigan Press, 1975), p. 13.
26 'Tibetans on Human Rights in Tibet,' p. 5.
27 Ronald Schwartz, 'Democracy, tibetan Independence, and Protest Under Chinese Rule,' *The Tibet Journal*, Vol. 17, No. 2 (Summer 1992), p. 3.
28 'The ABCs of Discrimination in Tibet,' p. 8.
29 Maurice Charland, 'Constitutive Rhetoric: The Case of the Peuple Quebecois,' *Quarterly Journal of Speech*, No. 73 (1987), pp. 133–50.
30 Gary A. Purse, 'Rearticulating British Subjects: Constitutive Rhetoric and the American Revolution,' unpublished manuscript, Department of Communications, Ohio University, Athens, OH, 1996, especially pp. 9–29.

Chapter Six

Tribalism and Elites in a Demotic State: The Case of Sri Lanka

A. Jeyaratnam Wilson

A THEORETICAL OVERVIEW

Broadly Arend Lijphart's four principles of consociational democracy were vaguely discernible in the inter-elite workings of Sir Lanka's political processes in the pre- and immediately post-independence phases, viz., the grand coalition, mutual veto, proportionality and segmental autonomy. None of the four were fully operative. Modified aspects of each were incorporated into political structures without much success. Coalition building as between Sinhalese and Tamils, especially, (the Muslim minority was not adversely affected) coloured elitist activity during the agitational phase of constitutional reform (1910–1934) and in the construction and composition of the Ceylon National Congress (1917–1923). In the transitional Donoughmore constitution (1931–1946), the Ceylon Tamils were isolated but in the latter phase (1943–1947), some active role came into play as a result of the election of a Ceylon Tamil representative to the Board of Ministers.

One or two Ceylon Tamils were included in the post-independent cabinets of 1947–1956, 1965–1970 and 1977 onwards, but they were not effective enough to impose even a contingent veto. There was, at most, consultation but seldom consensus or compromise.

A certain proportionality in representation was the basis of the independence constitution of 1948 but this was reneged on in the years immediately after when the Indian Tamils were disfranchised in 1948 and 1949.

Segmental autonomy was agreed to in the Sinhalese-Tamil pacts of 1957, 1960, 1965 and the District Development Councils legislation of 1978–1980 but while the leadership of one section of the Sinhala elite desired an end to the conflict, competition between rivals among them represented through their political groupings, the United National Party (UNP) and the Sri Lanka Freedom Party (SLFP) inhibited the leaders from delivering on their promises. Thus an atmosphere conducive to Lijphart's consociational ethos prevailed but failure resulted because of three factors, viz.,

a. the sharpness of intra-elite electoral competition;
b. the emergence of ultra-chauvinistic Sinhala forces whom the Sinhalese leadership utilised as excuses for their failure to deliver and;
c. the emergence of leading Buddhist monks and politically non-responsible Sinhala Buddhist personalities who made stirring appeals to the Sinhalese on the alleged dangers confronting them.

We have explained in the body of the text the reasons for the failure of Arend Lijphart's and S.J.R. Noel's consociational designs to take root in Ceylon. It could all be summed up in the phenomenon of the demotic state. A demotic state is a state where the vulgar numerocratic polity prevails manifested in the concept of the *staatsvolk*. In Malaysia this is represented by the phenomenon of *Bhumiputra* (sons of the soil).

If however we view the prospects for consociational behaviour from the angle of Hans Daalder's (1971) general approach, Ceylon could reasonably fit in, in that Daalder uses the term 'to characterize a certain pattern of political life in which the political elites of distinct social groups succeed in establishing a viable, pluralistic state *by a process of mutual forbearance and accommodation* (emphasis ours).

But then Daalder's amplification of his view in his succeeding paragraph modifies the possibilities, viz., 'a process of building up a new political society *from below* (our emphasis) to some degree by the consent of participating communities, in which deliberate compromises by elites carefully circumscribe and limit the extent to which political power can be wielded by one political centre.'

Daalder does not insist on Lijphart's four pillars but his latter proposition nevertheless could make it possible to fit consociationalism into a Sri Lankan Procrustean bed. Thus it may just be probable, to incorporate, to some extent, parts of Lijphart's theorisation with Daalder's.

Daalder's propositions suggest five intervening factors in Sri Lanka:

1 the internationalisation of the Ceylon Tamil question;
2 the pressure on Western governments from the Ceylon Tamil expatriate diaspora;
3 consequent on (1) and (2), states providing aid to Sri Lanka requesting the Sri Lanka government to resolve the conflict;
4 India's direct involvement; and
5 arising from the first four, offers by other states such as Norway, Sweden, Switzerland, Australia and Canada to mediate a settlement.

The prospects of foreign involvement imply a chance of reconciliation on the lines of Lijphart's segmental autonomy and Daalder's propositions.

Daalder's propositions have in some measure prevailed. Most Sinhala elites have accepted Sinhala and Tamil as official languages, no longer Sinhala Only. Further they have reconciled themselves to Sri Lanka being a multicultural society and by implication they are not committed any more to a monopolistic Sinhala Buddhist state. These no doubt need implementation but Sri Lanka has expressed a willingness to comply and will be under pressure from aid giving foreign governments. There is also the persistence of the internal armed Tamil struggle with all its damaging consequences. Where Daalder needs modification is that 'the new political society' will have to be largely structured at the elite level and not from below. The competing Sinhalese and Tamil elites need to structure a mutually acceptable framework. The generality of electors will then have to be persuaded to fall in line. Such a process takes long but no other rational alternative is available. Already peace movements, individual mediationary efforts, political party conferences and an all party select committee of Parliament are endeavouring to end the impasse.

THE EARLY POST-INDEPENDENCE PHASE (1947–1956)

Britain transferred power in 1948 to Don Stephen Senanayake, a Sinhala Buddhist statesman who commanded the confidence of most of the Sinhala middle classes and large sections of the peasantry (the rest backed the left wing) but with not much support from the most articulate of the other co-indigenous group, the Sri Lankan Tamils (Jeffries, 1962 and 1969). Nor did Senanayake have the trust of the Indian Tamils. The Muslims acquiesced as did a minority of the Sri Lankan Tamils.

To forge a unity of the diverse groups, Senanayake and his leading supporters organised the United National Party (UNP) in 1946. Its name indicated its goal. Essentially it was to become an amalgam of the westernised and conservative Sinhala Buddhist bourgeoisie with cooptees from the other communities (Wilson, 1979). But neither Senanayake nor any of his successors had, unlike Jawaharlal Nehru or Tunku Abdul Rahman, a wider vision on how a new multiethnic state should have political institutions as in India or ways and means of accommodating ethnic minorities as with the Alliance Party in Malaysia so as to ensure for some length of time a peaceful polity. There was in Sri Lanka's case an absence of consensus or any attempts to seriously forge inter-ethnic agreements based on an understanding of the problems of the different groups in the polyethnic state. A constituent assembly (India) or a consensus-style political grouping such as the Alliance party in Malaya (now Malaysia) could have helped to bridge gaps.

In the case of Sri Lanka, its leading statesmen did not have long term goals for either a new society or a new deal for the minorities. The rigours of neglect and repression of the Tamil minority could have been mitigated had adequate economic development ensured a better redistribution of wealth. As it happened a stagnant society and the available limited economic pie failed to provide employment and minimum comforts for the increasing Sinhala majority population. Numerocratically constituted governments could therefore be sustained only by depriving an expendable minority (Wilson, 1988).

On the first question as we shall explain and analyse, rather than effect compromises agreeable to the ethnic disputants (Sinhalese, Ceylon Tamils and Indian Tamils) on lines similar to Arend Lijphart's consociationalism, the Sinhalese leadership cultivated, principally, the numerically ethnic majority, the Sinhala Buddhists (Lijphart, 1979). Thereafter the national issue was which party was more favourable towards providing greater benefits to the ethnic majority? This became an auctioning game between the two main contending Sinhala parties: the United National Party which governed during 1947–1956, 1965–1970, 1977 and the Sri Lanka Freedom Party which, with its allies, held the government in 1956–1959, 1960–1965, 1970–1977.

Both parties promoted the Sinhala Buddhist political claim at the expense of the Ceylon and Indian Tamils and the Christian minority on such issues as the national flag, state-aided Sinhala colonization of the Tamil traditional homelands, the decitizenisation and disfranchisement of the Indian Tamils, Sinhala as the only state language, the nationalisation of the Christian denominational schools, standardization of admission marks to the universities to give an advantage to the Sinhala students over the Sri Lankan Tamils and the unilateral framing of two constitutions (1972 and 1978) without the cooperation of the major Ceylon Tamil grouping in Parliament (Wilson, 1988). Table 6.1 below provides a demographic picture of the multi-ethnic composition of the island's population:

Table 6.1: *Ethnic Data on Sri Lanka's Population.*

Peoples	Number	Percentage
Sinhalese (the ethnic majority)	10,985,666	74
Sri Lankan Tamils (the principal ethnic minority and co-indigenous with the Sinhalese)	1,871,535	12.6
Indian Tamils (nineteenth century arrivals)	885,223	5.6
Muslims* (majority Tamil-speaking with a minority being bilingual)	1,100,350	5.9
Burghers	38,236	0.3
Others	28,981	0.2

Source: Department of Census and Statistics, *Preliminary Release*, No. 1 (Colombo 1981).
*Note: the Muslims are for reasons of origin categorized as Moors (1,056,972, 7.1 per cent) and Malays (43,378, 0.3 per cent).
Note (1): the majority of Indian Tamils live outside the Tamil majority Northern and Eastern provinces.
(2): some 30 per cent of Muslims live in the Northern and Eastern Provinces while the rest are scattered in the Sinhala districts; there is a strong concentration of Muslims in the Colombo district.

Lijphart's model failed to eventuate because as stated earlier Britain transferred power to virtually a single person (D.S. Senanayake), the same as it did in other Asian colonies such as with M.A. Jinnah (Pakistan), Jawaharlal Nehru (and the Indian National Congress), General Aung San (Burma) and Tunku Abdul Rahman (Malaya, later Malaysia). In Britain's African colonies too, Kwame Nkrumah (Ghana), Jomo Kenyatta (Kenya), Julius Nyerere (Tanzania), Kenneth Kaunda (Zambia), Milton Obote (Uganda) and other such leaders were the immediate beneficiaries. They were dependable. This gamble paid off. These leaders headed stable political movements and at the point of transfer showed democratic inclinations, but only for a short while thereafter. Many African states took to one-party systems and executive presidential-type rule, while in Asia, the veneer of democracy prevailed with a few notable exceptions. Beneath the surface there were all the trappings of an authoritarian state as in Sri Lanka, Malaysia, and in India under the Gandhis.

D.S. Senanayake, as the last visiting reforms commission to the island (1944–1945) headed by Viscount Soulbury opined, would have been able to weld the communities together and share with the ethnic minorities the power transferred to him in a way as to win their confidence (Soulbury Report, 1945). Instead Senanayake followed a twin track policy – one that was pro-British in external affairs, and in internal affairs, an ethnic policy which alienated sizeable sections of Tamils (Ceylon and Indian).

The All-Ceylon Tamil Congress (TC) formed by G.G. Ponnambalam in 1944 was heir to the problems and frustrations of the Sri Lankan Tamils during the Donoughmore phase (Russell, 1982). In all of the one hundred and fifty years of British rule, the Sri Lankan Tamils remained a separate identity and a majority of them lived in their traditional homeland in the Northern and Eastern Provinces. They readily took to the English education provided in Christian missionary schools. Knowledge of the English language gave English-educated Tamils ready access to low and middle level jobs in the British colonial administration as well as to the professions – physicians, scientists, engineers, accountants and lawyers etc., both in Sri Lanka and in other British territories, particularly Malaya. It so happened, an accident of history, that a disproportionate number of Tamils obtained places in the administrations and professions. The Ceylon Tamil leader, Ponnambalam campaigned for fifty-fifty representation in the legislature and the executive. The Soulbury Commission (1944–1945) rejected this demand. Instead the Commission provided for various constitutional safeguards against possible legislative discrimination of ethnic and religious minorities. But there was no protection against administrative discrimination. Nor did Britain provide for a bill of rights. Such a charter would have acted as a contingent judicial veto.

THE CAUSES OF CONFLICT

Immediately after independence, the new state faced the urgent tasks of laying down its foundations. A farseeing liberal Sinhalese political elite could have, in 'Lijphartian' style sought an overarching accommodation with their Sri Lankan Tamil counterpart so as to avoid confrontational politics. This did not happen mainly because the Prime Minister (D.S. Senanayake) was pressured by Kandyan Sinhalese members in his party to enact a citizenship law which would exclude nearly a million Indian Tamil settlers from the franchise. These Indians, by and large had exercised their votes at the general election immediately prior to independence (in 1947) as domiciled people (de Silva, K.M., 1981 and 1986).

Senanayake as leader of his own United National Party was angry with the Indians. Seven of their MPs sat in the opposition while his own government continued to be a contingent coalition of unreliable political groupings (Weerawardena, 1952 and 1960). The Indian Tamils through their principal political grouping, the Ceylon Indian Congress (CIC) supported left candidates or Independents in all other constituencies where the UNP contested.

A final reason for Senanayake's actions, put forward by the dissident Tamil Federal Party (FP) which splintered from the parent All-Ceylon Tamil Congress in 1948, was that Senanayake and his UNP were seeking to erode the political strength of the Tamil contingent in the House of Representatives (Wilson, 1988). Therefore the exclusionary legislation enacted by the Senanayake government in 1948 and 1949 to deny the Indian Tamils their Citizenship and franchise rights was, the Tamil Federal Party insisted, but a first step towards accomplishing the Sinhala national design of converting the new state to a Sinhala numerocratic polity. To reinforce their argument the FP accused Senanayake of deliberately following land settlement policies in favour of the Sinhalese in newly irrigated schemes in the traditional Tamil homelands in the Eastern Province so as to dilute the Ceylon Tamil majority there.

The new state in addition to the discriminatory citizenship and franchise laws (1948 and 1949) proceeded to design a national flag based largely on the lion emblem of the last king of the Sinhala kingdom of Kandy; this was done by a committee comprising representatives of all communities; finally a national anthem was adopted. There was an absence of consensus in that sections of the Ceylon Tamil minority were opposed to the new flag (Wilson, 1988).

Senanayake's strategy during his prime ministership was to endeavour to avoid muddying the waters. For this purpose he formed a coalition government (Jennings, 1953). The coalition however was unstable. It was not merely disequilibristic but its recruits were not entirely representative of the Ceylon Tamils. They were Tamils who had yet to prove themselves. At the same time, the Sinhala component in the government led by S.W.R.D. Bandaranaike was unhappy with the pace of change in matters such as the national languages, religion (Buddhism) and in regard to enhancing the status of the Sinhala rural classes. Bandaranaike eventually broke with the UNP in 1951 and formed the Sri Lanka Freedom Party (SLFP).

Senanayake tried to contain discontent and to establish a level of harmony among the elites by careful manipulation of adverse political forces. He was adept in his statecraft in the short run but the ethnic problems remained unresolved. These plagued the new state.

The controversial issues were

a. on the adoption by the new state of an official language (Sinhala only) or of official languages (Sinhala and Tamil);
b. whether the state should control or nationalise education, the majority of primary and secondary schools being owned by minority Christian missionary organisations allegedly used by them for proselytisation;
c. on the state-aided colonisation of the traditional homelands of the Tamil-speaking peoples with mainly Sinhala settlers; to this was tied the demand for a restructuring of the state on federal lines; and
d. recognition by the state of Buddhism as the religion of the majority.

The question of the disfranchised Indian Tamils remained unresolved for a long time.

The language question was wrought with peril (de Silva, K.M., 1986). Whatever way it was to be resolved, there were the stark probabilities that the outcome would cause fissiparousness. The United National Party and D.S. Senanayake preferred a laissez faire policy. Their elites actually desired the continuance of the English language. In this way government and administration could be kept remote from the masses while the elite would claim to govern in the best interests of the latter. However, politicisation of the electorate had been going on apace since the grant of universal adult franchise by Britain's colonial administration in 1931.

Coupled with growth in political awareness was the introduction in 1944 of the scheme of free education from the kindergarten to the university. This brought in increasing numbers of educated unemployed Sinhalese and Ceylon Tamils into the work force. Along with free education was the decision by the government to switch the medium of instruction in the schools from English to the national languages, Sinhalese and Tamil. Free education in the national languages resulted in an exploding constituency of politically conscious young employables demanding the abolition of English as the official language (Samarasinghe, S.W.R. de A., 1984).

That this language movement would channel itself to Sinhala as the only official language was not anticipated by proponents of the national languages. The removal of English would facilitate the employment of the swabasha – trained (*swabasha* meaning one's own language). At the Sinhala elite level the expectation was that the Sinhala (and Tamil) – trained would have job opportunities in the bureaucracy which in turn could contain the discontentment. But the trickle of dissatisfaction ended in a flood of Sinhala chauvinism, all in a matter of a few years. The Sinhala-educated demanded that they be given employment in proportion to their population numbers.

Until 1955, the Sinhala and Tamil elites were agreed on the two languages being made official. There was at the time little manifestation of the Sinhala language becoming the vehicle of Sinhala chauvinism and Sinhala nationalism. The Tamils would indeed have preferred the continuance of English because they had mastered its use whereas the majority of the Sinhala-educated lacked adequate proficiency. But given the swelling tide, the Tamils went with the Sinhalese for the change to the national languages. The hope was that such recognition would settle itself at the administrative level, with the Sinhalese being satisfied to be governed in their own language. The consequences of an inter-ethnic controversy in which employment would become an issue was not anticipated.

The language movement however became soon fuelled by fears that the English language would continue with its pre-eminence and that in such a situation the Tamils would occupy the most advantageous positions (Smith, 1966). Sinhala nationalists further had the fear that their language would be relegated and would cease to exist in the context of the dominance of English (Maialasekera, G.P., 1955). They had serious concerns that the Tamil language, which they associated not merely with an ethnic minority in Ceylon but with neighbouring Tamil Nadu's teeming millions, would swamp their language (Nadesan, 1955). To the politicians awaiting the tide there was the expectation that a leap from Sinhala and Tamil to Sinhala Only would reward them with an enormous harvest of votes from among the Sinhala electors. This actually happened.

Sinhala militancy asserted itself during 1952–1954 through reports from royal commissions, an unofficial commission on the state of Sinhala Buddhism in the country and countrywide agitation coupled with pamphlet warfare and mediawide attention (Smith, 1966). In 1954–1955, the movement to make Sinhala the only state language gathered momentum.

In 1955, the Sri Lanka Freedom Party decided to adopt a platform of Sinhala as the only official language with a saving proviso for 'the reasonable use of the Tamil language'. In February 1956, the UNP led by the Prime Minister, Sir John Kotelawala (1953–1956) performed *a volte face* from its earlier stance of parity of status for the two languages to one of Sinhala Only. Thus Lijphart's and Daalder's proposition ceased to apply.

The general election of April 1956 was mainly concentrated on this language question and the SLFP with its allies emerged victorious (Weerawardena, 1960). Legislation was enacted in 1956 for Sinhala to be the only state language. This was reaffirmed in the autochthonous constitutions of 1972 and 1978 (Wilson, 1979 and 1980).

A place for Tamil was not given serious consideration. From a political point of view there was little need for electoral support from the Tamils as they had ceased to be a reckoning factor, the Sinhala numerocracy being adequate for ensuring the passage of legislation favourable to the Sinhala majority even if their political parties were divided on other issues (de Silva, C.R., 1982). Thus when Tamil was eventually given a place, as in the Tamil Language (Special Provisions) Act of 1958 and the Tamil Regulations of 1966, these were not meaningfully implemented. The majority of public servants, being Sinhalese, was not conversant with Tamil and they resisted attempts to introduce Tamil into the central administration. No government could therefore enforce provisions for the use of Tamil.

Furthermore the use of Tamil implied demarcation of the Northern and Eastern provinces as Tamil areas. This in turn implied a decentralization of power which a Colombo-centered bureaucracy was reluctant to undertake. Consequently the clauses in the constitutions of 1972 and 1978 for a limited use of Tamil remained dead letters. In 1987, under the Thirteenth Amendment to the Sri Lanka Constitution of 1978, Tamil was added as an official language but to date the Sinhala-dominated state has not taken the necessary steps to give effect to this change. The Tamil language had to be also recognised outside the Northern and Eastern provinces because of the large numbers of Tamils resident there. No other alternative was available for the state to transact official business with these Tamils. No steps were taken to ensure a transition. Table 6.2 gives the distribution of the Tamil population in the island:

Table 6.2: *Distribution of Sri Lankan Tamil – Population, 1981.*

In the Sri Lankan Tamil Majority Northern and Eastern Provinces	In the seven Sinhalese Majority Provinces	In the Colombo District only
1,358,188 (65.0 per cent of total Sri Lankan Tamil population)	828,812 (35.0 per cent of total Sri Lankan Tamil population)	165,952 (8.9 per cent of total Sri Lankan Tamil population)

Source: Department of Census and Statistics, Preliminary Release No. 1 (Colombo, 1981).

The question of the nationalisation of schools became strident after the victory at the 1956 general election of S.W.R.D. Bandaranaike's coalition, the Mahajana Eksath Peramuna (the People's United Front). The Front comprised the SLFP and its allies. Bandaranaike and his Minister of Education, W. Dahanayake resisted the demand on the score that enough funding was not available to finance a takeover of schools (de Silva, K.M., 1988).

Buddhist activists nevertheless persisted in pressing their claims. Although they did not make any advances during 1956–1959, they were successful when Mrs. Sirima Bandaranaike led the SLFP to victory at the general election of July 1960. During December 1960–April 1961, all denominational schools owned by Christian, Buddhist, Muslim and Hindu organisations were nationalised without payment of adequate compensation (Smith, 1966). The sum result was that the majority of schools owned and managed by Christian denominations were transformed into Sinhala Buddhist-oriented institutions. This also applied to those Christian-owned schools where a majority of students were Tamil Hindus or Muslims. They too derived similar benefits as the Buddhists. A few Christian-owned schools were permitted to remain private but under trying conditions. Thus education after 1960 became the near monopoly of the Sinhala dominated state.

The state control of education was a serious setback to the Ceylon Tamils. The Tamils of the Northern and Eastern provinces had thrived and progressed under the aegis of the Christian missionaries. These schools were adequately equipped and provided a well rounded education enabling the Tamils to successfully compete for places in the pre-1956 phase when the administration was in the English language. Now, not only had English been displaced, but the schools were owned by a Sinhala dominated state. The Ceylon Tamil leadership feared for these schools. The biased state gradually ceased to provide the equipment and education that the Christian missionaries had so readily given.

Tamil Hindus at first were receptive to the nationalisation for they too did not approve of the overweening Christian presence. But when the discrimination against schools in the Tamil areas became all too obvious, Tamil dissatisfaction and frustration began to be manifested in extra-constitutional agitation. The Tamil Federal Party (FP) which had won an overwhelming victory against the Tamil Congress in the general election of 1956 articulated this discontent. From 1956 to 1977 the FP won every general election and led civil protests and civil disobedience campaigns against the state. Lijphart's and Daalder's models were no longer relevant.

The education question would have quietened had not Mrs. Bandaranaike's 1970–1977 United Front government imposed a quota scheme to restrict the admission of Ceylon Tamil students to the professionally oriented faculties (especially medicine, engineering and science) in the universities (de Silva, C.R., 1984 and de Silva, K.M., 1984). This was indeed the last straw. When qualified Ceylon Tamils were required to obtain more marks than their Sinhala counterparts to gain admission, Tamil youth decided to take to violent protest. The immediate cause for the Tamil insurrection of 1976 and thereafter arises from this one single fact, compounded by the various other acts of discrimination over the years.

The launching of irrigation schemes since the nineteen forties in the dry zone areas of the island disturbing, as the table below indicates, the demographic composition of the Tamil-speaking Eastern Province became yet another area of serious contention (Manogaran, C., 1987). The Ceylon Tamils led by the FP since 1949 claimed the province as a component of the traditional homeland of the Tamil-speaking peoples. Sinhala-dominated governments consistently ignored Tamil protests and organized settlement schemes for Sinhala colonists in the irrigated areas, providing the latter with inducements from state funds. These state-aided colonization schemes were a potent cause for the Ceylon Tamil agitation for the re-structuring of the island state on an ethnic federal principle. Table 6.3 gives statistics of the increase in state-aided Sinhala settlers populating the Northern and Eastern provinces between the period 1946 (two years before independence) and 1981.

Table 6.3: *Sinhalese Colonisation of the Sri Lankan – Tamil Majority Northern and Eastern Provinces.*

Province	Population			Percentage Increase 1946–1981
	1946	1971	1981	
Northern	9,602	25,847	33,149	1048.1
Eastern	27,556	148,572	243,358	1674.7
Total	37,158	174,419	276,507	644.1

Source: Adapted from R.N. Kearney and Barbara Diane Miller, *Internal Migration in Sri Lanka and its Social Consequences* (London, Westview Press, 1987).

The special recognition granted to Buddhism in the constitutions of 1972 and 1978 were not as contentious an issue. However the underscoring of Buddhism served to confirm Ceylon Tamil fears that the Sinhala political leadership was determined on transforming a secular polity into a Sinhala Buddhist state. It lent force to the Ceylon Tamil demand for a federal structure and their demand to the right of self determination.

During most of the post-independence period, from 1948 to 1976, the Ceylon Tamil political leadership endeavoured to seek an accommodation with the Sinhala majority's governing party, both UNP and SLFP. But the desire and the will to negotiate understandings were one way. The Sinhala political elites failed to initiate dialogues; they burdened the Tamils with impositions – Sinhala Only, the state-aided colonisation schemes, discrimination in public sector appointments and admissions to the universities. On looking back, none of these policies paid off, for they had to, in the end, be modified if not reversed by the Sinhala-dominated state.

INITIATIVES FOR CONFLICT RESOLUTION

The entire period, 1948 to present times was ethnically speaking crises-ridden. A normal expectation would have been for statesman-like approaches to have been made by the ethnic majority's leaders. They failed to seriously consider the demands of the Tamil leadership. Their immediate response to the problem was to incorporate nominal representatives from the ethnic minority in their governments especially during the period 1947 to 1956.

Thereafter the Sinhalese leadership failed to act positively. Instead they considered initiatives from

a. intermediaries seeking to intervene on behalf of the ethnic minority often after a critical phase when the inter-ethnic situation had gone out of hand;
b. Indian efforts to provide good offices;
c. all party conferences attempting a consensus so as to ensure that a resolution of the Tamil demand would not become a party issue at a general election;
d. states other than India providing their good offices either because of Tamil expatriate pressure on the governments concerned (Australia and Canada) or because of such governments hoping for a settlement in order to stem the inflow of refugees (Switzerland and the United Kingdom); and
e. states compelled to act for humanitarian reasons (Norway and Sweden).

These external pressures were in line with attempts at promoting Lijphart's advocacy of segmental autonomy and Daalder's proposition on accommodation.

We will examine these initiatives to determine the extent of their success. The leaders of the Sinhala demotic polity could not provide the much needed start. Given the state of Sinhala public opinion, they would if they had attempted any rapprochement, been blamed for selling the pass. The dangers of imminent crises or instability to their governments compelled them to sign agreements and come to understandings. These were agreed to invariably under duress and were not the result of conviction. When the political situation improved in their favour or there was threat of backbench revolt or Sinhala mob protests, they reneged on their pledges.

In effect governments in Sri Lanka since independence countenanced the objectives of the Sinhala Buddhist polity in its inflexible stances, were reluctant to provide correct or positive leadership, concluded agreements when imperilled and backed down when there was unrest in their ranks, leaving the Tamils to

(i) exert pressure and extract undertakings from unwilling prime ministers;
(ii) resort to extra-parliamentary forms of protest; and
(iii) launch the violent armed struggle when non-violent strategies failed to yield results.

114

In the beginning cooptation was accomplished with ease for there was no dearth of Ceylon Tamils who would give in to

a. the lure of office for its own sake;
b. the prestige and power that went with a cabinet portfolio or;
c. as not seldom claimed, the opportunity to help the Ceylon Tamil community which opportunity it was felt should not be missed.

During the immediate post-independence phase, 1947–1956, these factors contributed towards Ceylon Tamil participation in UNP governments. The moot question was how representative were these Ceylon Tamil ministers.

Only one of them, G.G. Ponnambalam, Minister of Industries, Industrial Research and Fisheries for five years, 1948–1953, as leader of the All Ceylon Tamil Congress could be reckoned as having the support of a major segment of the Ceylon Tamils. But even he had his support base eroded because of his collaboration with governments allegedly unsympathetic to the Tamils. The other ministers were there because UNP governments generally wished to live up to their claim to be a national party. The latter reason prevailed when the UNP took office again in 1977 and was re-elected in 1989. Ceylon Tamils were appointed but they were not adequately representative as none of them were from the Ceylon Tamil heartland of the Jaffna peninsula. In the post-1977 period S. Thondaman, the Indian Tamil leader of the Indian-dominated Ceylon Workers' Congress (CWC) serves as a senior cabinet minister. He himself has however stated that he does not have effective power in the Cabinet as he is often outvoted by the majority of Sinhalese ministers (Wilson 1990). Lijphart or Daalder would presumably insist on a more qualitative representation than a nominal cooptation.

Pacts and understandings indicated a measure of willingness by Sinhalese prime ministers and presidents to resolve the thorny issue. But they invariably had to resign when their ranks threatened revolt or when even ministers in their cabinets wilted under populist pressures. All of these were examples of nominal efforts to obtain an overarching inter-elite accommodation in line with Arend Lijphart's theories.

However the trickling down to the masses of populist appeals could not be avoided. The electorate had in successive general elections, since the conferment of universal suffrage by Britain in 1931, become increasingly politicised. Along with politicisation, populist slogans that the Sinhala language and Sinhala Buddhism would be endangered and that devolving of power to the Ceylon Tamils was but a first step towards separation and a sell out had an impact on a demotic polity. Consequently the Sinhala leadership were like Barkis willing but the Sinhala electorate, like Cerberus could not be easily propitiated.

Some of the chauvinistic slogans of the period conveyed much meaning, such as sevala Banda, the 'slippery S.W.R.D. Bandaranaike' stigmatised for signing the Bandaranaike-Chelvanayakam Pact of 1957 (BC Pact) and allegedly responsible for *demelungta rata bedanawa*, that is dividing or sharing out the country to the Tamils, *demulung*, 'the Tamils', here being used in a pejorative sense. More vulgar was the doggerel *Dudlevqav buddav masala vadday* popularised after Dudley Senanayake signed the Dudley-Chelvanayakam Pact (DC Pact) of 1965. Dudley had a sensitive stomach. So he was contemptuously dismissed by the Sinhala mob, incited by Oppositional elements for the supposed presence in his abdomen of an edible Tamil cake (*masala vaday*).

Both the BC and DC Pacts were timely and could have been, if honestly implemented, contained the inter-ethnic dispute. Bandaranaike more than Dudley Senanayake understood better the concept of devolution. The Ceylon Tamil leader, S.J.V. Chelvanayakam of the Tamil Federal Party, was eager to try the experiment to the extent of laying aside temporarily his party's demand for a federal structure. Chelvanayakam had a prestigious standing among the Ceylon Tamils who were willing to entrust their destiny to their statesman of integrity. Though challenged by the rival All Ceylon Tamil Congress, Chelvanayakarn prevailed.

On the other hand S.W.R.D. Bandaranaike was plagued by an opposition orchestrated by the UNP with the Buddhist clergy in a significant role. The Prime Minister lost heart and using the excuse that the FP had queered the pitch for him by their protest campaigns against the imposition of Sinhalese letters on the number plates of private and public transport, declared in May 1958 that his 'pact was no more', a virtual abrogation.

The pact had provided for regional devolution with, among other powers, the right to control allocation of land under colonisation schemes (except major inter-provincial ones) and recognition of Tamil as the language of a national minority in Ceylon as a whole and as the language of administration in the Northern and Eastern Provinces. In the end Bandaranaike was able to enact into legislation only the language part of his agreement, the Tamil Language (Special Provisions) Act of 1958. The Prime Minister failed to introduce the necessary regulations under this act. The Federal Party refused to cooperate with him because he had pledged to present legislation for regional councils and for the Tamil language at one and the same time.

Mrs. Sirima Bandaranaike entered into an 'understanding' with Chelvanayakarn in April 1960. She agreed because she needed Chelvanayakam's FP support to defeat Dudley Senanayake's minority government of March 1960. The minority government was accordingly defeated on the Address of Thanks in April 1960. The general election of July 1960 which ensued gave Mrs. Bandaranalke a convincing majority and she reneged when pressured by militant Sinhala groups.

The 1965 pact with Dudley Senanayake was more circumscribed in that it stipulated that district councils, as distinct from regional councils under the BC Pact, would be under the direction of the central government. A regional council covered a whole province while a district council was for one of several administrative districts within a province. The area of decentralization was therefore limited in scope. Yet for all these difficulties, Chelvanayakarn consented. An elaborate draft carefully negotiated with the Prime Minister was completed. There was delay in that the Prime Minister procrastinated in the negotiations on the details. Senanayake was never convinced that district councils were the answer to Tamil dissatisfaction. When the district councils bill was eventually presented in 1968 to the Government Parliamentary Group, there was threat of a revolt from the government's backbenchers and the Prime Minister was constrained to withdraw the bill.

Unlike with S.W.R.D. Bandaranaike where the two parties parted with some bitterness, Dudley Senanayake gracefully ensured the withdrawal of the Federalists from the government parliamentary group. Dudley Senanayake too implemented one part of the DC Pact. The Tamil Regulations of January 1966 were virtually rammed through Parliament amidst riotous demonstrations outside Parliament led by the Leader of the Opposition, Mrs. Sirima Bandaranaike (SLFP) and her Communist (Moscow) and Trotskyist (the Lanka Sama Samaja Party, the LSSP) allies. Dudley Senanayake had also agreed in his pact to cease colonising the traditional Tamil homelands with Sinhala settlers. Henceforth preference would be given to Ceylon Tamils in the region and Indian Tamils from outside if a sufficient number of Ceylon Tamils were not available (Wilson, 1988).

The last of the efforts within Sri Lanka to resolve the conflict was initiated by this writer (Wilson, 1988). I persuaded President J.R. Jayewardene to take a long term view of the conflict and to see in it a historic opportunity for himself. The Tamil United Liberation Front (TULF) which had been mandated by the Vaddukoddai Resolution of 1976 and at the general election of 1977, when the Front won an overwhelming victory, to demand the creation of a separate sovereign state of *Thamil Eelam* agreed to my role as an intermediary.

Since the constitutions of 1972 and 1978 stipulated that Sri Lanka (the name for Ceylon being unilaterally changed to Sri Lanka without the consent of the Tamil minority under the 1972 constitution) is 'a unitary state', I used the model of the quasi-federal Provincial Councils of the unitary constitution of the Republic of South Africa. The District Development Councils (DDCs) that I suggested with devolutionary powers and decentralised government and with control over land settlement was approved by President Jayewardene and consented to by the TULF leadership. The latter stated that they were not regarding DDCs as an exchange for their separate state but as a significant advance in local self government. Legislation was enacted in 1980 despite opposition from the government's backbenchers.

The scheme could well have contained the conflict but President Jayewardene met with several obstacles. His ministers were reluctant to share their powers with the DDCs, government officials were unwilling to implement the legislation meaningfully and the Minister of Finance was not able to find the finances necessary for the functioning of the DDCs. Consequently the scheme ran aground. It was further overtaken by the insurrection of militant Tamil youths who after the anti-Tamil pogroms of July 1983 began prosecuting their armed struggle with greater vigour and a fierce commitment. Thereafter there could be no internal initiatives. The Indian government intervened from 1983 onwards as an interested party, and in the recent past, Australia and Canada as members of the Commonwealth, and Norway, Sweden and Switzerland have offered their of good offices' but these have not been accepted by the Sinhala-dominated Colombo government.

President Jayewardene committed one more serious error of judgment even after India's decision to intervene after July 1983. His government enacted in August 1983 the Sixth Amendment to the Constitution. Members of Parliament were required to swear their loyalty to the unitary constitution before taking their seats. Given the severity of the anti-Tamil violence and the enormity of the damage to Tamil persons and property, all MPs belonging to the Tamil United Liberation Front refused to take their oaths and in the process forfeited their seats. There could not have been a graver blunder, for the Sixth Amendment and the resulting vacating of seats by the TULF MPs enabled Tamil militant groups to take over the leadership of the Tamil movement from a moderate parliamentary party.

INTERNATIONALISATION OF THE CONFLICT

When chaos and lawlessness prevailed in July 1983, Mrs. Indira Gandhi pressured President Jayewardene in phone conversations from New Delhi to accept her good offices to mediate the dispute (de Silva, K.M., 1991 and Kodikara, S.U., 1991). In the week of the July 1983 pogrom, her Minister of External Affairs, Narasimha Rao, visited Colombo to assess the situation. In November 1983, Mrs. Gandhi's special emissary, Gopalaswarny Parthasarathy, hammered out in New Delhi a compromise agreement with President Jayewardene referred to as 'Annexure "C"'. The Annexure provided for the amalgamation of the Northern and Eastern provinces with a fair measure of devolution. Back in Colombo, President Jayewardene had second thoughts. The President convened an obviously delaying device, the All Parties Conference (APC). The APC, a medley of parties except for the largest Opposition party, the SLFP which boycotted the sessions, and members of the Buddhist clergy deliberated till the end of 1984 at which point the government announced its proposals. These were based on the DDC model. The TULF rejected the scheme and the stage was set for another attempt at Indian mediation.

The venue on this occasion was at Thimpu in Bhutan. The Thimpu talks of July–August 1985 too failed to produce a solution acceptable to both sides. The principal Tamil demand for the right to self determination was rejected by the Sri Lanka delegation. All the Tamil groups withdrew from the talks when word went round that the Sri Lankan army (ninety nine per cent being Sinhalese) had massacred Tamils in the north and east and in particular in the Tamil towns of Trincomalee and Vavuniya. The Sri Lanka delegation lingered on in New Delhi and in September 1985 negotiated the 'Terms of Accord and Understanding' under which certain powers were to be devolved to regional councils (the unit being the province, not a district) which would be supervised by the Executive President. The TULF rejected the scheme and explained to New Delhi that interference by the President would compromise their concept of autonomy.

The Thimpu talks were followed by the Chidambaram proposals of July 1986 which did not meet with Tamil aspirations (P. Chidambaram was a cabinet minister in Rajiv Gandhi's government and was from Tamil Nadu). Yet another delaying mechanism, this time under a different name, the Political Parties Conference (PPC) without representatives from the diehard Buddhist clergy convened in June 1986, without SLFP participation, to deliberate on the Chidambaram proposals. This was a waste of time, for the Tamils were not interested in the contents. However by November 1986, the Sri Lanka government's snail's pace progress had reached the stage when President Jayewardene indicated to Rajiv Gandhi at Bangalore that his government would seriously consider the Indian mediator's proposals of 19 December 1986. The Northern Province would be connected by a narrow corridor to the Tamil majority section of the Eastern Province to constitute one unit. That province would have separate autonomous Muslim and Sinhalese regions. The Liberation Tigers of Tamil Eelam (LTTE) which by now was the most powerful of the Tamil militant groups rejected the scheme. At this point the Sri Lankan government launched on 26 May 1987 a nearly successful 'Operation Liberation' with a view to regaining control of the Jaffna peninsula.

By early 1987, Rajiv Gandhi and India's foreign policy makers realized that the Sri Lankan government was not serious on implementing any meaningful scheme for the devolution of power. On the other hand 'Operation Liberation' was evidence enough of a single minded pursuit of a military solution. To New Delhi, the Sri Lanka government's grant of broadcasting facilities to the Voice of America in its territory, the lease of oil refining arrangements to the United States around the strategic port of Trincomalee, securing of military advisors from the private Keeny Meeny Services in Britain, from the states of Israel and Pakistan and supplies of arms from the Republic of South Africa were all evidence of policy goals not consonant with President Jayewardene's declared peaceful intentions.

Mr. Gandhi switched therefore to a direct policy of confrontation. In the circumstances of U.S., British, Israeli and South African involvement, India's vital interests were at risk. On 3 June 1987, as a first step, India despatched twenty Indian fishing vessels with food and oil for the people of Jaffna which the Sri Lanka navy turned back. The Sri Lanka government failed to note the ominous change in Indian policy. The following day in a show of strength, the Indian air force dropped food and medical supplies in Jaffna, again presumably as a token warning.

In early July 1987, India chose to impose its terms of a settlement on the Sri Lanka government. The Indo-Sri Lanka Accord of 27 July 1987 signed by Mr. Gandhi and President Jayewardene went far beyond 'Annexure "C"' (1983) and the Chidambaram Proposals (1986). In addition, India secured her vital interests.

The Accord went to a fair extent to recognise Ceylon Tamil aspirations. The two leaders agreed that the traditional Tamil homeland 'the Northern and Eastern Provinces (NEP) have been areas of historical habitation of Sri Lankan Tamil speaking peoples who have at all times hitherto lived together in the territory with other ethnic groups'. It provided for a temporary merger of the two provinces (the NEP) for an interim period. The Accord further sought to reproduce the quasi-federal aspects of the Indian Constitution.

Mr. Gandhi was satisfied with the agreement stating on 2 August at a public meeting in Madras that it 'secures everything that the Sri Lankan Tamils had demanded short of breaking Sri Lanka's unity', that 'approximately one-third of Sri Lanka's territory will be made into a single province where the Tamils will have a clear majority' and that they (the Ceylon Tamils) 'will have regional autonomy comparable to state governments in India' (Kodikara, 1990). India agreed to guarantee the implementation of the agreement under Article 2.14. This implied the assurance that India will enforce a cessation of hostilities and ensure the surrender of all arms in the possession of Tamil militant groups. For this purpose President Jayewardene invited an Indian Peace Keeping Force (IPKF) which however despite its enormous size of some 70,000 soldiers failed to secure the surrender of the weapons or put an end to the hostilities. In the end President Jayewardene's successor, President Ranasinghe Premadasa requested India to withdraw the IPKF which India agreed to, the mission having failed in its objectives. The IPKFs withdrawal was completed by 31 March 1991 but not in the friendliest of circumstances.

The other aspects of the Accord need not delay us here. These related to Sri Lanka agreeing that the strategic harbour of Trincomalee and all other ports of Sri Lanka will not be made available to a third power 'in a manner prejudicial to India's interests' and foreign broadcasting organisations located in Sri Lanka will not be permitted facilities to use these for military purposes hostile to India's strategic concerns (Koclikara 1991).

The question arises as to whether the provisions of the Accord and its translation into the Thirteenth Amendment of the Sri Lanka Constitution are any longer valid in the context of the renewal of hostilities between the Sri Lanka government and the Liberation Tigers of Tamil Eelam (LTTE). Dennis Austin and Anirudha Gupta (1990) are not hopeful stating that 'in the Sri Lankan world of the 1990s it is still an open question which will triumph – good or evil, democracy or violence'. Rita Sebastian, the well known Colombo journalist took a similar view when she wrote that 'even a decade of unprecedented violence has not made hardline Sinhala opinion relent in its refusal to share any meaningful power with the Tamils' *(Tamil Times*, 15 February 1992).

The Indian High Commissioner in Colombo, Nagendra Nath Jha, sounded more optimistic. He thought that 'like everybody else, the Sinhalese population too must be sick and tired of war...' adding that 'if that is so they (the Ceylon Tamils) need to be shown, given some assurance that they have a place in the sun' *(Tamil Times, op. cit.)*.

And as to the validity of the Accord itself he affirmed that 'it has not lapsed by any means' *(op. cit.)*.

What all this amounts to is that there is now a middleground of Sinhalese opinion, notwithstanding the opposition of leading Buddhist monks and Sinhala Buddhist pressure organisations, which is supportive of a Sinhala-Tamil reconciliation to which the LTTE itself is not opposed. The LTTE foreign affairs spokesman, Anton Balasingham, stated categorically that the LTTE 'would be prepared to give up its demand for a separate state ... if the Tamil people were granted a federal system....' And this, despite the statements of his leader Veluppillai Prathakaran and his representative in Western Europe, the Paris-based Lawrence Thilakar, that the LTTE will not settle for less than a separate state *(Tamil Times, op. cit.)*.

Thilakar however appears willing to consider alternatives. He, at first, requested this writer to provide the LTTE with a draft constitution similar to that of the constituent units of the (Russian) Commonwealth of Independent States'. For Thilakar however there seemed room for manoeuvre; for his office in Paris was agreeable to consider proposals for an improvement on the Thirteenth Amendment as advanced by Sinhala peace groups and in particular by the Indian Tamil senior cabinet minister, S. Thondaman. All these moves are indicative of a desire to effect an overarching Lijphartian/Daalder-type consociational accommodation that will produce a compromise settlement between the leaders of the two warring communities, without such an agreement having to be debated by the representatives of political parties of every hue.

The IPKF failed to win the confidence not only of the Tamil militant groups, with the exception of the Eelam People's Revolutionary Liberation

Front (EPRLF), but it permanently antagonised the majority of the Tamil people in the NEP. It is possible that for generations to come the Tamil people of Sri Lanka will not accommodate an Indian military presence. The alternative is a negotiated settlement with the Colombo government which will enable the two groups to coexist peacefully so as to make Indian intervention unnecessary or superfluous. The chances however are that the Colombo government will, because of Sinhala Buddhist opposition and the reluctance of Sinhala bureaucrats to cooperate, not be able to honour a demarcation of powers and as a consequence various Tamil groups will at times invoke India's monitoring role. India will therefore, despite Sinhala suspicion and even opposition, continue to be involved in Sri Lanka's affairs for a considerable length of time. The intervention will vary, depending on pressure from political forces in Tamil Nadu and the stability of governments in New Delhi.

In the consociational framework Sri Lanka has thus a third operative factor beyond the practicalities of overarching arrangements between the two ethnic groups. India will act as a catalytic promoter similar to the role of the US in the recent Arab-Israeli peace talks. The JVP on the other hand will be a disruptive force having abandoned its earlier ultra-Marxism for a populist anti-Tamil ultra-chauvinistic goal which combined with its antiIndian stance can have a potent impact on the traditional fears of the Sinhala electors.

It is this writer's view (confirmed by confidential information provided to me) that President Jayewardene decided to sign the Accord because he failed to obtain agreement from his seriously divided cabinet. Between 1983 and 1987, two distinguished outsiders, Dame Judith Hart of International Alert and Jyotendra Dixit, the Indian High Commissioner in Colombo, addressed the Sri Lanka cabinet with little success. Though the Accord provided for measurable Tamil gains and had the approval of the TULF which by the time the Accord was signed had ceased to be a relevant force in Tamil politics, President Jayewardene was probably confident that he and his party (the UNP) could prevail in the newly created NEP. The latter amalgamation had to within six months be approved in a referendum by the people of the Eastern Province. This referendum has been postponed on four occasions to date (1992) because of the war situation in the Eastern Province. The proposals providing for autonomy for the amalgamated NEP as well as for the other eight provinces were enacted as the Thirteenth Amendment to the Sri Lanka Constitution. We will explain the new framework using the NEP as the typical example, that province being the traditional homeland claimed by the Ceylon Tamils.

The NEP would have a single Provincial Council with a chief minister and a cabinet. There would (as stated earlier) be three lists of powers, central, provincial and concurrent, as in the Indian federation, except that these powers, were in the context of the unitary state of Sri Lanka, significantly different from India; however India agreed to underwrite the terms of the Accord (H.L. de Silva, 1991). The margin for manoeuvre in the interstices of devolved powers were minimal for the provincial councils but proper Indian supervision could have obfuscated any attempt by Colombo to impotentiate the devolutionary package. Furthermore the Accord compelled Sri Lanka to agree to Tamil and English as official languages in addition to Sinhala. The Sinhala Only Act of 1956 was to that extent modified. All these provisions were included in the Thirteenth Amendment to the Sri Lanka Constitution and in the Provincial Councils Act, both enacted in the latter quarter of 1987.

There was violent opposition from the Jathika Vimukthi Peramuna (JVP) while other opposition parties, in particular the SLFP, too voiced their protests. The JVP comprised mainly frustrated educated unemployed Sinhala youth. It was effectively organised in the late sixties/early seventies with a grassroots network and an ultra-Marxist program, one of its principal objectives being opposition to 'Indian expansionism'. The Organisation led the abortive insurrection of 1971 against Mrs. Bandaranaike's United Front government. It ceased to be a force for some years.

When the Accord was signed in July 1987, the JVP seized the opportunity of 'the surrender to India' to lead a populist uprising against President Jayewardene's government (for details on the JVP please see below). It reduced the government to desperate straits. In the end, the JVP leadership was apprehended and eliminated by Sri Lanka's military personnel in 1989. For the time being it is in low profile but its emergence as a serious threat in the future cannot be ruled out. The JVP refuses to enter the political mainstream unlike the LTTE which is willing to negotiate and could perhaps contest in elections in the NEP whenever held.

The fly in the ointment was the role of India's intelligence agency, RAW (Research and Analysis Wing) and the refusal of Velupillai Prabhakaran and his LTTE, the most powerful of the Tamil resistance fighters, to accept the Accord and to lay down arms. RAW had gone down a slippery slope of effectively creating suspicion and conflict between the Tamil militant groups. The LTTE feared that RAW sought their immobilisation. Consequently they turned vicious on the Indian Peacekeeping Force (IPKF). With the LTTE hostile, the IPKF failed in its mission (Austin and Gupta, 1990).

The prospect of resolving the issue now returned to an internal initiative by President Premadasa. The President negotiated with the LTTE for some thirteen months during 1989/1990 but failed to obtain an agreement. Hostilities resumed in June 1990 in what came to be called Eelam War 11.

The efflux of several thousands of Tamil refugees to countries in Western Europe and North America and the appalling violation of human rights has attracted the attention of Sri Lanka's aid givers. The states affected from the outflow of refugees, such as Switzerland and others, conscience stricken, like Norway and Sweden and members of the Commonwealth, pressured by expatriate Tamil lobby groups (in Canada and Australia) offered their good offices to mediate in the conflict. To date there has been no tangible acceptance from either side.

PROSPECTS FOR THE FUTURE

The Sri Lankan imbroglio is not beyond disentanglement. We have identified the weaknesses in the internal mechanisms which are not conducive to an amicable resolution of the conflict. At the heart of it has lain the demotic polity, in effect the successful manoeuvring of the Sinhalese electorate by militant and chauvinistic Sinhala lobby groups such as Buddhist priests, bureaucrats, haute elements of the feudal and prosperous Sinhalese elites and the frustrated educated unemployed among the Sinhalese. This is a sizeable constituency which cannot be readily satisfied. Social and political bribery could succeed to some extent but this has to be at the expense of the Tamils. The latter would have to be deprived of even what is their proportionate due. Such disproportionate sharing of a limited pie is one of the potent causes of conflict.

The senior Sinhalese leadership of both major parties realise that a compromise acceptable to the Tamils is the only way out for the island state. The Sinhala leadership as well as the only contemporaneously relevant Tamil force, the LTTE, are sceptical of India. The LTTE nevertheless prefers a controlled Indian presence at the mediating table. India might not be satisfied with such a limited role. There are ways however of meeting Indian concerns without compromising Sinhalese and LTTE stances. The two parties have therefore tentatively explored possible alternative mediators such as Norway and in a tangential role Switzerland. The Tamils could obtain an arrangement which will in effect be of a loose devolutionary structure.

At the present time the peace proposals are held up on the question of (a) the unit of demarcation, the Tamils generally insisting on the NEP as a single unit while some Sinhalese requiring a redrawing of the Eastern Province so as to excise the Sinhalese and Muslim sections and (b) the quantum of legislative powers to be devolved; on this the peace initiators, even the senior cabinet minister, S. Thondaman, have failed to realise that any amount of powers can be devolved but as long as executive powers remain concentrated in the Executive President and even though he can constitutionally delegate his executive powers to his representative, the governor of the province, devolution ceases to have meaning. For the provincial legislature will have power to pass any number of statutes within the powers allocated to them; but it will be the governor and the officials of the state bureaucratic apparatus that will execute legislation on the orders of the Executive President. There is therefore a hiatus here which leaves the chief minister and his ministers devoid of executive power and dependent on the governor, appointed by the Executive president, to execute the statutes of the legislature, a situation which led Professor Lakshman Marasinghe (a Sri Lankan Sinhalese) of the University of Windsor to observe: the reform package contained in the Provincial Councils Bill and Thirteenth Amendment is no more than the creation of an ethnically ascertained local government body exercising subordinate legislation.

It was his view that this reforms package 'proffered as an alternative to the Tamil demand for a separate state ... falls for short of Eelam....'

The problem therefore is to devise a meaningful federalism which will provide for an autonomous Tamil NER There are two pre-requisites here, a commitment by the Sinhalese elite, UNP and SLFP, to share power with the Ceylon Tamils. If the past is any indication, there is little or no evidence.

Secondly the respective Sinhala power elites are not secure in their political bases to effect comprehensive settlements. The rivalry and competition for the middle ground of Sinhalese voters make Sinhala governments feel vulnerable and threatened. This in part explains the abandonment of pacts and understandings.

Thirdly the consolidation of a military complex with its own vested interests in pursuing the LTTE in an all out search for victory may hinder the doves in the ranks of government. The military's sanguine hopes may not necessarily materialise in the context of the LTTE's commitment to the armed struggle and protracted civil war.

Fourthly neither side provides any hope of an outright victory. This means an indefinite bleeding war, continued violation of human rights and an ongoing stalemate.

As against these formidable obstacles to peace, the Sri Lankan President, Ranasinghe President, insists that he seeks a negotiated settlement. The Political Parties Conference which continues to sit to explore possibilities and the all parties Select Committee of Parliament are themselves manifestations of moderate Sinhalese opinion seeking a way out of the present impasse. And so are the mushrooming peace movements. In addition, the government of Sri Lanka is promoting the concept of Sri Lanka as a multi-ethnic democracy, no longer the monopolistic Sinhala Buddhist state that it was claimed to be in the past. Two important volumes were produced by Neville Jayaweera for the International Peace Research Institute, Oslo in 1990 and 1991. The 1990 Jayaweera Report recommended that though the 'framework is fragile', there are steps which can be taken to strengthen it (p. 89). The 1991 Jayaweera Report emphasised that 'in the case of President Premaclasa the evidence of a commitment to multiethnicity is abundant and unambiguous (p. 46).

In the end there are two possibilities. Sinhalese peace groups themselves could gain sufficient strength to influence the government to go for a compromise. If this fails, the war can bankrupt or reduce to financial straits the Colombo government compelling the latter to effect a compromise settlement. Lastly, as the Indian High Commissioner, Nagendra Nath Jha, stated in his interview to the editor of the Sunday edition of The *Island* (reproduced in the Tamil *Times, op. cit.*), India does not consider the Accord to have 'lapsed by any means'. Thus the necessary components of consociation are present. They may not be adequately activated in the course of the immediate future.

India will however continue to be the push factor. It is possible that in the end a meaningful ethnic federalism will result because of international pressures. On the other hand a conflict that will never end might prevail.

REFERENCES

Austin, Dennis and Gupta, Anirudha, *Lions and Tigers – Sri Lanka Crisis* (London, 1988).

Austin, Dennis and Gupta, Anirudha, *The Politics of Violence in India and South Asia: Is Democracy an Endangered Species* (London, 1990).

de Silva, C.R., 'The Sinhalese-Tamil Rift in Sri Lanka', pp. 155–74 in Wilson, A. Jeyaratnam, and Dalton, Dennis, *The States of South Asia: Problems of National Integration* (London, 1982).

de Silva, C.R., 'Sinhala-Tamil Ethnic Rivalry: The Background' pp. 111–24, in Goldmann, Robert and Wilson, A. Jeyaratnam, (1984).

de Silva, H.L., *An Appraisal of the Federal Alternative For Sri* Lanka (Dehiwela, Sri Lanka, 1991).

de Silva, K.M., *A History of Sri Lanka* (London, 1981).

de Silva, K.M., 'Indo-Sri Lanka Relations, 1975–1989: A Study in the Internationalization of Ethnic Conflict', pp. 76–106 in de Silva, K.M., and May, R.J., (eds), *Internationalization of Ethnic Conflict* (London, 1991).

de Silva, K.M., *Managing Ethnic Tensions in Multi-Ethnic Societies: Sri Lanka 1880–1985* (London, 1986).

de Silva, K.M., 'Nationalism and the State in Sri Lanka', pp. 67–76, in de Silva, K.M., Duke, Pensri, Goldberg, Ellen S., and Katz, Nathan, *Ethnic Conflict in Buddhist Societies: Sri Lanka, Thailand and Burma* (London, 1988).

de Silva, K.M., 'University Admissions and Ethnic Tension in Sri Lanka: 1977–1982' pp. 97–110 in Goldmann, Robert and Wilson, A. Jeyaratnam, *From Independence to Statehood: Managing Ethnic Conflict in Five African and Asian States* (London, 1984).

Jayaweera, Neville, *Sri Lanka: Towards a Multi-Ethnic Democracy, Report of a fact finding mission* (Oslo, International Peace Research Institute, 1991).

Jeffries, Sir Charles, *Ceylon: The Path to Independence* (London, 1962).

Jeffries, Sir Charles, *'O.E.G.': A Biography of Sir Oliver Ernest Goonetilleke* (London, 1969).

Kodikara, Shelton U., 'Internationalization of Sri Lanka's Ethnic Conflict: The Tamil Nadu Factor' pp. 107–14 in de Silva, K.M. and May, R.J., (eds), *Internationalization of Ethnic Conflict* (London, 1991).

Lijphart, Arend, *Democracy in Plural Societies* (Yale, 1977).

Malalasekera, G.P., 'The Language Problem, 1, 11 and III', *Ceylon Daily News* 10, 11, 12 October, 1955.

Manogaran, C., *Ethnic Conflict and Reconciliation in Sri Lanka* (Honolulu, 1987).

Marasinghe, M.L., 'Ethnic Politics and Constitutional Reform: The Indo-Sri Lanka Accord, *The International Comparative and Law Quarterly*, Vol. 37., No: 1988 (July).

Nadesan, S., *Ceylon's Language* Problem (Colombo, 1956).

Russell, Jane., *Communal Politics under the Donoughmore Constitution 19311947* (Dehiwala, Sri Lanka, 1982).

Samarasinghe, S.W.R. de A., 'Ethnic Representation in Central Government Employment and Sinhala – Tamil Relations in Sri Lanka: 1948–1981'.

Smith, Donald E., 'The Sinhalese Buddhist Revolution' pp. 453–88 in Donald E. Smith, *South Asian Politics and Religion* (Princeton, 1966).

Tamil Times, 15 February 1992 (Vol. XI, No. 3).

Weerawardena, 1. D.S., *Ceylon General Election* (Colombo, 1960) 47.

Weerawardena, 1. D.S., 'The General Elections in Ceylon 1952' in *The Ceylon Historical Journal*, Vol. 11, Nos. 1 and 2 (1952).

Wilson, A. Jeyaratnam, 'Buddhism in Ceylon Politics, 1960–1965' in Smith, Donald E., *South Asian Politics and Religion* (Princeton, 1966).

Wilson, A. Jeyaratnam, *Electoral Politics in an Emergent State: The Ceylon General Election of May 1970* (London, 1976).

Wilson, A. Jeyaratnam, *Politics in Sri Lanka, 1947–1979* (London, 1979).

Wilson, A. Jeyaratnam, *The Break-Up Sri Lanka: The Sinhalese-Tamil Conflict* (London, 1988).

Wilson, A. Jeyaratnam, *The Gaullist System in Asia: The Constitution of Sri Lanka* (London, 1980).

Wilson, A. Jeyaratnam, 'The Tamil Federal Party in Ceylon Politics', *Journal of Commonwealth Political* Studies (Vol. 4., July 1966).

Woodward, Calvin A., *The Growth of a Party System in Ceylon* (Providence, 1969).

Chapter Seven

Ethnic Conflict in Post Cold War Africa: Four Case Studies

Alexander Johnston

INTRODUCTION

For those who believe that conflicts of communalism and identity are the driving force of a 'new world disorder', the conflicts of Africa in the post-Cold War world offer gratifying confirmation. Communal conflicts of one sort or another are implicated in cases of state collapse and humanitarian disaster in Liberia, Rwanda and Somalia. Even in a relatively robust state like South Africa, which is underpinned by sturdy institutions, popular legitimacy and a structured competitive politics, the most serious threat to the orderly process of democratic transformation has come from a conflict with strong communal overtones. This chapter will discuss each of these cases in turn, but some general discussion will provide a contextual background.

Any attempt to discuss 'tribalism' in post-Cold War Africa has to take three problematic issues into account. These are; the difficulties of generalising about Africa; the question of historical perspective; and 'tribalism' itself as a term of discourse.

Generalising about Africa

The difficulties of generalising about Africa are well-documented and as recent discussions have shown, the onset of the post-Cold War World has not made them any easier. Even those contributions which seek to establish a systematic basis for generalisation, acknowledge the difficulties of doing so.[1] The experience of ethnicity in Africa has been varied and uneven, as have the strategies of coping with the phenomenon of communalism in all its varieties.[2] Although the spectacle of states collapsing amid appalling human suffering might impose a superficial picture of commonality on Africa's experience of communal conflict in the post-Cold War world, closer examination reveals a continuing narrative of variety and contradiction.

Perspective: globalisation and the longue duree

The politics of ethno-nationalism and tribalism in contemporary Africa have to be seen, logically enough, in contemporary terms. It is common cause that Africa has experienced a crisis of globalisation since the end of the 1980s. Under these conditions, the withdrawal of Cold War subsidy and support has coincided with importunate demands for restructuring and democratisation from Western governments and lending institutions. Intensified competition for foreign investment and a drastic decline in the already attenuated bargaining power of African states are aggravating factors. These things, along with indigenous demands for democratisation, have put strains on clientelist regimes beyond the capacity of at least some of them to cope. The contemporary context of new, or restated ethno-nationalist tensions and conflicts should be seen in this light.

But any review of post-Cold War tribalism in Africa should not confine itself to a current crisis. Specifically, it should not fail to note the current move by Africanists to emphasise the continuity and weight of indigenous historical experience in understanding contemporary Africa. Pointing to the influence of one academic in particular (Bayart, 1993) in this development, Clapham notes the importance of the long term – la longue durée – in encouraging this tendency to see African states '... in their own terms, as the product of their own societies, and not merely as the failed attempts to reproduce some model of government designed elsewhere.'[3]

Tribalism and Discourse

'Tribalism' has the ability to convey powerful images and messages, but its usage is diffuse, imprecise and frequently pejorative as noted in the introductory chapters to this volume. It has long gone beyond the bounds of any reasonably precise anthropological or ethnographic meaning. It can be met in the context of large, politically mature nation states, or of sub-national fragments without structured political identities or aspirations to nationhood and self-determination.

In the South African context for instance, some of the confusions surrounding the usage of 'tribalism' can be illustrated with reference to Afrikaners and Afrikaner nationalism. It is commonplace for Afrikaners to be described as a 'white tribe'.[4] Indeed, the label is often self-assigned, with the purpose of insisting on an identity which is not merely that of 'settler', but indigenous to Africa. Yet Afrikaners, with their cultural entrepreneurs, ramified ethnic coalition, and elaborate schemes of state-sponsored social mobility in an industrialising society, were among the great state builders of recent times. They are far removed from tribalism's more frequent associations with state destroying, by which sub-national groupings with no capacity, or perhaps even desire to create states of their own, obstruct the development of strong, legitimate, state authorities and structures.

Adding to this confusion, and in fact linked to it, is the question of pejorative usage. For Vail the issue is simple: 'If one disapproves of the phenomenon, it is "tribalism"; if one is less judgmental, "it" is "ethnicity"'.[5] Others might want to make a distinction between ethno-nationalism (rational, modern, state-building, driven by ideas like self-determination) and tribalism (irrational, atavistic, obstructive, or even destructive of modern state-forms). Even if such a distinction were sustainable in analytical terms it would not be easily sustainable in normative terms, given the appalling capacity for destruction of 'modern' ethno-nationalism. As a result, the social science usage of 'tribalism' in Africa (or elsewhere) is condemned, at least to some extent, to the vagaries of subjective dislike and/or weakly-grounded analytical categories.

CASE STUDIES

Mad Max and Marabouts: Conflict in Liberia

In December 1989, the invasion of Nimba County by Charles Taylor and the National Patriotic Front of Liberia (NPFL) plunged Liberia into civil war. The resulting carnage, social disintegration and institutional collapse have become emblematic of Africa's 'new tribalism'. Journalistic accounts have noted the shocking and bizarre signatures of the conflict, which include the youth of the combatants, their ritualistic behaviour, the role of drugs and popular culture, even cannibalism.[6] Popular commentary highlights Liberia as epitomizing Africa's potential for anarchy.[7] Three scholarly analyses of the Liberian conflict which will be considered here (Ellis, 1995; Richards, 1995; Reno, 1995), are broadly compatible in the accounts they give of these phenomena, but each has a distinctive emphasis in explaining Liberia's contribution to the aetiology of conflict in post-Cold War Africa.[8]

Taylor's invasion began as an attempt to oust the regime of President Samuel Doe which was marked by extremely low levels of political and bureaucratic competence, beginning with the 'functionally illiterate' president himself. The intensification of ethnic clientism (especially in the army) and a 'marauding' character in which brute force and personal enrichment at all levels of 'government' were also features of the Doe regime.

Both inside and outside the country, it was widely accepted that Taylor's invasion, 'would lead to a coup of a relatively familiar type' (Ellis, 1995: 174). Instead, collapse into anarchic conflict between fissiparous warring factions has been the result. These factions combine the qualities of ethnicized militias and freebooting armies which control the resources of

Liberia's clandestine forest economy. In their ethnic dimension, they are communal (and regional) defence and revenge groups. In their commercial incarnation, they use force to underwrite agreements between warlords and international commercial interests, control forced labour and (in the absence of payment) seek plunder on their own account. The costs of the Liberian civil war are generally reckoned to be (in mid-1996) over 150,000 dead, and over one million displaced (from a pre-war population of 2.5m). Some 300,000 of these refugees are across the border in neighbouring Ivory Coast and the remainder in the capital, Monrovia. The bulk of the country is in the hands of the warring factions, with Taylor's NPFL predominant, while a 12,000 strong peace-keeping force, drawn from members of the Economic Community of West African States, controls Monrovia. Since between 1989 and early 1996, thirteen peace accords were made and broken,[9] it is difficult to view the prospect of lasting peace with any confidence.

There is a large measure of agreement among the principal explanatory accounts of this human disaster. All three note the pervasive influence of realpolitik practised by regional powers Nigeria, Ivory Coast and Burkina Faso. The motives include personal ties respectively influencing presidents Houphouet-Boigny and Compaore of Ivory Coast and Burkina Faso. Nigeria's hegemonic aspirations in the region and francophone determination to resist them while sponsoring French commercial interests are also important. There is unanimity too, on the studied passivity of the USA, beyond the barest minimum of order-keeping concerns. The control of logging, iron ore and agricultural resources is seen as the essential prize for which the warlords and international concessionaires are competing.

It is, however, in their treatment of the role of ethnicity in the conflicts that the shared perspectives of these three accounts bear most upon a discussion of 'tribalism' in contemporary Africa. In fact, Reno has little to say directly about ethnicity, concentrating more, as we shall see, on the emergence of, 'an alternative institutionalization of sovereign authority' (Reno, 1995: 111). For their part, both Ellis and Richards make it clear that while ethnicity is an essential medium of the conflicts, it provides neither a primary motive for the participants' actions, nor a political discourse which would make them intelligible in terms encouraging resolution.

> As with the Krahn-Mandingo/Gio-Mano rivalries, the Krahn-Mandingo split in ULIMO did not have its origins in any generalized ethnic hatreds, but in the factionalization of ambitious politicians seeking to carve themselves a following. All of Liberia's current ethnic feuds started at the top and spread downwards. To a great extent, all have been manufactured by people hungry for power, using violence as a means of political recruitment. (Ellis, 1995: 183).

Richards distinguishes between two types of ethnic tension in Liberia (and in the latter of the two, Sierra Leone). The first refers to clientist tensions between the Krahn people (4–5% of the pre-war population), who were favoured by President Doe (himself a member of that group) and others, notably Gio and Mano. Secondly, there is anti-Mandingo feeling directed at members of this Guinean-based trading diaspora, which in turn has sparked defensive organization into militias.

Despite this, Richards concludes that neither the NPFL in Liberia, nor the insurgent Revolutionary United Front (RUF) in Sierra Leone, was in origin an ethnic movement. He argues: 'Ethnic tension is ... seen as an opportunity for, rather than as a cause of, rebellion in Liberia and Sierra Leone.' (Richards, 1995: 141). What is clear from both accounts is that ethnicity is not linked in Liberia to any discourse of self-determination or regional autonomy. Nor is there any trace of the ethnic entrepreneurs who create political movements out of shared culture and language. In fact as Reno confirms, the 'movements' which vie for advantage in Liberia have neither political platforms nor demands. (Reno, 1995: 118).

Agreed as they are on the motivations of realpolitik and commercial rivalry, along with the purely instrumental role of ethnicity, each author brings his own emphasis to explaining the anomie and anarchy. Reno's perspective on Liberia looks beyond state decay: '.. to a simultaneous non-bureaucratic process of state-building, an alternative institutionalization of political authority, heavily dependent upon external resources for survival.' (Reno, 1995).

In this way, external resources (mercenaries, commercial interests) replace the bureaucratic and military organs of state, which leaders like Taylor cannot afford, and could not in any case control, even if the revenue was there to subvent such an inevitably clientist regime. Under this ingenious, if self-limiting strategy, Taylor divests himself of most of the responsibilities of statehood, including inherited debts, obligations of social spending, payment of state functionaries and even respect for international boundaries. This is one possible response of a decaying patrimonial system to a crisis composed of importunate donors, reduced resources, and demanding of ethnic, regional, and bureaucratic constituencies. Despite the contemporary conjuncture for what Reno calls the 're-invention' of patrimonial states, its true context is: '... a longue durée that resumes many of the strategies of late pre-colonial and colonial rule in parts of Africa.' (Reno, 1995: 112).

Ellis also points to the pre-colonial African past in seeking an explanation beyond the political for Liberia's disintegration. In this context, his focus is on religious and spiritual aspects of Liberian culture and society. Ellis notes the importance of secret societies (Poro and Sende, being the most important) and claims that their ritualistic and cultic influence has survived the erosion of their formal power, which has accompanied the development of the modern state in Liberia. Until Liberia's disintegration, this influence was felt in: '... occult, but nevertheless ordered rituals in which the power represented by violence and the capacity to dominate are represented symbolically, including sometimes by human sacrifice.' (Ellis, 1995: 193).

Three points made by Ellis are particularly noteworthy here. The first is that the character of the violence in Liberia (its political incoherence, its ritualistic forms) can be partly explained, not only by the survival into the present of a pre-modern spiritual inheritance but, crucially, the decay of the controls which previously kept such cultic influences in check: 'Ritual murders are no longer carried out by officers of established cults, but by unqualified adolescents.' (Ellis, 1995: 194).

Secondly, the ritualized quality of the violence is enhanced, rather than diminished by trappings of modernity, especially media which record and transmit them. Thirdly, although a reader might deduce from Ellis' account that the spiritual dimension of the violence is a barrier to the emergence of a coherent discourse of political conflict, in fact: '...the construction of a coherent system of spiritual communication may accompany the building of a coherent political order. In these circumstances, representations of power expressed in a spiritual register may not be seen as a-political but as the necessary accompaniment to a political project.' (Ellis, 1995: 196).

For his part, Richards tends to emphasize the dimension of dystopic futurism which journalistic accounts convey so vividly from the fronts of conflict and inform the more apocalyptic passages of commentaries and forecasts like Kaplan's (1994). Richards views the conflicts of Liberia and Sierra Leone as more than, 'obscure post-colonial 'tribal' conflict.' For him, they are dramas of peripheral modernity in which part-educated youths, marooned by state collapse and the disappearance of educational and formal sector opportunities play a central role. Encouraged by a variety of influences ranging from Libyan-inspired populism to the violence of global popular culture, along with a variety of role players from warlords to neighbouring heads of state, these youthful brigands, once mobilized are very difficult to control.

Rwanda

The extremity of the violence in Rwanda has been arresting, even by the destructive standards of ethno-nationalist conflict in the post-Cold War world. Between April and July 1994, about 500,000 people were systematically slaughtered in a long-prepared and methodically carried out genocidal campaign. The victims were mainly members of the Tutsi minority (perhaps 14% of the pre-1994 population), but many were members of the Hutu majority. Hutu's designated as moderate in politics and accommodating towards the minority were done to death by their 'own' militias, at the urging of propagandists and on the instructions of the government and civil administration. The systematic killing was brought to an end only with the overthrow of the Hutu government by an invading army of Tutsi exiles. They were organised by the Rwandan Popular Front (RPF), which had its origins in a previous generation of escapees from mass slaughter, who had been a key military element in Uganda's various conflicts. The triumph of the RPF prompted an accelerated flood of Hutu refugees across Rwanda's borders with Tanzania, Burundi and Zaire. By the end of 1994, an estimated two million were in exile while perhaps five million in all had been displaced inside or outside the country during the year.

The drift to ethnocide in Rwanda took place in the presence of a number of factors which largely define post-Cold War Africa. They include economic decline and prescriptions for adjustment by the International Monetary Fund; pressure to democratize by western states and donors, global and regional international organizations as well as, in this case, neighbouring states; hesitations and prevarications by the UN over the prospects of intervention; ambiguous motivations for French intervention; the equivocal role and status of international humanitarian non-governmental organizations.[10] These things brought global forces to bear on a domestic political situation which has been punctuated by recurrent ethnic violence since 1959, three years before independence from Belgium. In that year, the oligarchical rule of the Tutsi minority, which had been encouraged by the racial ideologies and policies of indirect rule of both German (1894–1919) and Belgian (from 1919) colonists, was overthrown. As a result, the stratified system of ethnic relations which had hitherto favoured the Tutsi, was reversed.

Despite their majority status, the guardians of this 'Hutu revolution', have never felt able to risk strategies of accommodating the Tutsi minority as a way of consolidating their rule. On the contrary, periodic massacre (1963, 1973) and vicious racial ideologies have been their responses to the threat of subversion from Tutsi exiles. The threat became a reality from October 1990, when the RPF (which was founded in 1979) launched an invasion from Uganda. The twin threat of this externally-based insurgency and the well-meaning efforts of regional and global actors to force power-sharing reforms on the Hutu regime, provided the provocation for Hutu militants to put into operation the systematic plans for slaughter to which their demonising propaganda about the ethnic 'other' had long predisposed them.

Ethnic violence in Rwanda appears to satisfy popular expectations of 'tribalism' in no uncertain measure. These expectations (in the eyes of academic critics) are of 'deep-seated ancestral enmities' and 'immutable givens' of race and ethnicity (Lemarchand, 1994: 588), of conflicts which are 'given in nature' (De Waal, 1994, 3), reflecting 'historical inevitability' and 'patterns of repetition'.[11] There are presumptive qualities of longevity and durability to the Rwandan conflict. There is an apparent symmetry of opposition in two groups which are thoroughly alienated from each other and a reciprocity of rejection. The spasmodic nature of the violence suggests irrationality, as does the bizarre nature of the propaganda by which the Tutsis are demonised. Although the 1994 atrocities were planned with meticulous care, they were often carried out with rudimentary weapons, which carried associations of primitivism. Despite, or more probably because of Rwanda's popular association with a tribalism which is immutable, irrational, monstrously destructive and given in nature, academic denials of this allegedly primordial nature are insistent and vehement. According to De Waal, 'Anthropologists and historians unite in deriding the description of Hutu and Tutsi as 'tribes' and even as 'distinct ethnic groups'. For Lemarchand, writing of both Rwanda and Burundi:

> Only by ridding ourselves of this essentialist view of primordial identities can we begin to appreciate the fundamental changes that have shaped the contours of collective selves. (Lemarchand, 1994: 588).

It is frequently pointed out that Hutu and Tutsi speak the same language, share the same customs (Lemarchand, 1994: 588) and religion. Johnstone (1994: 25) describes Rwanda as 'the most thoroughly Christianized country in Africa'.[12] Despite the claims of racist propaganda and the enduring mythology of the 'Hamitic hypothesis' (De Waal, 1994: 3) physiognomy is not a good guide to identifying the two groups. Regional and clan affiliations ensure that neither the Hutu nor the Tutsi camp is monolithic (Lemarchand, 1994: 588; De Waal, 1994: 3). Further evidence that Rwandan society is not irrevocably divided is adduced in the facts that Hutu moderates were a sufficiently serious obstacle to the extremists' genocidal agenda to be a priority target in the first wave of violence, that the RPF espouses a non-sectarian ideology of pre-colonial unity and that, 'Before April 6 (1994), Rwanda had one of the most vigorous human rights movements in Africa.' (De Waal, 1994: 3–4).

Taking all these things into consideration, De Waal goes so far in his rejection of primordialism to make the claim that 'Rwanda is – or was – one of the true nations in Africa.' (De Waal, 1994: 3). For her part, Johnstone insists that, 'The Hutus and the Tutsis are not "tribes" but the symbiotic social components of the small and fertile volcanic hill countries of Rwanda and Burundi'. (Johnstone, 1994: 25).

The rejection of primordialism has two principal planks. The first commands a wide measure of agreement. The responsibility of the German and Belgian colonial powers for intensifying the Tutsi hegemony over the Hutu and codifying these identities by administrative means, is not in dispute. (Lemarchand, 1970: 62–3 and 72–9). The second, the question of relations between Tutsi and Hutu in pre-colonial society is less easy to establish. In De Waal's view;

A century ago the colonists found a powerful and relatively decentralized kingdom, consisting of three groups determined largely by occupational status, and a large number of clans, determined by landholding. They were not even distinct 'ethnic groups'. (De Waal, 1994: 3)

A note of contradiction creeps in however, when in discussing RPF ideology, he says that they hark back to the mythical origins of a unified Rwandan people 'conveniently skating over the Tutsi oppression of the Hutu in historical times.' (De Waal, 1994: 3). For his part, Lemarchand confines himself to noting that the groups did exist 'before the advent of colonial rule' and that they coexisted 'in relative harmony' (Lemarchand, 1994: 588). Stephen notes a tendency in writings which relate present atrocities to Rwandan history, to portray an 'almost idyllic' pre-colonial society and complains that such accounts fail to question seriously, 'the evidence for the standard picture of a settled and violence-free pre-colonial era. This is a valid point, but the substantial historical works which have influenced the discourse on the roots of the present conflict are, in fact, quite cautious and measured on the subject of pre-colonial ethnicity.[13]

Catherine Newbury's researches focus on Kinyaga, the south-western periphery of the pre-colonial Rwandan state, over which central authority was extended rather late, only in the last quarter of the nineteenth century. Although she pays due attention to the influence of the colonial period in shaping ethnic identities, she describes how it was during the reign of Rwabugiri (c.1865–1895) that 'the lines of distinction between Hutu and Tutsi began to be altered and sharpened' and 'the category Tutsi assumed hierarchical overtones which heretofore in Kinyaga had been of minor significance'.[14] The principal medium for this development was the imposition of central power by the appointment of chiefs for the region. So although she rejects any primordial origins for Tutsi and Hutu identities as they exist at present (M.C. Newbury, 1988: 13–4), she describes a pre-colonial past of 'fluid' ethnic identities, expressing 'separation' and 'stratification' which were correlated with political, social and economic changes (M.C. Newbury, 1978: 26).

David Newbury achieves a notable balancing act in discussing the contribution of colonial and pre-colonial influences in the formation of ethnic groups. He pays tribute to the 'newness' of ethnic identities shaped under colonial rule by initiatives of both the colonists themselves and African actors who sought to exploit the new context of power relations to their own advantage. At the same time, he acknowledges that the developments; '...solidified the more pragmatic fluidity which characterised the broader and more multifaceted situational identity structures of a previous era' (D.S. Newbury, 1991: 230).

Thus, while in content and function, the ethnicities which are the legacy of the colonial era may be new, the social process of identity formation

pre-existed them and 'ethnic consciousness is not exclusively a construct
of the twentieth century' (D.S. Newbury, 1991: 230 no. 8).

Somalia: The Nationalist Mirage

Perhaps the principal contribution of Somalia to any review of sub-national
conflict in the post-Cold War world, is to offer evidence of Africa's
contrariness. Not only does Somalia fail to conform to the conventional
patterns of sub-national conflict – regional, ethnic, religious or linguistic –
but the parties to the conflict belong to 'what was previously acclaimed as
one of the very few nation states in Africa'.[15] The beginning of scholarly
wisdom on the subject is that:

> Somalia is different because virtually all the people within the
> boundaries of the Somali Democratic Republic share a common
> tradition. They speak the same language, respond to the same poetry,
> derive their wisdom (and their experience) from the camel economy,
> and worship the same God.[16]

Clapham makes the point even more strongly by invoking the pedigree of
the state in Somalia. According to him, the Somali state '... followed a logic
of indigenous rather than colonial statehood, such as might well have been
recommended by an advocate of a truly African process of state formation.'
In fact, it represented a people separated by colonisation democratically
united 'to form what could plausibly be regarded ... as Africa's sole
indigenous nation state.' (Clapham, 1995: 72–3).

A nation state Somalia may indeed have been, but by January 1991, the
state had collapsed into warlordism, anarchic pillage and bankruptcy, to be
followed by famine and secession. The pathological effects of Somalia's
collapse have by no means been confined within its borders. Somalia has
all too graphically demonstrated the threadbare resources of order-keeping
in the post-Cold War world, especially in the more marginal reaches of the
'new world order'. The limits of superpower resolve, the inadequacies of
international organisations and the dilemmas of humanitarian aid have all
been exposed in Somalia. Indeed, the failures of international order-
keeping are widely believed to have caused the multilateral paralysis which
allowed the Rwanda disaster to happen. The sense of malaise pervades
more than Western foreign policies and international organisations,
however. In the case of Somalia, the very appropriateness of the state is
called into question as the basis of providing order for that territory and
that population.

Such has been the extent of Somalia's institutional collapse and so
intractable have the subsequent conditions of anarchy been that, clearly, the
absence of ethnic divisions has counted for very little. If the Somalis indeed
constituted a nation, it was not one which could easily express itself in

stable statehood. This unpromising verdict can be attributed in the first place to two flaws in the make up of the Somali nation. These are the problems of irredentism and regional relations, and the system of clans into which the Somali nation is divided.

The Somali state was created by voluntary association out of the colonies of British and Italian Somaliland at independence in 1960. This left significant Somali populations in three other territories; Kenya's North-eastern Province, the Ogaden region of Ethiopia and Djibouti (formerly French Somaliland). As a result, state and nation-building in post-colonial Somalia have been inextricably bound up with irredentism, along with regional rivalries and insecurities. Somalia presents a 'classical' case of irredentism,[17] involving ethnic fragments across the border and organised national movements struggling to achieve unification with the mother country. More importantly, the national identity and purposes of the Somali state were to a large extent defined by the goal of adding lost territories and populations to it.

This irredentist project had a number of destabilising effects on the goals of state and nation-building in Somalia. As far back as 1969, the military coup of that year demonstrated the dangerous effects that irredentism and clan divisions could have on each other. Among the military discontents which led to the coup, was resentment at the government's policy of detente with Ethiopia and Kenya over the irredentist issue:

The army, heavily Darood in composition and led by a Darood officer, could be expected to react unfavourably to the detente foreign policy of an Issaq prime minister. The Darood community spills across the Ethiopian and Kenyan borders, and so the Darood have a special stake in Somali irredentism.[18]

Central to the failure of state-building in Somalia was the disastrous miscalculation which induced President Siad Barre to take advantage of the revolutionary upheavals in Ethiopia to enforce by war (1977–1978), Somali claims to the Ogaden desert and people. Since, 'the pursuit of Somali nationhood was inseparable from the aspiration for the unification of all the Somali peoples, and hence from conflict with Ethiopia' (Clapham, 1995: 79), there was doubtless an element of inevitability about the onset of war. But in any event, the outcome was disastrous for Somalia. Military defeat discredited Siad Barre to the extent that his regime was never on a solid basis thereafter. The fragmentation of the opposition and his own increasingly ruthless, but eventually self-defeating, tactics of manipulating clan divisions allowed him to cling to power for nearly 13 years. But compared to the achievements of his early years in power (Clapham, 1995: 79), these years were no more than a lengthy postscript dedicated to nothing more than survival.

'I believe neither in Islam nor socialism, nor tribalism nor Somali nationalism nor Pan Africanism. The only ideology to which I am firmly committed', the president reportedly said, 'is the ideology of political survival'. (Laitin and Samatar, 1987: 159).

Perhaps fittingly, the last act in the struggle to unseat Siad Barre was precipitated by diplomatic manoeuvres which combined the legacy of Barre's irredentist adventure with Ethiopia's struggle against its own secessionists in Eritrea. Having given sanctuary to Somali National Movement rebels in Ethiopia, as part of the continuing Somali-Ethiopian conflict, the Mengistu government expelled them in 1988, as part of detente policies designed to give breathing space on the Somali frontier in order to concentrate forces on the Eritrean front. Once over the border and into their homeland, however, the SNM fighters embarked on an offensive whose momentum Siad Barre was unable to reverse.

CLANS IN SOMALIA

The essential, indeed the defining element in the sub-national conflicts of Somalia is the clan structure of Somali society. This complex network of kinship and lineage groups has its basis in the agro-pastoral origins of the Somali economy. The political, economic and social changes of the post-colonial era have worked to erode some aspects of clanship (and the contextual cultural values which helped the clan system to work), while assuring the survival of others. At the same time the whole system has been put to altered purposes in serving emerging class and governing interests. More specifically, as the clan structure of Somali society has adapted to the nation state, central rule, representative government and Western codes of law and practice (Doornbos and Markakis, 1994: 84), the traditional values and institutions which provided for conflict resolution and social justice in a stateless society were eroded (Samatar, 1992: 629–30). In a complementary development, clans and clanism have become politicised as part of clientist strategies to ensure the survival of regimes and individuals. As part of this process, the very notion of what constitutes a clan has been subject to change.

Central to the clan structure of Somali society has been the fact that the clans lack the internal coherence which elsewhere, political and cultural entrepreneurs work assiduously to create in ethnic and national blocs. Each of the six 'clan families' into which Somalis are divided is, 'in turn divided into clans, subdivided into sub-clans, sub-sub clans and so forth'.[19] The level at which sub-national conflict takes place has varied throughout the post-colonial years. Lewis sees the 1969 coup as a reversion to conflict at clan and sub-clan level. The extended clan family blocs which, Horowitz argues, are 'to a considerable extent artifacts of the modern political system' (Horowitz, 1985: 524), temporarily lost their significance. In the aftermath of the coup however, Adam points out how the Siad Barre regime

...ignited civil war at the level of the six super units. This has created the subjective characteristics of 'nationality' within the former loose clan families, one manifestation of which is that each clan family has created its own political party (or parties) as well as armed militias. (Adam, 1992: 12).

Yet, as Prendergast's account of today's complex and baffling conflicts makes plain, this level of conflict has by no means been superseded:

The main potential locus of military activity centres on Mogadishu in a Hawiye intra-clan conflict that sporadically pits the Abgal and Hawaadle loosely allied on one side and the Habr Gedir and some Murosade militias co-ordinating military campaigns on the other.[20] (Prendergast, 1995: 268).

Against this background of complex divisions, changing social structure and fluctuating levels of conflict, the prognosis for re-building state institutions and re-establishing central authority is not good. Indeed, something which unites most commentators on contemporary Somalia is the belief that this goal may well not be the right one for the Somali people at this stage. Prendergast claims that only the most powerful warlords, Ali Mahdi and the late Mohammed Farah Aideed, and the United Nations want the restoration of central state authority. Clapham argues for a new political order made in keeping with the decentralized nature of pre-colonial Somalia. Bryant warns that an obsession with restoring state sovereignty will only trigger a new round of war between the major factions. Peterson and Barkely emphasise the importance of balancing 'modernised' institutions with a house of traditional authorities which would build a legitimate arena for settling clan rivalries into the political system. In a similar vein, Adam talks of an evolving indigenous consociational democracy.

TRADITION AND TRIBALISM: THE AMBIGUOUS 'ZULU' FACTOR IN POST-APARTHEID SOUTH AFRICA

South Africa's transition to democracy took place under the threat of sub-national conflict, which was portentous enough for the country to be included in a scholarly collection on 'collapsed states', under the heading 'states in danger of collapse'.[21] Although the interregnum period of negotiation and democratization was very costly in human lives, such apocalyptic possibilities as institutional collapse and chaotic fighting were avoided.

South Africa's transition, however, did not take place unmarked by sub-national conflict. The challenge posed by the Inkatha Freedom Party to the ANC's dominance of African popular politics brought an ethno-nationalist dimension to the heart of South Africa's 'new' politics of constitutional negotiation and open electoral competition. Inevitably, given the country's history and the enigmatic nature of the IFP, this rivalry brought with it the spectre of tribalism.

Probably nowhere else in the world does the term 'tribalism' provoke such academic and political mistrust as it does in South Africa. This is hardly surprising. Under apartheid policies, state-sponsored ethnicity was allied to a ruthless system of racial discrimination, backed by brutal force. Inevitably, these associations have coloured academic treatments of ethno-nationalism. Even the ethnic factor in white political mobilisation came under sustained assault from neo-Marxist historians who were determined to demystify ethnic identity in terms of class politics.[22]

Although as its title suggests, it rejected any primordial status for ethno-nationalism, Leroy Vail's landmark collection (Vail, 1989) reflected a cautious change of academic mood. Although some of his fellow contributors continued to show a marked distaste for ethno-nationalist phenomena, on the whole the editor's judicious verdict set the tone.

> ... granted that it is virtually certain that the nation states of southern Africa are going to continue as institutionalized governing states in tension with those whom they govern, it will be necessary for the region's politicians and scholars alike to work towards accommodating ethnicity within these nation states. (Vail, 1989: 18).

This recommendation has been reflected in scholarly choices and priorities in the years since it was delivered. Ethnicity is on the academic agenda in a way it could not have been under apartheid, but Vail's injunction has proved less in harmony with political developments. however. In South Africa, the ANC's implacable opposition to 'accommodating ethnicity' in any constitutional form has remained unbending. Only in grudging, ad hoc and marginal ways is it prepared to acknowledge the force of ethnic identities. For instance, by agreeing to a provision in the interim constitution for a Volkstaat Council to debate the merits of giving territorial expression to Afrikaner self-determination, the ANC, in effect, offered the fig leaf of a fair hearing, before inevitably rejecting the idea as impractical.

Whatever tactical adjustments and gestures the ANC is prepared to make towards accommodating non-African identities, however, no such tolerance is shown in the direction of ethno-nationalist sentiments harboured by any part of the country's African population. It is in this context that the IFP's challenge to the ANC is stigmatized (and anathemized) as 'tribalism'. Central to the ANC's concerns in its clash with the IFP are the questions of the IFP's appeal to Zulu ethnic identity and its vigorous defence of the prerogatives and interests of traditional authorities in KwaZulu-Natal. In the context of over a decade of political rivalry, the ANC has treated the

IFP's challenge not so much as legitimate political competition, but as a tribalist challenge, not only to the democratic transformation, but also to the very integrity of the state.

In the first place, the IFP's roots as a modern political movement lie in the homelands system and the resources – patronage and control of local security forces – which quasi independence put at Inkatha's disposal for the purposes of political mobilisation.[23] This central aspect of the IFP's provenance reinforced the ANC's already conspicuous prejudice against any form of ethno-nationalism. Matters were made worse by revelations of collusion between Inkatha and apartheid security forces and the IFP's association with the white right in a negotiating alliance between 1992 and early 1994.

Secondly, the geographical concentration of support for the IFP in KwaZulu-Natal and its avowed constitutional positions, between them add another layer to the IFP's politics of ethnic identification. The IFP vigorously promotes federalism as its preferred constitutional option, but its political discourse frequently invokes the idea of self-determination and its constitutional blueprints have had a markedly confederal flavour. When these things are added to the militant chauvinism of Zulu ethnic mobilisation (and, it might be added, the historical associations of white Natal politics with separatist sentiments), the result is chronically ambiguous discourse[24] which leaves observers puzzled and opponents suspicious. Under these circumstances, it is hardly surprising that the IFP's challenge to the transition process as defined by the ANC and the National Party, should acquire secessionist overtones.

Since the mid-1980s, the ANC and the IFP have been engaged in a bitter and sporadically intense low-level civil war for territorial and political control of KwaZulu-Natal. When negotiations for a new political order began in 1990, a constitutional dimension was added to this contest, in which (as noted above) the IFP emerged as the champion of maximum regional autonomy and the ANC as the leading proponent of the central state. Both the violence and the constitutional wrangling have extended two years beyond the holding of democratic elections and the assumption of power by an ANC-dominated government.

A third element in this power struggle – one which has, in truth, been present from the beginning – has emerged in this post-election phase as the force which shapes and drives the conflict in its present form. That is the struggle to define and accommodate 'traditional' elements (of culture, identity, authority) in a democratic transition. The problem of reconciling traditional and modern elements in a new, democratic political culture is one that was only belatedly and sketchily recognised as one of the contradictions facing South Africa's political elites.[25] (Johnston, 1994: 192–3). The contradiction has, unfortunately, been sharpened and distorted by its associations with ANC/IFP rivalry in KwaZulu-Natal, particularly the violence and spectre of secession. In this way, the issue of 'tradition' has become central to questions of 'tribalism' and ethno-nationalism in South Africa.

TRADITIONAL LEADERS IN THE NEW SOUTH AFRICA

It is probably inescapable that traditional leaders face long-term erosion of their status and powers. But the institution of traditional leadership has been more flexible and resilient and the development of a national political system has been more hesitant and incomplete than many would have predicted in the early 1990s. Traditional leaders have fought a vigorous rearguard action, appropriating for themselves a significant role in an emerging political culture which is itself sufficiently patchy and ill-defined to be open to determined claimants.

There are about 800 traditional leaders in the whole country and 300 in KwaZulu-Natal. Given the numbers of those who owe them allegiance, they can be substantial brokers of electoral and other influence and, when grouped either nationally or provincially, they can form substantial pressure groups.

They are not merely archaic and atavistic resisters of impersonal forces of 'modernisation'. Enough of them, through entrepreneurship and relations with institutions of government, are themselves bringers and interpreters of modernisation to their communities, for them to be a more dynamic and ambiguous force than the 'feudal' stereotype which recurs in the rhetoric of their detractors.

Correspondingly, their ability to strike relationships with political parties on terms of incorporation, like the KwaZulu-Natal amakosi (tribal chiefs) and the IFP, or the much less well-defined and increasingly ambiguous partnership between the Congress of Traditional Leaders of South Africa (Contralesa) and the ANC, gives them direct political leverage.

TRADITION AND TRIBALISM IN KWAZULU-NATAL

The claims and prerogatives of traditional leaders in KwaZulu-Natal permeate most, if not all conflict issues and they have come to be the most representative feature of the Zulu nation which the IFP proclaims. 'Tradition' also brings its own flavour to 'modernised' political debates – like federalism vs the unitary state, or the defence of pluralism and civil society – where one would not expect to find it. An illustrative list of issues involving disputed aspects of traditional authority in KwaZulu-Natal indicates the scope of the problem.

One group of issues revolves around relations between tribal chiefs and their communities. 'Unpopular', 'reactionary' or 'oppressive' chiefs figure prominently in ANC accounts of KwaZulu-Natal's civil war. In the IFP's version, an anti-chief revolution led by young militants and orchestrated first by the UDF and since 1990 by the ANC itself, has been the main offensive front in a war to eliminate all substantial opposition to the liberation movement in the province. Chiefs are indeed central to the conflict. Their power to grant or withhold political space for parties and movements to mobilise is crucial to the question of political tolerance. Measures taken by successive homeland, provincial and national governments to arm or disarm chiefs, are among the most controversial law and order issues of recent years. In both cases, the significance of actions taken by chiefs is bitterly contested by the parties.

A distinctive feature of the problem of traditional authority in KwaZulu-Natal is the fact that the forces of tradition are deeply divided. The monarchy and a minority of the amakosi are at odds with the majority of the chiefs, a division which is signalled by the former's rapprochement with the ANC and the latter's closeness to the IFP.

This division has led to numerous 'contests of authenticity' where each side disputes the other's claims in matters where ceremonies, offices and appointments are seen to invest individuals or groups of people with authority and legitimacy.

These authenticity disputes have a bearing on another front of conflict, the negotiation of institutions of government for KwaZulu-Natal. The negotiations for a provincial constitution were greatly preoccupied with the rival claims and statuses of the monarchy and the amakosi, as was the controversial provincial act for the setting up of a House of Traditional Leaders.

The salience of issues of traditional leadership casts the political world of KwaZulu-Natal in forms which are difficult to analyze and contradictions which are difficult to resolve. This is especially true in the case of the authenticity contests which loom so large in the conflict between the ANC and IFP. Among them have been rival Shaka Day celebrations and controversy over whether or not there is any such post as 'traditional prime minister' in royal tradition. The essential complement to this disagreement is whether or not Chief Buthelezi is a legitimate claimant to the post, if it does indeed exist. The status of the king's royal council and of its most frequent spokesman, Prince Sifiso Zulu is also at issue.

Given that its continuity was ruptured in the destruction of the Zulu kingdom by the British, that its long subjection to the demands of colonial and minority rule was a corrupting influence and its association with the homelands system has been profoundly subversive of its legitimacy, it is hard to believe that there is a coherent enough body of 'Zulu tradition' against which rival claims to be its authentic custodians can be decided definitively. Indeed, it is precisely this context of cultural discontinuity and dispersal which encourages the colonisation of political debate by authenticity contests.

The fractured and corrupted condition of Zulu tradition is inextricably linked through the IFP's mobilising strategies to ethno-national claims made on behalf of the Zulu nation. Yet the potential for self-determination of this putative nation is limited by well-founded doubts over not only its territorial and economic viability but even of its own cultural and political cohesion. In addition, the attractions of continued association with the South African state are formidable. As a result there is chronic ambiguity in the IFP's discourse

The IFP is committed to being a party which is 'truly modern and at the same time truly African'. There is little real evidence, however, that it has enthusiastically embraced the task of exploring what this might mean. The party has seemed content to hold apart the two worlds, one of traditional culture and ethnic self-determination, the other of secular democracy, whose existence is implied in its own slogan. At the same time, the IFP assumes the roles of broker and interpreter between them. This, in turn, is a de-racialised version of the roles it claimed to play between black and white in the last decade of minority rule.

If the IFP stands for the preservation of the integrity of traditional authority as the flagship of ethno-nationalism, the ANC's position is less easy to summarise. In many respects, the phenomenon of traditional authority contradicts the secular and democratic (though admittedly malleable) agenda which the ANC professes. This is especially so where the links with ethno-nationalism and tribalism are made explicit by the IFP. On the other hand, traditional authority can neither be ignored, nor wished out of existence.

A party which is called the *African* National Congress cannot lightly disdain, never mind destroy, such a characteristically *African* phenomenon as traditional authority. The ANC has, in any case, a disposition to incorporate potentially troublesome constituencies altogether, or at least detach them from political competitors, rather than confront them. Its critics see in this a residual one-partyism, while its admirers praise its nation-building flavour. In any case, the Zulu monarchy and KwaZulu-Natal's traditional leadership between them present an exposed flank on which the IFP could be engaged in a war of manoeuvre. For these and other reasons, the ANC's attitude to traditional leaders is a lot more complex than its more militant rhetoric about the unacceptability of 'feudalism' might suggest. At various times, and in the versions of its various mouthpieces, the ANC sends conflicting signals about its attitude to traditional authority. Sometimes the principle of traditional leadership is condemned, at others it seems acceptable, provided the chiefs are 'progressive' and validated by the ANC. The association of chiefs with political parties is condemned, but this principle sits uneasily with the fact that the ANC has its own lobby of traditional leaders in Contralesa.

The result of all these contradictions is a tense and absorbing tussle in which the IFP seeks to fuse the concerns of tradition and ethno-nationalism, while the ANC strives as assiduously to delink them.

CONCLUSION

In all four of the African states discussed in this chapter, communal identities have played a part in the conflicts of the post-Cold War years. To this extent it is justifiable to talk about a 'new tribalism', if only at a very broad level of generalisation. But each conflict situation presents a different profile of tribalism and together they offer an intriguing balance of similarities and differences.

In Liberia and Somalia, according to their various chroniclers, the state is no longer worth fighting for. This has an important bearing on the political meaning of tribalism. According to Reno's account, in the post-modern dystopia of Liberia (and Sierra Leone), the state has ceased to exist as a respectable member of international society, with even the facade of obligations to other states and its own people. Indeed, the conception of a 'people' to go with a state seems to have been lost. All these things have been replaced by ad hoc understandings with other states, foreign businesses and mercenaries. At this level of state, or quasi-state organisation, the need for even the pretence of a binding identity as Liberians is gone. This has been replaced by sub-national ethnic identities (which appear to be weak and instrumental), the solidarities of criminality and generational groupings of the young, as described by Richards. If one lesson of the Liberian experience is that states collapse when the resources which made clientelist strategies possible are withdrawn and there is no critical mass of ethnic or cross-ethnic identity to sustain them, there is also another exemplary effect. That is, such identities will not develop when the prize – the state – which is the incentive for the creation of 'imagined communities' is not worth the effort of cultural and political mobilisation necessary to bid for it.

The case of Somalia has been similar in the central respect that once the underpinnings of Cold War aid were removed, it was no longer possible to sustain the repressive and clientelist balancing act which enabled Siad Barre to survive so long. And once the state went into free fall, it was no longer worth the effort to piece together a people to match a vanishing institutional personality. Somalia's warlords have practised similar post-collapse strategies to Charles Taylor's in Liberia, involving pragmatic understandings with outside forces. The emphasis, however, has been on aid agencies rather than companies and freelance adventurers. But see one account which documents relationships between fruit companies and warlords (ROAPE, 1995). Where Somalia differs from Liberia, is in the possession of a structure of communal identities. The relationships between clan families, clans and sub-clans may be fiercely complicated (and contested), but they have a kind of coherence and durability which communal identities in Liberia appear to lack. These qualities might make the task of reconstruction easier, or, given the ferocity of the rivalries more difficult. The myth of common Somali nationhood might help, but commentators seem agreed that whatever is reconstructed in Somalia, it is unlikely to be a post-colonial 'nation state' on the conventional model.

At one level, tribalism in Rwanda represents a more recognisable attempt to elaborate communal attachments into an ethno-national project for capturing and controlling the state apparatus, maintaining it in some form consistent with official membership of international society. But the projects by which Hutu militants have tried to demonise and then exterminate their Tutsi fellow citizens, have been malign, bizarre and extreme to a degree which defies rational discourse of ethno-nationalism. It is an extremely depressing observation that the Rwandan state held together, at least until June 1994, but this merely enabled those acting on its behalf and on its instructions to commit crimes beyond the reach (or possibly even ambition) of the disintegrating fragments of Liberia and Somalia.

As might be expected, South Africa, with its comparatively durable state institutions and emerging culture of constitutionality, is the only one of the four African states discussed here to display an ethno-nationalist project which has been kept within the bounds of legitimate political competition. But the nature of this project – the IFP's exploitation of the politics of identity – is fraught with ambiguity. The IFP attempts to be the voice of the Zulu nation, of democratic pluralism and federalism, of tribal authorities and traditional African society, not to mention the champion of free enterprise and deregulated capitalism. It is never very clear how the Zulu identity by which the IFP sets such store is to be accommodated; by self-determination, by federal self-expression, by the protection of tribal authority within a largely modernised state.

Part of this ambiguity can be attributed to the need to appeal to several constituencies, which include rural Africans, urban Africans, whites and external funders. For demographic reasons and in the face of ANC hegemony in popular African politics everywhere in South Africa except KwaZulu-Natal, the IFP has to go for a wide-spectrum appeal. Another reason for ambiguity is concealment of long-term strategies. The ANC's hostility to the accommodation of the ethnic factor and the exigencies of being in what amounts to permanent negotiating mode probably encourage the IFP to play its cards close to its chest. The IFP also, it is probably fair to say, has a self-image as the outsider in South African politics, misunderstood, wilfully misrepresented, unjustly accused. This self-image also contributes to a reticence about ultimate objectives.

Other things have to be considered, however, in accounting for the ambiguity of the 'Zulu factor' in post-apartheid South Africa. Although the

IFP may draw up confederal blueprints, indulge in hyperbolic rhetoric which celebrates self-determination and brands the ANC as an implacably centralising and monopolistic force, the attractions of continuing association with the South African state are strong. What is more, the costs of separation from it – even to the extent that the IFP's constitutional proposals have consistently envisaged, would be high. The state in South Africa, that is, is well enough developed for a variety of possibilities to be explored in accommodating the politics of communal identity and the IFP has done this, without committing itself unambiguously to any of them. But as the inevitable ratification of the national constitution draws near, at this stage still without the participation of the IFP in the constitutional process, the days of such ambiguity are numbered. When constitutional finality is achieved, the narrowing focus of IFP concerns from the pursuit of ethno-nationalism and self-determination to a concern for the conventions and interests of traditional tribal life (which, as this chapter shows is already far advanced) is likely to continue.

REFERENCES

Adam, H.M., (1992), 'Somalia: militarism, warlordism or democracy?', *Review of African Political Economy*, 54, 11–26.

Adam, H., (1995), 'The politics of ethnic identity: comparing South Africa', *Ethnic and Racial Studies*, 18 (3), 457–73.

Adam, H. and Giliomee, H., (1979), Ethnic Power Mobilized: Can South Africa Change? New Haven, Yale University Press.

Africa Rights, (1994), Rwanda: Death, Despair and Defiance, London, *Africa Rights Publishers*.

Allen, C., (1995), 'Understanding African politics', *Review of African Political Economy*, 22 (65), 301–20.

Austin, D., (1993), 'Reflections on African politics: Prospero, Ariel and Caliban', *International Affairs*, 69 (2), 203–22.

Bolton, J.R. (1994) 'Wrong turn in Somalia', *Foreign Affairs*, 73 (1), 56–66.

Bryden, M., (1995) 'Somalia: the wages of failure', *Current History*, 94 (591), 145–51.

Bayart, J-F., (1993), The State in Africa, (London: Longman).

Business Day (Johannesburg) 16.4.96, 'Anarchy as aid groups flee Liberia' (*SAPA/AP report*).

Carter, G. and O'Meara, P., (1985), African Independence: the First Twenty-Five Years, (Bloomington: Indiana University Press).

Chazan, N. (ed), (1991) Irredentism and International Politics, Boulder, Lynne Rienner.

Clapham, C., (1994), 'The longue duree of the African state', *African Affairs*, 93 (372), 433–9.

Clapham, C., (1994) 'The Horn of Africa, a conflict zone', in Furley (1995) 72–91.

Davies, R., (1979), Capital, the State and White Labour in South Africa 1900–1960, (New Jersey: Humanities Press).

De Villiers, M., (1987), White Tribe Dreaming, (Toronto: Macmillan).

De Waal, A., (1994, 'The genocidal state', *Times Literary Supplement*, 1.7.94, 3–4.

De Waal, A. and Omaar, R., (1995), 'The genocide in Rwanda and the international response', *Current History*, 94 (591), April, 156–61.
Doornbos, M. and Markakis, J., (1994), 'Society and state in crisis: what went wrong in Somalia?', *Review of African Political Economy*, 59, 82–8.
Economist, 'Making no peace', 20.11.93.
Ellis, S., 'Liberia 1989–94: a study in ethnic and spiritual violence', *African Affairs*, 94 (375), 165–97.
Furley, O., (1995), Conflict in Africa, London, Tauris Academic Studies.
Horowitz, D., (1985), Ethnic Groups in Conflict, (Berkeley: University of California Press).
Horowitz, D., (1991), A Democratic South Africa? (Berkeley: University of California Press).
Ingham, K., (1990), Politics in Modern Africa: The Uneven Tribal Dimension, (London: Routledge).
Johnson, R.W. and Schlemmer, L., (eds), (1995), Launching Democracy in South Africa: the First Open Election, (New Haven: Yale University Press).
Johnston, A.M., 'The political world of KwaZulu-Natal' in, Johnson and Schlemmer (1995).
Johnston, A.M., (1994), 'South Africa: the election and the transition process – five contradictions in search of a resolution', *Third World Quarterly*, 15 (2), 187–204.
Johnston, A.M. (1996), 'The clash that had to come: African nationalism and the 'problem' of traditional authority' KwaZulu-Natal Briefing 1, 11–15.
Johnstone, D., (1994), 'Making a killing', *In These Times* (Chicago), 26.12.94, 25–7.
Johnstone, F., (1976) Class, Race and Gold: A Study of Class and Race Relations in South Africa, (London: Routledge).
Kaplan, R., (February) 'The coming anarchy', *Atlantic Monthly*, February, 44–76.
Laitin, D., and Samatar, S.S., (1987), Somalia: Nation in Search of a State, (Boulder: West View Press).
Lemarchand, R., (1994), 'Managing transition anarchies: Rwanda, Burundi and South Africa in comparative context', *Journal of Modern African Studies*, 32 (4), 581–604.
Lemarchand, R., 'Power and stratification in Rwanda: a reconsideration', in Skinner (1973).
Lemarchand, R., (1970), Rwanda and Burundi, (London: Pall Mall Press).
Mair, L., (1974), African Society, (Cambridge: Cambridge University Press).
Mamdani, M., (1996) 'From conquest to consent as the basis of state formation: reflections on Rwanda', *New Left Review*, 216, 3–36.
Maré, G. and Hamilton, G., (1987), An Appetite For Power: Buthelezi's Inkatha and South Africa, (Johannesburg: Ravan Press).
Neuberger, B., 'Irredentism and politics in Africa' in Chazan (1991), 97–109.
Newbury, M. C., (1988), The Cohesion of Oppression: Clientship and Ethnicity in Rwanda 1860–1960, (New York: Columbia University Press), 1988.
Newbury, M.C., (1978), 'Ethnicity in Rwanda: the case of Kinyaga', *Current History*, 48 (1), 17–29.
Newbury, D.S., (1991), Kings and Clans: Ijwi Island and the Lake Kivu Rift, 1780–1840, (Madison: University of Wisconsin Press).
Newbury, D.S., (1980), 'The clans of Rwanda: an historical hypothesis', *Current History*, 50 (4), 1980, 389–403.
Observer (14.4.96) 'Teenage rebels go on cannibal rampage'.
Observer (18.8.96) 'Only a programme of enlightened re-imperialism...'

Observer (27.6.93) 'Peace makers at odds'.

O'Meara, D., (1983), Volkskapitalisme: Class, Capital and Ideology in the Development of Afrikaner Nationalism (Johannesburg: Ravan Press).

Peterson, C.M. and Barkley, D.T., 'Saving Somalia', *In These Times* (Chicago), 4.4.94.

Plaut, M., (1994) 'Rwanda: looking beyond the slaughter', *The World Today*, 50 (8–9), August–September, 149–53.

Prendergast, J., (1995) 'When the troops go home: Somalia after the intervention', *Review of African Political Economy*, 22 (64) 268–73.

Reno, W., (1995) 'Re-invention of an African patrimonial state: Charles Taylor's Liberia', *Third World Quarterly*, 16 (1), 109–20.

Richards, P., 'Rebellion in Liberia and Sierra Leone: A crisis of youth?' in Furley, (1995).

ROAPE (1995), 'Banana wars', *Review of African Political Economy*, 22 (64), 274–5.

Rothchild, D., 'State-ethnic relations in middle Africa', in Carter and O'Meara, (1985).

Samatar, A.I, (1992), 'Destruction of state and society in Somalia: beyond the tribal convention', *Journal of Modern African Studies*, 30 (4), 625–43.

Sesay, M.A., (1996), 'Civil war and collective intervention in Liberia', *Review of African Political Economy*, 23 (67), 35–52.

Skinner, E.P., (1973), Peoples and Cultures of Africa, (New York: Doubleday).

Stephen, M., (1995), 'Ethnocide: discourse and perceptions', *Review of African Political Economy*, 65, 367–71

Thakur, R., (1994), 'From peacekeeping to peace enforcement: the UN operation in Somalia', *Journal of Modern African Studies*, 32 (3), 387–410.

Vail, L., (1989), The Creation of Tribalism in Southern Africa, (London: James Surrey).

Weekly Mail and *Guardian* (Johannesburg) 30 August–5 September 1996, 'Good News for Liberia at last'.

Welsh, D. (1996), 'Ethnicity in sub-Saharan Africa', *International Affairs*, 72 (3), 477–91.

Zartman, I.W., (1995), Collapsed States, Boulder, Lynne Rienner.

NOTES

1 See Allen, C. 'Understanding African Politics' in the *Review of African Political Economy* Vol. 22 (65). September 1995.

2 See D. Austin, 'Reflections on African politics: Prospero, Ariel and Caliban' in *International Affairs* 69 (2) 203–22; K. Ingham (1990). *Politics in Modern Africa: The Uneven Tribal Dimension* (London: Routledge); D. Rothchild, 'State-Ethnic relations in middle Africa' in G. Carter and P. O'Meara (Eds.) (1985). *African Independence: The First Twenty-five years* (Bloomington: Indiana University press).

3 See C. Clapham (1994). 'The longue duree of the African state' in *African Affairs* 93 (372), p. 434.

4 See M. De Villiers (1987) *White Tribe Dreaming* (Toronto: Macmillan).

5 See L. Vail (1989) *The Creation of Tribalism in Southern Africa* (London: James Surrey), p. 1.

6 See the *Observer* (London), 14/4/96, 'Teenage Rebels go on the rampage.'

7 See the *Observer* (London) (18/8/96). 'Only a programme of Enlightened Imperialism' and R. Kaplan 'The coming anarchy' in *Atlantic Monthly* February 1994, 44–76.

8 See S. Ellis, 'Liberia 1989–1994: A Study in ethnic and spiritual violence' in *African Affairs* 94 (375), 165–97, 1995; P. Richards, 'Rebellion in Liberia and Sierra leone: A crisis of youth' in O. Furley,(ed) (1995). *Conflict in Africa* (London: Tauris Academy Studies); and W. Reno, 'Re-invention of an African patrimonial state: Charles Taylor's Liberia' in *Third World Quarterly* 16 (1), 109–20, 1995.

9 See *Business day* (Johannesburg) (16/4/96). 'Anarchy as aid groups flee Liberia' (SAPA/AP report).

10 For these factors see A. De Waal and R. Omar, 'The genocide in Rwanda and the international response' in *Current History* 94 (591), April 1995, 156–61; A. De Waal, 'The genocidal state' in the *Times Literary Supplement* (1/7/94), 3–4; M. Plaut, 'Rwanda: looking beyond the slaughter' in the *World Today* 50 (8–9), August-September, 1994, 149–53; and R. Lemarchand, 'Managing Transition Anarchies: Rwanda, Burundi and South Africa in comparative context' in the *Journal of Modern African Studies* 32 (4) 581–604.

11 See M. Stephen. 'Ethnocide: discourse and perceptions' in *Review of African Political Economy* 65, 367–71, 1995.

12 See D. Johnstone, 'making a killing' in *These Times* (Chicago) (26/12/94), 25–7.

13 See M.C. Newbury, 'Ethnicity in Rwanda: the case of Kinyaga' in *Current History* 48 (1), 17–29, 1978 and D.S. Newbury (1991). *Kings and Clans: Ijwi Island and the Lake Kivu Rift, 1780–1840* (New York: Columbia University Press).

14 See M.C. Newbury (1988). *The Cohesion of Oppression: Clientship and Ethnicity in Rwanda 1860–1960* (New York: Columbia University Press), p. 21.

15 See M. Doornbos and J. Markakis, 'Society and State in crisis: what went wrong in Somalia' in the *Review of African Political Economy* 59, 82–8, 1994.

16 See D. Laitan and S.S. Samatar (1987). *Somalia; Nation in waiting* (Boulder: Westview Press), p. vii.

17 See B. Neuberger, 'Irredentism and Politics in Africa' in N. Chazan (1991). *Irredentism and International Politics* (Boulder: Lynne Reinner).

18 See D. Horowitz (1985). *Ethnic Groups in Conflict* (Berkeley: University of California press), p. 523.

19 See H.M. Adam, 'Somalia: militarism, warlordism or democracy?' in the *Review of African Political Economy* 54, 11–26, 1992.

20 See J. Prendergast, 'When the troops go home: Somalia after the intervention' in *Review of African Political Economy* 22(64), 268–73.

21 See I.W. Zartman (1995). *Collapsed States* (Boulder: Lynne Reinner).

22 See F. Johnstone (1976) *Class, Race and Gold: A Study of Class and Race Relations in South Africa* (London: Routledge); R. Davies (1979). *Capital, the State and White labour in South Africa 1900–1960* (New Jersey: Humanities Press).

23 See G. Mare and G. Hamilton (1987). *An Appetite for Power: Buthelezi's Inkatha and South Africa* (Johannesburg: Ravan Press).

24 See A.M. Johnston, 'The Political World of Kwazulu-Natal' in R.W. Johnson and L. Schlemmer (eds) (1995) *Launching Democracy in South Africa: the first open election* (New Haven: Yale University Press).

25 See A.M. Johnston, 'South Africa: the election and the transition process–five contradictions in search of a resolution' in *Third World Quarterly* 15 (2), 187–204, 1994.

Chapter Eight

Tribalism and Nationalism in Turkey: Reinventing Politics

Nergis Canefe

INTRODUCTION

> Only a horizon ringed about with myths can unify a culture.
> Friedrich Nietzsche (*The Birth of Tragedy*, p. 136)

Ideologies are guides to political action. They furnish the individual with a sense of identity, purpose and a sense of belonging (Adams, 1993; Meszaros, 1989). Ideologies are also bodies of knowledge, describing how the world is as well as prescribing what it should be (Mannheim, 1936). They are thus embodiments of political traditions which often include contradictory and conflictual strands. Probably one of the most dynamic and expanding ideological positions that surfaced during the last quarter of the twentieth century is tribalism reconstructed in the form of ethnic violence. Until the collapse of the Eastern Bloc, social movements informed by tribalist ideologies were pushed to the fringes of mainstream politics as archaic formulations of communalism. In other words, while conservatism, Marxism, liberalism, nationalism, anarchism, fascism and even religious fundamentalism were accepted as ideologies, ethnic movements were wrongfully situated in the backdrop of semi-utopian longings without a legitimate political appeal. It is only after the fact that ethnic and communal ideals established their hegemony across the new regimes of the ex-communist world that tribalism gained saliency as an important system of ideas (Kupchan, 1995).

Tribalism is a *bona fide* political idiom even though it is in the precarious position of sitting on the thin line separating utopia from ideology.[1] As an anti-modernist critique, the tribalist dictum resorts to the glorification of collective memory as a means to reclaim the center-stage for those standing at the margins of the modernist history. In the meantime, the tribalist preoccupation with re-writing history rarely outpaces the inertia propagated by the sterilization of history in civic/secular accounts of the past. Like many other contemporary treatise of home-coming and political righteousness, tribalist yearnings tend to resume the totalitarian aspects of modernist ideologies. They thus establish the backbone of the leading resurrectionist ideologies of the twentieth century. If so, why is it that tribalism has primarily been associated with utopian redemption.[2]

Tribalism is a doctrine which applies across the board and entertains a wide range of political options which can be deceiving if taken for their face value. It reconstructs the past in an effort to imagine a different future. While doing so, it utilizes a utopian mode of thinking for the re-articulation and legitimation of a new ideology with strong populist features. In the end, its idealization of the past for the criticism of the present provides the nomenclature for historical essentialism and exclusionist identity politics. In this context, tribalism can be categorized as an outdated utopia only if we do not pay attention to the political power it generates and the grassroots support it enjoys. In the modern history of Europe, such strategies of denial of populist force and the political nature of fascism have been resorted to, only to worst the grimmest of outcomes (Gellner and Ionescu, 1969; Talmon, 1960). In this case then, it is timely to think about tribalism not as a fossilized scenario of communal redemption but as a modern ideology that hinges upon utopianism.

As an ideology with strong popular appeal, tribalism thrives upon its promise of a utopian exodus that would bring us into unknown territories through the act of remembrance. This sought out memory then justifies tribalist doctrines' search for new truths and historical claims made by and for a chosen community. Communal identity is, however, a tricky stronghold in that it simultaneously harbors conservative and contentious components. Consequently, the communitarian politics of tribalism essentializes and calcifies cultural identity in order to bring forward change. This peculiar aspect of tribalist politics is best illustrated by its propensity for political violence fed by the zero-sum-game mentality of 'one of us' or 'one of them', or in other words a distinct reference to the 'other.' Turning different social groups and culture-communities against one another and the resulting instances of political violence are then justified as the 'necessary purification' of outsiders, traitors, etc. In the meantime, not all tribalist political scenarios lead to violence and terror. There has to be a set of specific alliances in place which not only enables the leading cadres and militants of the tribalist movement to have access to military training and supplies, but also legitimizes and purports the acts of violence committed by the members of the movement.

In the following pages, the utopian origins of Turkish secular nationalism and their re-invocation by ultranationalist Turks will be discussed in an attempt to reveal the conditions that lead to peculiar alliances between authoritarian forms of nationalism, fascism and ethnicity. In Republican Turkish history, the communitarian ethics of tribalism challenging the liberal mores of civic nationalism led to recurrent waves of ethno-religious resurgence. By representing a united front of particularist values and communitarian demands based on assumed blood line and religious brotherhood, the Turkish extreme right re-defined the boundaries of and membership criteria to the national polity. In this context, the targeting of the religious minorities and in particular heterodox Muslim Alevi communities by the ultranationalist militia is an important illustration of the growing tide of tribalism in Turkish politics.

HISTORICAL BACKGROUND: THE ENIGMA OF 'THE TURK' IN KEMALIST TRADITION

The political tradition of the modern Turkish nation-state strives for the erosion of ethnicity in the semantics of state-civil society relations while resurrecting it at state-level decision and policy making. In turn, in their contestation of the official absence of ethno-religious distinctiveness as part of the ordering principles of Turkish politics, the two sides of ethno-religious revivalism, that of tribalist/Turkist ultra-nationalism and ethno-religious resurgence of minority populations such as Kurdish nationalism, employ forms of utopian communitarianism. Critics of ethno-nationalism might argue that these movements do not belong within the matrixes of modern politics (Hobsbawm, 1990; 1963). Nevertheless, tales of ethnic roots, myths of the Origin and ancient cultural heritage circulated in the service of tribalist movements are not necessarily ideological fossils of pre-modern eras. What is new within the framework of contemporary political formulations is the alliance between the secular and civic nation-state apparatus and selected tribalist movements that inform agendas of targeted political violence.

Depending on the specificities of the process of nation-building, religious or secular, aristocratic or proletarian, bureaucratic or populist, etc. nationalisms can all serve the very same purpose of consolidating the image of a nation as a distinct conglomeration (Renan, 1990). In the meantime, scholars of nationalism generally divide the vast domain of nationalist movements into 'territorial/civic' and 'ethnic' nationalism (Smith, 1986). As we have seen throughout, the nation is a bounded and contractual political community that abides to laws and legal institutions in the civic model. The uniformity, standardization, universal applicability and legitimacy of these laws reflect the sovereign powers of the territorial state. In contradistinction, according to the ethnic model of nation-building, common origins, descent and cultural peculiarities mirrored onto chronicles of the national history provide the foundations for the territorialisation and institutionalization of nations (Rothschild, 1981). The retention of ancestral ties, myths, ethnic symbols of solidarity and uniqueness makes this kind of nationalism into an 'organic formulae' for the attainment of political legitimacy. Ethnic nationalism appeals to a hierarchy of cultural, linguistic and religious properties. In many instances, it elevates customs and traditions into rules, creating an official religion of the state, and developing national languages out of regional dialects during the delineation and fashioning of the nation (Smith, 1986: p. 138). Finally, the ethnic conception of nationhood exhibits strong demotic and plebeian characteristics and cherishes populism via 'inviting the masses into history' (Nairn, 1976; 1975).

The young Turkish state initially espoused civic territorial nationalism as its official ideology. Under the leadership of Ataturk, with the foundation of the Republic in 1923, modernization of the Nation of Turks was to happen along the lines of the motto of the French Revolution: Equality (of all ethnic groups and religions under the neutralized rubric of Turkish national citizenship), Fraternity (of all ethnic groups and religions following the promise of Turkish nationalism within the sanctified borders of contemporary Turkey) and Liberty (from Imperial/colonial invaders and through modernization and state-centered economic development).[3] However, the actual social, economic and political transformations were actually moulded according to the principles of German romantic nationalism. Kemalist ideology created and elevated the myth of 'Peoplehood' not as a civic/secular construct, but as a peculiar combination of elements that pertain to motherland, blood and religion. It gave life to the image of the proud and self-assured Turk, who could have been anybody along the presumed ancestral line running between ancient Turkic tribes of the Middle Asia, the Hittites and Urartus of Anatolia – omitting the Ottoman period and the legacy of Christian minorities – and the amalgam of immigrant communities arriving from Balkans and the Caucases based on their religious and linguistic loyalties (Bora, 1995; Karpat, 1985; 1982). Consequently, the official facade of secular-civic Turkish nationalism became a mask that hid the strong ethnic orientation of the nation-building process. However, being a 'Turk was indeed an enigmatic formulation since it was built upon mythical foundations that constructed a mixed lineage. There was a surreal quality to some of the cultural products of state-sponsored, Turkish ethnicity such as the Sun-Language theory which links Turkish to so many unrelated civilizations based on presumed migration routes all leading to the land-mass of present day Turkey. And the creation and promulgation of what might be called a demotic Turkish state as a result of the endless efforts of ethnographers, musicologists and anthropologists travelling to the distant villages of Anatolia looking for the 'purest' rules of Turkish grammar as preserved by an 'ancient people'. These seemed to sharpen the ideological divisions within the Turkish society as to where the 'roots' of communities lie. Finally, at the surface level until the 1980 coup, the determined secular gestures of the state apparatus certainly silenced the religious revivalism that cherished the Ottoman pan-Islamic heritage despite the development of pan-Arabism etc. In the meantime, whether translated into Turkish as it was done during the initial years of the

Republic, or still sang in its original Arabic verse, the daily prayer song *ezan* was still calling all the (Sunni) believers to the 'houses' (mosques) of Islam financed by the Ministry of Religion (Cakõr, 1990). Still, state-sponsored Turkish nationalism remains an oddity that is neither religious nor ethnic, but more of a construct as described by Benedict Anderson's quintessential formulation of an 'imagined community' (Anderson, 1983).

In terms of political practice, what separates ethnic nationalism sharply from its territorial/civic counterpart is that in the former, the territorial demarcation of the nation usually takes place under the leadership of a particular strata identifying themselves with a specific ethnic heritage. In turn, the historical predominance and cultural-political authority of the emergent state's core *ethnie* dictates the form and content of social institutions and political traditions of the whole national polity (Smith, 1981). Under such circumstances, the bureaucratic incorporation of *other* communities or 'ethno-religious minorities' into the myths and symbols of the nation-state is the only guarantee for the success of nation-building. The more the civic, legal and territorial elements dominate the agenda of nationalism, the more opportunity for conflicting interests to unite behind similar political and economic causes despite separate histories and identities. The elite cadres of the Kemalist Revolution were aware of the dilemmas surrounding an exclusively ethnic formulation of nationality (Landau, 1984; Ozbudun, 1981; Mardin, 1966). That is why, in the midst of an abundance of myths, symbols, historical memories and divergent political loyalties espoused by different communities residing within the same state boundaries, they chose 'hybridity' as the perfect solution. However, they still had to name their product. The naming of the ultimate subject of Turkish nationalism was also an invitation for the extreme right-wing political movements to join the state apparatus in its search for the 'Turk'. The utopian elements of state-sponsored Turkish nationalism was thus linked to the ultranationalist Turkist movement.

TURKISH ULTRANATIONALIST RIGHT: OLD IDEALS, NEW ALLIANCES

The political movement referred to as 'ultra-nationalist right' has taken various forms in the Republican history of Turkey. In its early phases, the emphasis was on an imaginary pan-Turkism with imperial yearnings whereas in the post-monoparty area (1946-present) the most active branches of the movement became nationalist-idealist and concentrated on the 'motherland'. Particularly since the 1960s, under the banner of defensive nationalism against both the 'inside and outside enemies of the Turkish people', the once-elite ideology of ultra-nationalism gained unprecedented popular currency (Landau, 1974). Not only did it become a considerable oppositional force in the political arena but its ideals fueled

157

political violence ranging from street-level skirmishes to planned massacres of targeted ethno-religious communities. At the height of the movement, during the 1970s, the ultranationalist movements leading members were also able to partake in government under the roof of National Action Party (later National Labour Party). The 1980 coup banned the original party and at least temporarily terminated the careers of many of its members. The military regime of the 1980 coup also shot down the youth organisations, professional associations and brotherhoods espousing the ultra-nationalist ideology. However, the revived version of the original party – National Labour Party – as well as the re-established network of organizations began to threaten Turkish public life again in 1990s due to their explicitly violent and repressive merits. It is true that since the collapse of the Soviet Socialist regime, the Turkists of Turkey turned their attention more to the 'outside Turks' and their salvation. However, they continue to target specific groups and communities as enemies of the 'Turkish people' and purport civic violence in the country. If the chosen villain was the 'Communist-Alevis' previously, it is the 'traitor-Kurds' today. Interestingly enough, the 'new ultranationalist right' suffers from what might be called an organizational amnesia. The current leaders of the movement deny any responsibility for the killings performed by trained Turkist militants particularly targeting traditional Alevi communities in Eastern part of Turkey. Instead, especially at the party platform, they show painstaking efforts to absorb the ethno-religious minorities that were once victimized into the mythical line of Turkic ancestry. While doing that, however, the movement moulds and divides various ethno-religious minorities into 'the original Anatolian Turks' and 'others'. Thus, it continues to deny the heterogeneous cultural heritage of the people residing within the borders of Republican Turkey.

The historical roots of the ultra-nationalist right in Turkey goes back to the pre-Republican period (pre-1923). The leading ideology of the new Republic, that of Kemalism, dealt very harshly with the earlier forms of pan-Turkism in order to establish the official ideology of a secular and Turkey-based civic nationalism. Needless to say, the Kemalist cadres themselves resorted to compulsory Turkification of the minority populations and later allowed Sunni Islam to become the unofficial 'state religion'. However, during the early years of the young Republic, differences between extreme Turkish nationalism and official Turkish nationalism resulted in the political demise of the latter along with other contentious voices that rivalled the Kemalists.

The most momentous change affecting Turkish domestic politics in the immediate post-Ataturk era was the move of the People's Party (later re-named as the Republican People's Party) was to allow the change from mono-party to multi-party parliamentary system in 1945 (Helvacioglu, 1996; Landau, 1981, 1974; Karpat, 1972). New parties were set up and each began to establish branches across the country. Ultra-nationalist of the Republican era had already begun to intensify their activities in the eve of the World War II. Ultranationalist journals started to be published from 1938 onwards, and close contacts were established between statesmen, businessmen, public servants, teachers, university students and youth organisations sympathetic to the extreme nationalist ideas. Still, it was not until the 1946 general elections that their ideological stand gained political legitimacy.

The early Turkish ultra-nationalist movement enjoyed substantial intellectual support of German Nazism.[4] Yet, this favorable atmosphere did not last very long. After Germany's defeat in the war, the Turkish government severed its ties with Germany and also changed its stand towards the Turkist collaborators of the National Socialist regime in war-time Germany. In an attempt to re-establish their legacy in Turkish politics, the Turkist/ultranationalist circles organized large-scale anti-Communist rallies in Istanbul and Ankara in 1944. Consequently, most of the leaders of the movement were arrested and brought to trial on the basis that racism was to be condemned as countering the fundamental principles of the Republic of Turkey.[5] In a speech following this, the President stressed that nationalism and Turkism were not acceptable. Furthermore, he publicly accused Turanist ultranationalists of forming secret societies perilous to Turkey.[6] After various sentences had been passed, however, the Military High Court of Appeals dismissed all the charges on October 1945. In the wake of the transition to the multi-party system, the tide has changed. In the new political order of liberalization led by the Democratic Party (*Demokrat Parti*), ultranationalists were placed as a buffer as a remedy for the rising paranoia of the Soviet threat in Turkey. Their generic call for 'chasing the Red menace out of Turkey' thus began to be praised rather than discouraged by the Turkish state authorities. Having had the opportunity to be engaged in massive propaganda during their trials, the ultranationalist right used this new situation fully to their advantage. They used claims of national solidarity to channel the reaction and frustration of the masses caused by economic and social difficulties of the Cold-War era. During its popularization and legalization as an alternative political movement, Turkish ultra-nationalism also acquired a conservative/reactionary dimension favoring traditional and religious values in its opposition to the radical/ revolutionary agendas of left-wing movements. Still, the political and social environment would not ripen to steer large sectors of the population toward fascist doctrines well until the 1970s. Despite the initial approval of their ideological blueprint, the ruling political elite was ill-inclined to allow the creation of an independent fascist/nationalist party with statist-protectionist tendencies that could rival their own political status and outdo their burgeoning economic nationalism. Consequently, the Democratic Party closed down the leading ultranationalist organization – the Turkish Nationalists Association – in 1953.

Ironically, the organization of ultra-nationalists (Turkists) into a fascist political party and their acquisition of a growing audience were indeed facilitated by the rapid social change and increased politicization of the public under the Democratic Party rule. Initially, it gave them a legitimate voice in the opposition criticizing the oppressive policies of the government. For instance, the junta that led to the military coup of 1960 included a number of Turkist officers – notably Colonel Alpaslan Turkes – who has been sentenced and acquitted in the 1944 trials. Referred to as the Fourteen, however, this group opposed the ultimate transfer of power to civil hands, and instead called for the establishment of a permanent authoritarian administration. As a result of their opposition to the civil political forces, they were exiled and purged from the reformist cadres of the '1960 Revolution'. Meanwhile, their exile crystallized the political leadership of the ultranationalist movement. Turkes and his friends kept in close contact while in exile and looked for alternative courses of political action. Returning from exile in 1963, the ultranationalist politicians took over the Republican Peasant National Party and Turkes was elected as the party commissar. Soon, Turke's actions and political views split the RPNP and he declared himself as the chair in an extraordinary party congress in 1965. In 1969, the RPNP was renamed as the Nationalist Action Party and was the first official party openly entertaining the fascist ideological blue-print.

In summary, the movement persevered and indeed grew exponentially between the banning of the Turkish Nationalists Association in 1953 and the establishment of the Nationalist Action Party in 1969. Its rapid progress can be explained on the basis of the methods of organization and political indoctrination used by its cadres. During the period between 1945 and 1970, ultranationalist activities took place at three different levels: the media, grass-roots, and wide-spread professional organisations and networking. Already in the aftermath of the WWII, a large number of journals were published by the pre-war Turkists.[7] Gradually, the ultranationalist press ceased to be an isolated side-line. Ultra-nationalist ideas found their way into the mainstream media due to the skilful pen of writers and columnists affiliated with the movement. Secondly, in order to facilitate activism and grassroots support, demonstrations and rallies were organized against the communists. The content of what was meant by 'communist' changed according to the demands of the times, but the political slogan of protecting 'Turkey and Turks from outside enemies' preserved its zeal. These demonstration-cum-riots generally occurred with the tacit approval of the government due to its strong anti-Communist stand and in fear of Marxist-Leninist revolutionary activities. As a result of this tacit coalition, the ideology grew into the political elite circles. By the 1970s, Turkists were active in state bureaucracy and legal organisations. They protected themselves from possible official censoring by admitting religious or traditionalist/nationalist right-wing politicians close to the government and administration into their organisations. Finally, in their efforts to construct a network that cuts across social classes and occupational categories, they established a plethora of organisations. The most important ones were the Confederation of Nationalist Workers Unions, The Association of Idealist Policemen, The Association for the Cooperation of Idealist Public Servants, The Association of Idealist Teachers, the Association of Idealist Tradesmen and Artisans, The Association of Idealist Peasants, the Association of idealist Journalists, and the Association of Idealist Financiers and Economists. The NAP also organized fractions among the Turkish workers in Germany and enjoyed the flow of dues and donations in foreign currency. Their active involvement in the educational sector led to wide-spread propaganda efforts undertaken by sympathizing school teachers which fueled the street-level political violence of the late 1970s among student militants.

The National Action Party (Milliyet Hareket Partisi) led by Turkes was founded by the generation of Turkists who initiated the multi-faceted political activities during the 1945–1970 period. Its official ideology was formulated with reference to the political guidelines provided by the early phases of the Turkish nationalist movement. The main principles of the party ideology, which remained primarily intact till the present day, can be summarized as Turanism[8] (Turkey presents the political and the mythical land of Turan presents the natural borders for Turks), racism (the 'Turkish blood versus the alien blood debate'), militarism (the banner of the warrior nation of the Turks and promotion of political violence in order to protect Turks from their 'inner enemies'), anti-communism (alliance against the left and absolute refusal to share a political platform), traditionalism (alliance with religious circles), hierarchical command chain and single authority totalitarianism (obedience to the command to kill, if necessary) and finally, state-corporatism as opposed to liberal capitalism (communitarian spirit).[9] The original party symbols were chosen to be three crescents on a red background and the Grey Wolf. Both emblems had mythical-nationalist significance. The Grey Wolf symbolizes the unity of all tribes of Turkic descent as a people. The original tribes of Central Asia were personified by the character of the Grey Wolf who is a supreme fighter among fighters.

The party doctrine was named as the idealist path and included strands of nationalism, idealism, moralism, scientism, socialism, peasantism, liberalism mixed with a balanced dose of individualism, developmentalism, populism, industrialism and technologism (Turkes 1988, 1979). In the midst of this amalgam of influences, the state was defined as the highest organized form of a nation and democratic rule and governance was defined as an unrealistic and unnatural goal to be attained. The polity to be guided and ruled by the party was divided into the six sectors of workers, peasants, tradesman and artisans, salaried workers, employers, and liberal professionals. The ultranationalists tried to identify themselves

161

with all sectors of the population in various spheres of social and political life.[10]

In his speeches and statements, the party's long-time charismatic leader Alpaslan Tyrkes referred to the Turkish nation as a leader and a master among all other nations.[11] He defined an aggressive and combative nationalism which would be all-inclusive of the Turkish lineage, but Turkish lineage only. The NAP further broadened its base with the acceptance of Sunnite religious ideals as part of its official doctrine (Bora et al., 1990; Landau, 1974). On various occasions, the NAP cadres openly stated that they would need to cleanse the national state of all minorities to attain the ideal purity. The party's hostility to minorities was not only an ideological but also a tactical issue due to its active participation in elections and it was used selectively. In areas with national and sectarian differentiation and identifiable minority communities (Kurds, Alevis, Christian minorities), minorities were presented as the foremost enemies along with the 'Communists'. As a result, the poor and oppressed sectors of Sunni and Turkish elements of the society were stirred against the minorities as a remedy for their misery.

After the victory of the Justice Party in 1965, the ultranationalist circles received increasing support from the government as a useful force to suppress the oppositional and revolutionary left-wing movements in the universities and on the street. They began to be identified as auxiliary forces of the state. The adoption of the totalitarian and militant organizational structure by the NAP coincides with this period of state-induced tolerance for militant nationalism. The NAP headquarters were directly linked with the organs of the growing fascist movement such as the youth branches, idealist associations in different sectors of the economy, schools, neighbourhood units, government offices and subsequently with organized commando camps established for the education of political militants. The young militant cadres trained after 1965 were primarily members of the *Association of Hearths of Ideal* (*Ulku Ocaklarõ Dernegi*). In high schools, the NAP started Organization for Young Idealists, which was then linked to the above-mentioned commando camps. After the 1971 coup, these camps were officially closed and yet training with firearms resumed in secret. The AHI grew rapidly and its chapters spread throughout the country. Following the charges by the government in 1978, it dissolved itself only to be re-established as the Association of Idealist Youth (AIY). AIY continued its operations until 1980 from which point onwards it was taken over by the Path of Ideal Association situated in Nevsehir outside the jurisdiction of martial law to escape prosecution.

In terms of their place in the political spectrum, at the 1965 election, NAP was able to receive only 2.2 per cent of the votes. It increased its votes only to 3 per cent in the 1969 elections. After another small gain in 1973, however, NAP achieved a major leap in 1977 elections when it received

nearly a million votes and gained 16 parliamentary seats. 1977 is the year
which also symbolizes the Maras Massacre of left-wing Alevi Kurds and
Alevi Turks led by the youth militants of NAP.[12] NAP had already played a
very crucial role in the establishment of the first Nationalist Front
(Milliyetci Cephe) coalition government in 1975 and it had received two
ministers in the Justice Party-led coalition. In the second Nationalist Front
Coalition Government of 1977, NAP secured five ministers amounting
nearly to one third of its deputies. NAP's political rise was accompanied by
the strengthening of its militant organisations and increased support for
terrorism as a result of various forms of glorification of violence by party
politics. The NAP then claimed to assist the state-forces in their 'job'. These
and similar statements underlined the vision of the state as a repressive
political mechanism rather than as a platform for democratic governance.
In both of the Nationalist Front governments, the center-right Justice Party
protected and supported the NAP as a force against democratic opposition
and leftist political challenge. Throughout the seventies, armed confronta-
tions initiated by NAP militants in the streets and the rising toll of political
assassinations were tolerated and dismissed by the government and state
authorities based on the assumption that they were undertaking the
'necessary cleansing measures' against leftist militants and revolutionary
youth. This policy of tolerance for political violence if not approval of it
caused splits inside JP and raised severe criticism of the leadership in their
support for the fascist organisations gathered under NAP. Still, during its
tenure in the government, the NAP took over numerous public posts and
was thus given a chance to exploit state resources for its own interest by
staffing public positions with its own militants. The surveys after the 1980
coup in prisons reveal the extraordinarily high percentage of public servants
in NAP-related charges (Bora et al., 1990).

The violent practices by NAP related organisations increased in scale and
density from 1974 onwards. First, it targeted the leaders and members of
leftist youth organisations. During the mandate of the second Nationalist
Front Government, the target became the members of professional
organisations such as the Confederation of Revolutionary Workers Unions,
and the Teachers Association of Turkey. Later, assassinations of leading
intellectuals, university professors and journalists began to take place.[13] The
assassination of Dogan Oz, assistant prosecutor in Ankara, and Cevat
Yurdakul, director of Security in Adana, aimed in particular for the
intimidation of state officials who dared to take a stand against NAP-
initiated violence. The negative public reaction to the commando units of the
youth organization did not curtailed NAP's activities either. Serving as strike
forces of the party, most of the members of these youth themes were recent
emigres from small economically deprived villages to large cities. They sought
to realize their aspirations and resolve their identity problems under the
leadership structure which urged them to conduct armed political opposition.

Among all of its activities during the 1970s, the political massacres of Malatya, Sivas and Kahraman Maras led by NAP militants against Alevi Kurds and Turks as quintessential representatives of the Communist threat/ traitors deserve special attention. The upheavals leading to the massacres were left unattended by the state forces. Neither were there fair trials following the massacres. Rather, these events were treated as 'social turmoil' which meant that among an 'unidentified mob', there was not enough evidence to identify the attackers. Meanwhile, numerous documents drawn from the party headquarters after the 1980 coup proved that most of the attacks were dictated and/or protected by the party leadership.[14]

ALEVIS IN TURKEY: ENEMIES OR ALLIES?

Though the institutionalized and officially recognized sect of Islam in Turkey is Sunniism, Anatolia has long been a landmark for challenging religious heterodoxies. One of the oldest versions of Islam practiced by a large number of historical communities across Turkey is Alevi Islam. In vernacular Turkish, members of Alevi communities are known as *Kōzōlbas* (redhead) based on the legend that they worship fire but really because they decorate their heads with red scarfs during their religious ceremonies symbolizing the martyrdom of Prophet Ali and his son Hyseyin. The term Alevi is also interchangeably used to denote a variety of Shi'i and dervish sects. In reality, Bektashi dervish orders and other heterodox versions of Shiism are quite separate from the Alevi religious denomination. Alevi religious doctrine is a unique and geographically specific combination of Shii Islam, Persian Mazdeism, Christian iconography and central Asian shamanism (Bumke, 1989; Markoff, 1986).

There are close to 20 million Alevis living in Turkey, of whom a minority are Kurdish.[15] Due to inadequate documentation, as well as the dissembling and reticence of Alevi communities in revealing their ethno-religious identity in fear of harassment, the mapping of Alevi communities and population estimates depend largely on ethnographic case studies. They are not listed in the national census as a separate community due to the fact that Turkish censuses do not allow listings based on religious denomination since 1965. Even before 1965, sectarian divisions within Islam were not encouraged and thus overlooked on purpose while different Christian populations had a chance to claim their faith (McCarthy, 1983).

Alevi communities were historically targeted as the enemies of the Ottoman Empire based on their support of the Shi'i Persian Empire in the sixteenth century (Kehl-Bodrogi, 1996; Camuroglu, 1992; Kaleli, 1990). Since the Persian Empire lost the battle, Alevis have been gradually incorporated into the Ottoman imperial system. Nevertheless, their religious beliefs have always been subject to suspicion and derision due

164

to their critical stand against the Sunni establishment. The fact that Alevis have been treated with contempt also during the Republican era, however, can not be explained by the mistrust they might have invoked under the Ottoman reign. In fact, Alevi communities were devoted supporters of Kemalist regime of secularisation (*laiklik*) since it created a public space for heterodox communities to be recognized and treated as equal citizens (van Bruinessen, 1996; Oz, 1990). Still, no matter what end of the political spectrum they stand, there has been a firm consensus in Turkish politics that being an Alevi embodies more than believing in Prophet Ali and practicing unorthodox religious rituals. For the Marxist-Leninist as well as the democratic tradition, it symbolizes genuine social rebelliousness, an authentic adherence to the principles of equality and justice, as well as a perpetual position of opposition against blind state authority.[16] Kemalist-nationalists, after years of disregard and indifference, announced 'the Alevi' as the remedy for the rise of Islamic fundamentalism (Birikim, 1996; Bora, 1990). For the ultra-nationalist cadres, before 1980s, Alevi beliefs and religious ceremonies were judged to be not only heretic to Islam but also alien to the 'Turkish culture'. After the 1980 coup and particularly during the 1990s, with a strange twist, Alevis began to symbolize the 'original Turkish Islam' and were elevated by the ultranationalists to the status of the most veritable representatives of ancient Turkic peoples in Anatolia. Among the Sunni fundamentalist groups, however, the belief that Alevis are indeed inferior to both Sunnis and Shiis and that they allegedly engage in defamatory religious ceremonies, incest, and do not fast or clean, remained unchanged.[17]

Regardless of centuries-old negative stigmatization, Alevis regard themselves as legitimate and proud practicers of Islam. In the meantime, they do not observe the five fundamental requirements prescribed by Sunni Islam. Their way of *shahadat* (statement of faith) contentiously includes the name of Prophet Ali as God's messenger and conveyer, the performance of prayer to *Allah* five times daily (*namaz*) is not ascribed and mosques are not accepted as the holy place to pray[18], alms-giving (*zekat*) is not a common practice, and the month-long fasting in the month of Ramadan (*oruc*) is replaced by a special 12 day fast in the month of Muharrem commemorating the death of Ali's son Hyseyin, and *Hajj* (pilgrimage to Mecca) is not considered a holy duty. Instead, Alevis cherish an unorthodox form of belief based on the oral inheritance of religious knowledge within select families (*ocak*). In addition, radically different from Sunni religious practice of outcasting women from any public religious events, Alevi women have the right to be actively present in all religious ceremonies and ritual gatherings (*semah*).[19] Due to their communal nature, Alevi religious beliefs are ingrained into various cultural practices. Their communal celebrations (*Cem*) incorporate dances and songs performed to pay respect to historic religious leaders and the holy persona in the community. Nonetheless, when living among other ethno-religious communities, Alevis tend to be very discrete about their beliefs and religious practices. They, like the Nestorian or Yezidi communities in the region, traditionally resorted to dissimulation (*takiya*) in order to avoid discrimination and harassment. *Takiya* is an accepted practice among Shii and heterodox Muslim sects as a mode of survival in an hostile religious environment (McDowall, 1992, pp. 56–9).[20] It has been commonly practiced among the Alevis who speak Anatolian dialects of Turkish whereas it is considerably harder for Alevis with Kurdish ethno-linguistic identity to do so. As a result, particularly during the 1990s, Alevi Kurds have been singularly identified and targeted as 'alien elements' in the Turkish culture by militant sectors of the ultranationalist movement. Still, the 1990s created the social and cultural environment within which the Alevi identity itself became the stronghold of the struggle for democratic rights and *takiya*, for the first time in decades, began to be an outmoded custom.[21]

During most of Republican Turkish history, Alevi communities have been the underdogs of the state-sponsored ideology of Turkish secularism with its obvious Sunni bias regardless of their loyalty to secular democratic principles.[22] They did not have the bargaining power for religious rights or freedom of press until very recently. They have also been disproportionately affected by large-scale urban-rural migration since the 1950s, as a result of which many have been exposed to rapid socio-economic changes. Under such circumstances, the economic underclasses of Alevi populace in cities were largely devoted to the ideals of social and economic prosperity promised by the vast array of left-wing movements ranging from democratic socialism to militant-revolutionary Marxism. In turn, this peculiar combination of religious heterodoxy, a tendency to concentrate in close quarters and select neighbourhoods, and, progressive and sometimes rebellious idealism made Alevi communities into easy targets for the extremist right. Particularly in the 1970s, Alevi communities of central and east Anatolia have been devastated by ultranationalist reprisals of the pre-1980 coup period. For the trained militant forces of the Nationalist Action Party, impurities of religion, 'culture' and blood further contaminated by the 'communist ideology' was enough of a cause to engage in ethno-religious cleansing in the form of organized political violence. Back in 1967, 40 Alevis from Sivas were set upon and killed during a football match in Kayseri by Sunni civilians associated with ultranationalist organisations (McDowall, 1992, p. 59). 11 years later, the political tension finding an ethno-religiously specific expression led to the burning down of Alevi neighbourhoods associated with 'communists' in Kahraman Maras in 1978. This event is remembered as the Maras Massacre, and it has left more than one hundred Alevi civilian population dead. The right-wing militants engaged in the killings were active members of the Grey Wolves (youth branch of the National Action Party). Nonetheless, they were quitted in the court based on insufficient evidence and lack of witnesses to testify. Following the Maras Massacre, the majority of the Alevi communities left the city seeking refuge either internally or outside the country.

During the 1980s, following the 1980 coup and the mass imprisonment of youth militants along with the temporary banning of political parties, extremist activities shifted grounds from left-wing versus right-wing politics to the political assassinations undertaken by Sunni-Muslim revivalists (fundamentalists) or underground Marxist-Leninist guerilla organizations. The militant branch of the ultranationalist camp gradually embraced the ideological formulation of the synthesis of Turkism and Sunni Islam (*Tyrk-Islam sentezi*) and used its political energy to promote the interests of 'outside Turks'.[23] The exodus of ethnic-Turks from Bulgaria as well as the tensions between Azerbayjan and Armenia kept the movement busy and yet led to internal fractions. The Islamist branch became more and more keen on asserting their own ideals and identity and therefore staggered the fruitful alliance of the 1980s between fascism and religious fundamentalism. On June 2, 1993, primarily led by an Islamist-Turkist mob, some of the country's leading poets, literary figures and ethnographers gathered in Sivas for a culture festival were burnt alive in the hotel they were staying.[24] The celebrations were to commemorate the legacy of Pir Sultan Abdal, the 16th century Alevi poet and religious leader in Sivas. The mayor of the city as well as the police force and fire-extinguishers were not involved while the mob marched forward to the hotel that accommodated the guests coming from out of town and torched the building. In fact, security forces arrived at the scene after the fire was well under its way. This delay in intervention is explained in terms of the antagonism between the city's Islamic fundamentalist mayor and the Kemalist-secularist governor, as well as the understaffed police force at the time waiting for the army troops to arrive in order to reach secure numbers to face the mob (Kaleli, 1994). In any event, the pre-meditated and well-planned fire left 35 people dead and 90 people wounded.

A comparative analysis of the Maras and Sivas Massacres reveal that, regardless of the ethnic component of the Alevi communities, that is to say, whether the communities identify themselves as Turkish or Kurdish Alevis, they have been subjected to pre-meditated instances of organized political violence. Before the 1980s, these events were primarily led by the militant camp of the ultranationalist movement. As we reach towards the end of the twentieth century, the ultranationalist extremist groups are allied with the military sects of Islamic fundamentalism such as Aczmendis that led the Sivas massacres. In both instances, lack of governmental intervention and the blind-eye approach or the delayed reaction of the security forces facilitated the killings and created an environment which legitimizes organized political violence. In the case of the Maras Massacre, for example, the political *status quo* in the aftermath of the events was such that in 1989 local elections, Okkes Kangar, a right-wing politician affiliated with the 1978 Massacre, was elected to the city Council. Similarly after the Sivas Massacre, the state courts did not undertake a full-fledged examination of the incident which could have resulted in the trial of the Mayor. Instead, the spokespeople of the leading political parties have given apologetic speeches blaming the victims of the Massacre for attempting to cause religious cleavages in the secular Turkish state. After the Sivas Massacre, as a political gesture, the Ministry of Religion was advised by the Turkish Parliament to establish an Alevi Chapter. However, such verbal honorariums did not suffice to relieve the wounds inflicted upon Alevi communities.[25] The Ministry of Religion continues to be devoted to the rise of Sunni Islam and re-imbursement of mosques and religious schools out of public tax money.

Since the 1980 coup, the ultranationalist movement adopted a Kemalist gesture re-defining the ideals of the Republic of Turkey in accordance with their Turanist/Tribalist yearnings. The official re-writing of Turkish history since the 1930s sterilizing the existence of Alevi, Christian or Kurdish sectors in the society set the background for NLP/NAP's reproachment with state-sponsored Turkish nationalism. NLP/NAP unilaterally assumed the positions of spokesmanship for Turkish nationalism and sanctified love-of-country (Bora et al. 1990; Parla 1986). Establishing alliances around this particular theme not only strengthened the political position of ultra-nationalists, but also gave them a privileged position in their relations with the Kemalist army.

The NAP/NLP/NAP line of politics provided a legitimate center for the ultranationalist tradition in Turkey. While being members of a political party, however, the ultranationalist cadres acted and continue to act under the pretense that tribalist-Turkist nationalism is an supra-political idiom which can be cherished by all regardless of their political affiliation. This was indeed the recipe that guaranteed the survival of dispersed party membership through and after the 1980 coup. The 'anti-Communism' thesis combined with etatism and militarism kept the ultranationalist movement at a close bay to the authority of the state both during the parliamentary and the military phases of Turkish politics. Alevi communities became almost the 'natural' victims of the state-ultranationalist alliance since, at least until the 1990s, they were neither Turkist nor Sunni-Islamist. Instead, they symbolized a secular, modernist and/or revolutionary and generally anti-Turkist political force. Thus, NAP/NLP-led violence against Alevi communities was best to be ignored since it embodied many of the ideological elements espoused by the Turkish state apparatus itself. It was only after the split within the re-established NAP between Islamic fundamentalist and Turkist camps that a fraction of ultranationalist militants took a position against the state rather than with the state. One of the results of this new political positioning was the Sivas Massacre, which unfortunately created nothing more than a deafening bureaucratic silence. The new *status quo* in Turkish politics is not only Turkist but also increasingly Islamist. As such, it is capable of absorbing a wider ranger of essentialist movements than that was possible before. If Turkist-tribalist political violence was the quintessential product of state-ultranationalist alliance, Turkist-Sunni fundamentalist terror appears to be the new offspring of the mythic-utopian orientation in Turkish politics that denies the ethno-religious heterogeneity of the national polity.

CONCLUSION

Following the military coup of 1980, the activities of NAP were banned and the party was dissolved by order of the National Security Council in 1981. Its property was confiscated and many of its members and affiliates were brought to court and sentenced. However, in 1982, Turkes and other leading members of the NAP requested acquittal and their wish was granted in 1985. Sympathisers of NAP and former party members first joined several newly established right-wing parties and then re-united their power at the 1985 Grand Congress of the Nationalist Democratic Party.

The still-active Nationalist Labour Party (renamed as Nationalist Action Party again) was formed in 1985 as a continuation of the original NAP. At the outset, the NAP-related political violence subsided after the 1980 trials and sentences. However, many of the leading militants of the NAP cadres formed new alliances with Islamic revivalists and fundamentalist militants while in jail during the 1980s. The major trend in the 1990s was thus a rapprochement between the members of religious fractions, National Salvation Party and the ex-Grey Wolves. Initially, the leading Motherland Party's political basis and electoral agenda were satisfactory at a time when there were still a ban on the older political parties. However, combined with the NAP's loss of popularity, the burgeoning parties on the right soon established their own followers. In this new political environment, NLP/NAP eventually enjoyed a revival of nationalist politics, only to be stronger than before with the help of Islamic fundamentalist organisations.

It is true that NLP/NAP militants no longer play into the role of states private militia against the Communists. In other words, ultranationalists lost the unlimited tolerance for its extremist activities in exchange for creating a buffer zone for the central government. However, with the continual rise of the Kurdish problem in the East, the ongoing struggle for civil rights of the Alevi populace primarily in Middle Anatolia, and the undeniable popularity of Sunni fundamentalism, the NLP/NAP formulations of tribal lineage and ethno-religious purity and superiority might soon take the lead in terms of quick solutions to deep-seated economic and social problems. At present, Turkist-Islamist ideologies of ethno-religious purity particularly threaten the livelihood of Alevi Kurdish communities.

The radical emotional charge of tribalist political projects comes from a strong sense of self-justification. The utopian impulse fueling them and their re-formulations of identity is dependent upon the construction of a new past as the point of origin, as where history begins. More specifically, tribalist politics anchors communitarian self-righteousness in a mythical point of ancestry. Due to their entanglement in the labyrinths of an illusionary past, political revisions introduced by tribalist agendas then create artificial categories that divide and hierarchize the citizens of a multi-cultural and poli-ethnic state. In the end, the utopian impulse of tribalism speaks of 'revenge' in the disguise of rejuvenation. Its verbatim fabrication of diaries of the past engenders daydreams and landscapes which eradicate the value of human life in the daily mayhem of politics. As such, the utopian elements in contemporary forms of tribalism lead to a dangerous misplacement of politics in its struggle to re-invent it. The biggest peril posed by essentialist identity politics such as tribalism is that in their inauguration ceremonies, they recapture the authoritarian moments of modernity.

NOTES

1 It is true that utopia and ideology possess different discursive characteristics. Ideology constitutes an example for the 'authoritative' discourse – a privileged idiom of beliefs, values and categories stripped from their contextuality – (Bahktin, 1981: p. 424). In contradistinction utopian declarations are utterances that claim of authorship, political will and ethical choice and projection, even when they speak of the salvation and redemption of the whole of 'humanity.' Secondly, while identity assumes primarily an integrative function, utopias stimulate variations of and a departure from the status quo. Concomitantly, in the anti-modernist battle of identity politics that privileges the particular against the universal, utopian mode of thinking has a superior position compared to the ideological blueprint.

2 A simple comparison between common-place analogies used for ideology – such as distortion, reversal, mirror image, illusion–, and those depicting the utopian impulse – such as imagination, dream, escape, denial, construction or longing – is suggestive of a strong affinity if not complementarity between ideology and utopia. In both cases, fabrication is the ground-work that gives rise to the final discursive product. Meanwhile, ideology is usually formulated as a peculiar kind of fabrication that speaks the language of the *real*, whereas utopian forms of articulation categorically reject direct referencing of reality. This binary framework is primarily indebted to the Marxist/post-Marxist tradition of critique. Accordingly, utopia has been trivialised as a deceiving construction of the mind that stands outside of history. Particularly, structuralist Marxist readings of utopia postulate that ideologies are full-blown growths of nascent utopian forms into an idiom designed to legitimise structures of authority and social order. Such readings of the relationship between ideology and utopia stigmatises utopia as hindrance to the healthy growth of a true-consciousness to be experienced by a designated historical agent (Engels, 1959; Marx and Engels, 1964; Althusser, 1970).

170

3 For further debate on the contents of Kemalist ideology and the 'Kemalist Revolutions', see Koker (1990), Landau (1984), Kazancigil et al. (1981), Kushner (1977) and Karpat (1973).

4 'During the course of the Second World War, various circles in Turkey absorbed Nazi propaganda; these were pro-German and admired Nazism, which they grasped as a doctrine of warlike dynamism and a source of nationalist inspiration, on which to base their Pan-Turk and anti-Soviet ideology.' (Landau, 1974: p. 194).

5 Among them was the influential figure of Nihal Atsäz.

6 The group brought under trial included the young officer Alparslan Tyrkes who later became the leader of the movement under the title of 'Leader of Turkic Tribes' (*Basbug*).

7 The main journals supporting ultranationalist ideas included *Bozkurt* (The Grey Wolf – a leading symbol of ancient Turkic tribes of Middle Asia–) and *Tanrädag* (name of the Tien-Shan mountain range believed to be the land of ancient Turkic tribes). At the end of the Second World War, the Turkist poet and writer Necip Fazäl Käsakyrek started the publication of an aggressive nationalist magazine, *Byyyk Dogu* (The Great East). The magazine as well as the association carrying the same name simultaneously attacked secularism, westernization, freemasonry and Jews (Landau 1974; Darendelioglu 1968) The organization later disbanded to avoid prosecution and was re-established as *Yeni Byyyk Dogu* (New Great East) but the magazine continued to be published. Following the Second World War, quite a few new periodicals appeared supporting the ultranationalist and pan-Turkist causes. The majority of them were influenced by Nazi themes of race and racial superiority. The most well-known and scholarly of those, *Tyrk Kyltyr* (The Culture of the Turks) started publication in 1962. It was followed by Turk Birligi (the Union of Turks) in 1966, introduced as a 'nationalist, cultural and artistic monthly – the voice of Turkism in Anatolia, the Caucauses and Azerbayjan –' (quoted in Landau 1974, p. 197). In many of these publications, Sunni Islam was reconciled with Turkism, a combination which later led to the doctrine of Synthesis of Turkism and Islamism (*Tyrk-Islam Sentezi*) during the 1980s. As a result, Christian as well as non-Sunni Muslim minorities were identified as the outsiders of a 'true Turkey' whereas outer Turkic peoples were cited as the brethren of the Turkish nation.

8 Landau defines pan-Turanism as '[a] movement that aimed at the union of all Turkic, Mongolian and Finno-Ugric peoples.' (Landau, 1974: p. 193) Turanism has a different ideological make-up compared to pan-Turanism since it aims at bringing all Turkic peoples together but in the land of Turkey. In other words, it is infected by a tautology. Turanism was and still is espoused as the semi-official state ideology concerning Muslim and ethnically Turkish minorities in the Balkans (Bora, 1995).

9 There are striking similarities between the party programs of nationalism socialism in Germany and Italy, and their Turkish ultranationalist counterpart. (Landau 1984, 1974).

10 Concerning the workers, however, NAP opposed unionisation as a political movement and proposed a single hierarchical union structure with obligatory membership. (Bora et al. 1990).

11 Published in 1965, Tyrkes' book *Dokuz Isäk* ('Nine Lights') summarized these principles in a very succinct language.

12 The geographical distribution of the NAP votes prior to the 1980 coup exhibited a significant regional imbalance. In the provinces heavily populated by

Kurds (Bingol, Bitlis, Diyarbakir, Mardin, Mus, Siirt and Van), the average NAP
vote was less than 1 percent. Similarly, in most developed regions of Turkey
(Marmara and Aegean), NAP votes remained far below their national average.
Only in the central region (Central Anatolia and parts of Eastern Anatolia, and
areas north of Cukurova) the votes were brought up to rates exceeding 10
percent. Some of the cities in that category are Yozgat (22.9%), Erzincan
(19.0%), Elazig (18.7%), Kahraman Maras (15.5%), Sivas (13.2%), Corum
(12.7%), Gaziantep (11.1%), Tokat (10.6%), Cankiri (17.0%), Kirsehir
(14.2%), Kayseri (13.2%), Nigde (13.0%), Adana (11.3%), Nevsehir
(11.0%), and Konya (10.7%). All of the above listed cities and their districts
have significant Alevi and/or Kurdish minority populations (Bora et al., 1990;
Landau, 1984).

13 Abdi Ipekci, Kemal Turker, Cavit Orhan Tutengil, Bedrettin Comert, Bedri
Karafakioglu, Necdet Bulut, Umit Doganay were killed and Mihri Belli survived
the assassination attempt. These were established scholars and writers who
worked and supported democratic institutions and legal jurisdiction in Turkey.

14 In response to these findings, claims were laid by fractions of party membership
that acceptance of violence was not unanimous but an individual choice.
However, the political history of NAP openly defeats the truth-value of this
proposition.

15 1980 estimates given for the Alevi population in Turkey as a whole (including
Turkmens, Yoruks, Zazas and Alevi Kurds) is between 10 to 18 million
(Andrews, 1989; McDowall, 1982).

16 In particular, Alevi religion is identified with the songs and poetry of Pir Sultan
Abdal, a sixteenth century mystic and social rebel executed by the Ottoman
authorities. Pir Sultan Abdal's and other Alevi religious poets' ideas about
freedom and social justice foregrounded Alevi inspirations for equality in the
contemporary Turkish society.

17 Although there is a belief cherished among the Sunni majority that Alevi boys
are not circumcised, this is proven to be largely an allegation in support of the
Sunni belief that Alevis are not 'clean'.

18 Alevi villages are distinguished by the absence of mosques unless the
government authorities forcefully established one in exchange for public
services and educational facilities. They are also frequently decorated by trees
and tombs as objects of veneration, covered with colourful rags tied in tight
knots – an expression of the continuing Zoroastrian influences in their religious
practices.

19 Alevi women are known to be unveiled and work along their husbands outside
of the house in rural areas.

20 A customary form of takiya practiced by Alevi men during the military service –
18 months for the unqualified soldiers – is to pray (*namaz*) and fast at Ramazan
(*oruc*) along with Sunni soldiers in the army barracks.

21 There are also strong diaspora communities formed by Alevi political refugees
in many Western European cities. In fact, these were the centers of vanguardism
that led to the current revival of Alevi identity (Kehl-Bodrogi, 1996).

22 Especially with the post-1980 imposition of compulsory religion classes in the
state-run public educational system, Alevi children have been subjected to
indoctrination of Sunni Islam as a superior belief system. (Cakir, 1990).

23 The identity crisis in Republican Turkish politics is dictated by the interplay
between the counter-forces of three main principles: Turkism, Islamism and
Modernism. While the Kemalist-secular cadres prioritized Turkist and Modernist
elements in Turkish society, politics and culture, both ultranationalists and

Islamic fundamentalists relied on a doctrine of *Tyrk-Islam Sentezi* that links ethno-centric definitions of 'Turkishness' with the Islamic heritage of Turkey (Helvacioglu 1996; Bora et al., 1990; Parla, 1986). The definitive formulation of this Synthesis was announced in 1984 under the roof of the conservative-nationalist freemason organization *Aydänlar Ocagä* (The Guild/Fraternity of Intellectuals), which is known as the Opus Dei of Turkey (Saylan, 1987). The printed version of the Synthesis was written by the first president of the *Aydinlar Ocag*, Ibrahim Kafesoglu (Kafesoglu, 1985).

24 The 'List of the Dead' included Asäm Bezirci, a well-known writer and literary critic and a member of the PEN, musician/singer Nesimi Cimen, play-wright and literary critic Metin Altäok, folk musician/singer Muhlis Akarsu, literary critic and writer Behcet Safa Aysan, musician/singer Edibe Sulari, and, poet Ugur Kaynar, journalist and caricaturist Asaf Kocak.

25 Amnesty International Reports suggest that arbitrary arrests, torture under custody and varying forms of public harassment of Alevis are steady entries in the Human Rights Records of Turkey.

Index

175

Index